THE HUMAN PUZZLE

The Human Puzzle

Psychological Research and Christian Belief

DAVID G. MYERS

A Harper/CAPS Book

Published in San Francisco by
HARPER & ROW PUBLISHERS
NEW YORK   HAGERSTOWN
SAN FRANCISCO   LONDON

1817

in association with The Christian Association

To Carol

FIRST EDITION

Designed by Janice Stern

Library of Congress Cataloging in Publication Data

Myers, David G.
   THE HUMAN PUZZLE.

  (Christian perspectives on counseling and the
behavioral sciences)
  "A Harper/CAPS book."
  Includes index.
  1. Christianity—Psychology. I. Title.
II. Series.
BR100.M93 1978   201'.9   77-15873
ISBN 0-06-065558-5

78 79 80 81 82 10 9 8 7 6 5 4 3 2 1

22765

CONTENTS

v

Preface to Harper / CAPS Series

Throughout much of this past century, Christianity and psychology have been viewed as enemies. Religion has been a taboo topic for most psychologists, with a few notable exceptions such as William James and Gordon Allport. Psychology has been viewed with suspicion and fear by many in the Christian community. Within recent years, however, increasing numbers of individuals with personal commitment to the historic Judaeo-Christian faith have entered the counseling and behavioral science fields. Increasing numbers of ministers have received psychological training.

Several associations involving Christians in psychologically-related fields have emerged, including the national Christian Association for Psychological Studies (CAPS). At the same time the American Psychological Association has recognized the legitimate study of psychology and religion with creation of Division 36, Psychologists Interested in Religious Issues. The Society for the Scientific Study of Religion has also blossomed into an international association with nearly 2000 members. Although Division 36 and S.S.S.R. are composed of members with a wide variety of Christian and non-Christian commitments, the trend is clearly toward the legitimizing of the study of psychology/religion relationships. In addition to these associations, several journals have been developed to provide outlets for those wishing to publish theory and research. Within conservative Christian circles are the *Journal of Psychology and Theology,* and the *CAPS Bulletin*. Other prestigious journals include the *Journal for the Scientific Study of Religion* and *Zygon*. There is a new willingness and perceived need to consider the ethical implications of research and practice as a result of the new knowledge that has been gained in the behavioral and biomedical sciences. Few behavioral scientists are willing to accept the notion that their research is totally objective, and many clinicians are questioning the validity of the detached, completely objective therapist model.

All of this is not to say that most psychologists are interested in religion, or most Christians are comfortable with psychology. Neither is probably true. However, for a growing number of Christians and non-Christians, the rigorous study of relationships between psychology and religion in general (and Christianity in particular) is an important and legitimate activity.

To date, there has been no systematic publishing outlet for those committed to the Christian belief system wishing to write on a professional level on Christianity/psychology relationships. Among most religious publishers the tendency has been to popularize the writing due to market considerations. Secular publishers have tended to severely downplay or omit any explicit religious dimension. *Christian Perspectives on Counseling and the Behavioral Sciences* is the first series to appear that is both explicitly Christian in orientation, written on a professional level, and yet readable by psychologically-educated lay persons. Professionals in counseling and the behavioral sciences will benefit, as will pastors. The books in the Series will be valuable as supplementary texts in upper division undergraduate courses, seminary and graduate programs.

The purpose of the Series is to describe and analyze relationships between psychology and the orthodox Christian belief system. At the same time, the Series will be investigational and exploratory. For example, individual authors will undoubtedly take different views on the basic issue of whether it is even possible to "integrate" Christianity and psychology. The Series will encourage examination of behavioral science findings and their implications for understanding the Christian faith, as well as look at the implications of Christianity for the behavioral sciences. The topics explored will range from more general theoretical concerns to specific phenomena and issues.

Books in the Series do not represent the views of Christian Association for Psychological Studies in any formal way. They reflect the individual authors.

CAPS is a national organization of Christians working in psychologically-related fields, including psychology, psychiatry, sociology, counseling and social work. It also encourages participation and membership by members of the ministry. It was begun formally in 1955 in Western Michigan as a predominantly regional group. CAPS holds an annual convention, publishes a quarterly *Bulletin*, sponsors regional meetings throughout the United States several times each year, and publishes a membership and referral directory. Members are asked to indicate agreement with the basic pur-

poses and statement of faith of the association. Further information can be obtained from the Executive Secretary, 26711
Farmington Road, Farmington Hills, Michigan 48018. A prior publication of monographs, *SELF ESTEEM,* can also be ordered from
the Executive Secretary.

We are pleased to publish *The Human Puzzle* as the first book in
this series. Dr. Myers has done an admirable job of covering a vast
amount of research information from various subdisciplines of psychology, distilling and conceptualizing it in a coherent way, and
then drawing cogent implications for the understanding and practice of the Christian faith. *The Human Puzzle* will undoubtedly be
provocative at some points. Dr. Myers has not shrunk from tension
points, but has encouraged us to explore and face up to both the
data and the Christian faith. Some of the practical implications
that he has pointed out in the sections on superstition and prayer,
and behavior and belief should be stimulating and helpful. His discussion of the complex issues of the mind-body relationship and
freedom and determinism is thorough and compelling, though his
resolutions are not easy. His initial discussion of religious and scientific explanations of human nature is especially appropriate as a
beginning point of understanding for this Series.

Craig W. Ellison, Ph.D.
Series Editor

Preface to *The Human Puzzle*

Twenty-four centuries after Socrates' sage advice to "Know thyself" we are enjoying the excitement of new explorations into human thought and action. Sensing that public awareness lags years behind this new research, I have distilled from our leading psychology journals the discoveries and ideas which have most fascinated me. I also suggest how these new research findings connect with Christian belief, and I propose some practical implications of this integrated picture of human nature.

Sometimes this research will challenge the church with new questions and insights, and sometimes Christian beliefs will challenge the assumptions and values of behavioral scientists. Nevertheless, my general contention is that the emerging scientific picture of the person is similar to a very ancient picture—one based on the holistic understandings of the Hebrew people. I doubt many readers will agree with all of my integration. By indicating how I am struggling to relate psychological discoveries to Christian faith I hope at least to stimulate readers to consider how these facts and ideas bear upon their own thinking.

Who are my readers? Two imaginary groups looked over my shoulder while I wrote. The most important group was lay people and undergraduate students. For them I sought to avoid technical jargon and the assumption of special knowledge, but I have not assumed they are stupid. Science is most easily popularized if it is oversimplified. I have endeavored to be brief without being unfair, to move swiftly and simply through complex material without oversimplifying. Only the reader can judge how successful I have been.

The second group of imaginary readers consisted of my expert colleagues in psychology and theology. None of them will be totally happy with what I have written. At points they will want to say, "with the exception of," or "but on the other hand," or "there is more to it than that." Yet I hope that even this group will find something new here—a new way of looking at familiar ideas and perhaps even a few new ideas. I have found excitement in identifying common links between various areas of recent research and in relating these to Christian belief. I hope that some of this enthusiasm is contagious.

This intellectual task of synthesizing data into genuine understanding and then integrating this understanding with theological presumptions about human nature is a large agenda for one small mind such as mine. Interdisciplinary synthesis requires reaching beyond one's own professional competence, and I may have bitten off too much. But with the accelerating accumulation of knowledge, it seems essential that some people work at distilling and synthesizing this knowledge, lest our minds dry up even while we flounder in the sea of facts. I have worked at this task partly because I see so few others in my field doing so. Sad to say, there are few theologically interested psychologists and few of these are also active scientists.

Sometimes I will tread with rather large boots over intellectual minefields of great antiquity, and no doubt I will trigger a few explosions. Without the help of many friends and fellow scholars, most of them nonpsychologists, I would have tripped even more. The original impetus to prepare much of this material was an invitation to deliver lectures on psychology and religion to the eight faculties of the Association of Reformed Colleges. These several hundred people offered me countless insights and criticisms, and much encouragement as well. The support and stimulation I received under a Lilly Endowment faculty development grant also aided my efforts.

Some of what I have written also has emerged from interactions with Hope College students over the past ten years. Although they are too numerous to mention by name, a special thanks is due the exceptional participants in a recent seminar on "Psychology and Theology."

A number of other people, most of them present or former colleagues at Hope College, have read parts or all of the manuscript and contributed ideas and criticism. To Les Beach, Martin Bolt, Wayne Boulton, Elton Bruins, Roy M. Carlisle, Jane Dickie, Craig Ellison, Francis Fike, Lars Granberg, James Hurley, John Hollenbach, Charles Huttar, Dirk Jellema, Arthur Jentz, Christopher Kaiser, Craig Lammers, Thomas Ludwig, James Motiff, Richard Mouw, Jan Myers, Jack Nyenhuis, Robert Palma, Frank Roberts, Michael Rulon, John Shaughnessy, John Stewart, Hendrika Vande Kemp, Henry VanderGoot, Marlin Vander Wilt, Alan Verhey,

Ralph Vunderink, Helen Westra, Garret Wilterdink, and Nicholas Woltersdorff, my thanks. Extra thanks are due my friends Robert Coughenour (biblical studies), Sang Lee (theology), and Merold Westphal (philosophy), each of whom generously devoted many hours to reading and discussing selected chapters. Although none of these people agree with everything I have written, they have given me a sense of that for which the Christian and liberal arts college is uniquely well suited—the integration of learning and the integration of learning with faith. "The reason why an intellectual community is necessary," Robert M. Hutchins wrote shortly before his death, "is that it offers the only hope of grasping the whole." This has been my experience.

Like many other research psychologists, I am indebted to the taxpaying public for support. My thinking, research, and writing has been facilitated by eight grants and fellowships over the past thirteen years, mostly from the National Science Foundation. This book displays some of the fruits of our country's investment in the human sciences. It should go without saying, however, that I alone am responsible for its religious content.

Four other very special people have been a particular help. Maxine Mesbergen and Phyllis Vandervelde not only typed several drafts of this manuscript with their usual efficiency and perfection, but also provided helpful suggestions.

Steven Hoogerwerf's intellectual and technical assistance has been invaluable. Never before have I encountered a student who has so capably challenged and informed my thinking, particularly on philosophical matters.

Although I cannot credit my wife with such traditional services as typing and proofreading the manuscript, checking the footnotes, or even keeping the children out of my hair, her theological reading and thinking has been an enormous influence. After many hundreds of hours of conversation I no longer know where Carol's ideas leave off and mine begin.

David Myers
February, 1978

Introduction

Most books on psychology and religion relate religious thinking to the writings of the old personality theorists, many of them long dead. These writings are rich in speculative insight but stingy on fact. This book is not concerned with the speculations of personality theorists or with what psychologists have said about religion. It instead looks at human nature from the perspectives of psychological research and Christian belief.

It begins by considering the relationship of Christian and scientific explanations of persons. For example:

Are psychologists more irreligious than faculty in most other academic disciplines? If they are, does this symptomize an inherent conflict between Christian and scientific understandings of human nature?

If someone offers a sensible naturalistic explanation of a spiritual event, say of conversion, what effect should this have on a religious understanding of that event?

What is the Christian's proper relationship to secular research—to be an enthusiastic participant in it or to develop instead a uniquely Christian psychology?

To what extent do the assumptions and values of psychologists influence their description and interpretation of events?

The remainder of the book relates Christian belief to four different areas of research. First, scientific and Christian perspectives on the relationship of mind and body are considered:

What do recent insights of biopsychology concerning the evolutionary emergence of mind, the genetic foundation of our individual differences, and the correspondence between our brain states and our emotions, thoughts, and actions contribute to our understanding of human nature?

How does the human image emerging from biopsychology relate to the human image discerned by biblical scholars and theologians? Are we to think of ourselves as composed of two essential substances—body and soul?

What practical implications follow from one's view of mind and body?

The relationship between people's attitudes and their actions is considered next:

How much do people's attitudes and beliefs affect their behavior? Do people who profess belief in Christian doctrine act differently than those who do not?

To what extent do people's actions mold their subsequent attitudes and beliefs?

Can the conclusions of research on attitude and action be integrated with the biblical understanding of religious knowledge and with theological insights concerning the nature of faith? What practical implications follow for church renewal, for worship, and for Christian nurture?

If genuine satisfaction is to be derived from the areas in which scientific and biblical perspectives seem to be converging, then areas of apparent disagreement must also be probed. One such area concerns the implications research on superstitious thinking has for popular understandings of the power of prayer. For instance:

To what extent is human thinking distorted by biases, errors, and causal illusions? Do the illusions of human thought ever penetrate religious belief?

Is there an objectively observable connection between praying and subsequent events? What has been the counsel of serious Christian thinkers regarding the power and purpose of prayer?

What benefits and what dangers are there in becoming sensitive to possible intrusions of superstition into Christian belief?

The final section considers a deep problem which inevitably surfaces in discussions of psychology and Christian faith: the nature of human freedom.

What does a deterministic world view say about human freedom? What does the Christian conception of God's providence, sovereignty, and grace suggest about human freedom? What are the implications of research concerning genetic and environmental influences upon behavior and of research concerning a person's conviction of personal freedom? Is there a place in the Christian and scientific conceptions of human nature for making individuals ultimately accountable for their acts?

What are the practical implications of the Christian beliefs in divine sovereignty and human responsibility and of the psychological research on environmental and personal control?

Struggling to better understand human nature is a worthy venture, not only for its own sake but also because doing so can draw us closer to our Creator and can enable us to appreciate better the awesome mystery of his being. "We cannot have a clear and complete knowledge of God," noted John Calvin, "unless it is accompanied by a corresponding knowledge of ourselves."[1]

Are scientific and biblical insights sufficiently congenial that we can distill from both of them a clearer knowledge of ourselves? The human image that emerges will challenge some conventional assumptions about human nature. If discomfort results from wrestling with these difficult issues, we might remember, with C. S. Lewis, that

in religion, as in war and everything else, comfort is the one thing you cannot get by looking for it. If you look for truth, you may find comfort in the end: if you look for comfort you will not get either comfort or truth— only soft soap and wishful thinking to begin with and, in the end, despair.[2]

1. John Calvin, *Institutes of the Christian Religion*, I, XV, 1 (John T. McNeill, ed., Ford L. Battles, trans.) (Philadelphia: Westminster Press, 1975), p. 183.
2. C. S. Lewis, *Mere Christianity* (New York: MacMillan, 1960), p. 25.

PART I

Religious and Scientific
Explanations of Human Nature

CHAPTER 1

Christian Belief and the Human Sciences

Among recent developments in American culture, two trends are unmistakable. The first is a decline in the authority of traditional religion. Since 1967, a majority of Americans have sensed that religion is losing its influence on American life. Their perceptions are correct, for religious interests and participation have suffered steady erosion. Church attendance declined from 1958, when 49 percent of Americans went to church each week, until reaching 40 percent in 1971, where it stayed through 1975. In 1957, 81 percent believed that religion could provide the answers to problems facing society; this figure had declined to 62 percent by 1974.[1] Even among young people who describe themselves as "very religious," one-third now express little or no confidence in the Church or organized religion. Evidence from college campuses reveals a "dramatic decline" in church attendance between 1952 and 1969, and national surveys indicate that during this period the decline in attendance was sharpest for people under thirty.[2] Downward trends are even more striking in Western Europe, where the Gallup Organization reports that "something approaching a collapse of faith may be occurring."[3] It remains to be seen whether upward trends set in motion by the recent growth in American evangelical groups will be enduring (weekly church attendance did rise by 2 percent during 1976) or whether this religious renewal is another short term fluctuation in what some scholars believe is a "long gradual decline" in church attendance and traditional orthodoxy.[4]

Simultaneous with the decline in traditional religious commitment since the mid-1950s has been an increased interest in the human sciences. Consider the following statistics on the growth in American psychology:

During the past thirty years, membership of the American Psychological Association has grown from two thousand to over fifty thousand.

3

By the early 1970s psychology had become the most popular major among college students. In the ten years since 1964 the number of bachelor's degrees in psychology nearly quadrupled. This increase was approximately twice that of the humanities and natural sciences.[5] The 150 introductory psychology textbooks now comprise the largest college text market.

Best estimates indicate there are thirty-four applications and 4.6 applicants for every opening in graduate clinical psychology programs. These ratios are almost double those reported for medical schools.[6]

There are now more people in graduate school studying psychology than there are psychologists in the American Psychological Association.[7]

Since beginning publication in 1967, *Psychology Today* has been one of the fastest growth magazines on the popular market and now has a circulation well over one million.

This remarkable surge in the public's fascination with psychology seems to be leveling off (even as the decline in American religious interests has now leveled off). Reactions against objective analysis of persons are growing, and within the discipline itself one hears more frequent doubts regarding the importance of current research. Furthermore, the rise of psychology during the 1960s and the decline of organized religion during this same period may be just a coincidence. Still, it is tempting to speculate that *one* factor contributing to the decline of religion among young Americans *might* be the increased prominence of secular understandings of the human situation, including those proposed by psychology. The more liberal, mainline denominations, which are relatively open to insights from the human sciences, are, perhaps also coincidentally, the very denominations which happen to be shrinking, while the more insulated, conservative denominations are the ones which are thriving.[8] Indeed, many religious people view the rise in psychology with alarm, sensing here a threat to cherished beliefs. Their distrust is reciprocated by the many psychologists who agree that psychology and religion are incompatible.

Education in secular perspectives may, indeed, undercut religious commitments. College-educated Americans are much less likely to declare their religious beliefs "very important" to them than are grade-school-educated Americans (although they are just as likely to attend church). Moreover, religious beliefs and behavior typically undergo considerable erosion during the college years. During 1975, 40 percent of freshmen but only 23 percent of seniors reported they attended church weekly. And 10 percent fewer seniors than freshmen believed in God and in life after death, and expressed a religious preference.[9] Time in college tends also to be associated with increased intellectual interest and with decreased religious orthodoxy.[10]

Many would conclude from these observations that there is an inherent conflict between science and religion. Surveys of students indicate that from the 1920s to the late 1960s there has been a steadily increasing perception of conflict between science and religion.[11] Research, however, reveals that faculty members in the natural sciences do not, in fact, show less personal religiousness than other faculty members. It is rather among faculty in fields such as psychology and sociology, where knowledge claims seem to overlap those of religion, that personal religiousness becomes quite low.[12] For example, nearly half of college psychology faculty members express no personal religious commitment—a substantially higher disinterest in religion than in fields such as chemistry and business, where content is less likely to bear on religious assumptions.[13] Among the listed faculty supporters of InterVarsity Christian Fellowship, one could staff several university natural science departments, but not social science ones. Although some contend that "natural science has been the bridge on which many have crossed over to unbelief," it seems more correct to implicate the social sciences.[14]

This widespread agnosticism among psychologists may be due to the attraction of psychology for people eager to challenge the cultural orthodoxy.[15] Or it may be that engaging in psychological explanation of behavior tends to make religious explanation less plausible and to rob it of spiritual significance. One of religion's functions has been to interpret the mysterious and unexplainable aspects of our nature. The psychological account of human nature can therefore be seen as pre-empting the religious account. The principles of psychology are more easily substituted for religious beliefs than are the principles of natural science. Because religion and psychology overlap, it sometimes seems that one is trying to elbow the other out.[16] Given this apparent tension, psychologists may choose loyalty to their science, believing it to possess more credible answers to life's questions.

This polarization of psychology and religion points to the importance of building bridges between the two—for the benefit of both. On the one hand, theology can help shape the philosophical perspective and value structure of the science of psychology. On the other hand, what God is teaching in science can sometimes suggest a second look at conventional interpretations of Scripture. Furthermore, the credibility of religious language is enhanced by translation into ideas meaningful to contemporary culture. Just as Paul was a Jew to the Jews and a Gentile to the Gentiles, so today the Word seeks expression within the terms of the particular cultural context. The incarnation is the archsymbol of God meeting humanity on its own level, neither conforming to human culture nor remote from it. This is the Reformation spirit—ever reforming our understandings according to God's continuing revelation.

SCIENCE AND RELIGION

Most people think the history of science and religion suggests anything but this sort of congeniality between the two. We conjure up images of Galileo before the Congregation of the Index, of the reaction against Darwin's ideas at the Scopes trial, and of continuing hostility from many quarters of the church to what is seen as encroaching naturalism. Many students see psychological explanation of behavior and beliefs as being in competition with religious understanding: if one is true then the other is presumed false. Scientific and religious categories of explanation appear to be on opposite ends of a teeter-totter—as one goes up, the other comes down. This view is so widespread, especially with regard to the newer human sciences, that it becomes vital for us to have a correct understanding of the relation between scientific and religious explanation.

Contrary to this popular presumption of science-religion antagonism, some historians of modern science have noted that "Western science was cast in a matrix of Christian theology."[17] Many of the founders of modern science—among them Pascal, Bacon, Newton, and Boyle—drew encouragement from the Bible. Britain's Royal Society was founded predominantly by scientists whose Christian world view helped make the new science possible.[18] Many of these scientists were Puritans who believed God said of his creation, "It is good." Never could they search too far in the book of God's word or the book of God's works, for they believed both endeavors led one to praise the power, wisdom, and goodness of God. Whatever God found worth creating they found worth studying, as part of their ordination as creatures with responsible dominion over the earth. Their obedience to the source of truth motivated them to explore the material world, not disdain it, and to accept humbly whatever facts the creation should offer. They believed that whatever they discovered ultimately was God's and that they owed no ultimate allegiance to any human authority. Here, then, were grounds for celebrating science, not for vilifying it.

R. Hooykaas contrasts these biblical ideas about God and nature with Greek assumptions which were prevalent prior to the seventeenth century. If, as Plato supposed, the universe is not created, but rather eternally existing and imbued with divinity, then science should obey the dictates of deductive reason. By contrast, the Christian view is that "nature is not a deity to be feared and worshipped, but a work of God to be admired, studied and managed." The Christian's reluctance to deify nature made science "subject to data and facts, things given and made, whether they are rational or not."[19] As will be emphasized in the next chapter, philosophers of science have recently been noting that science is not so purely objective and free of dogma as this view supposes. But it is nonetheless true that, in its early years, science became less dependent on dogma as the conviction grew that the Book of Nature and the Book of Scripture both merited serious scrutiny.

Biblical thought continues to be conducive to science. Kenneth Hardy has documented the amazing production of scientists and scholars by midwestern Protestant colleges.[20] Despite their intellectually diverse, non-elite students, a number of these institutions have consistently ranked among the nation's top sixty colleges and universities in the production of Ph.D. scientists—a phenomenon Hardy partly attributes to these Protestants' assumption that the world is orderly and meaningful and to their strong sense of personal dedication in exploring it.

Yet people today are not as consciously aware of the Christian basis for excellence in science as were the fathers of modern science. We have lost our sense of what T. F. Torrance calls "science as a religious duty." Once assimilated into the culture, the scientific spirit has gained its own momentum, diminishing our awareness of how faith in a sovereign Creator, whose very nature is truth and light, nourishes the scientific spirit.

Natural / Supernatural Dichotomy

Many people today think science undercuts religion. In the prescientific era evidence for God was found everywhere—in anything which defied natural explanation, in, for instance, the unexplainable flashes of lightning and claps of thunder. People no longer attribute events of nature to supernatural magic. Man today "can manage his world and his future as men could not in the past. He can irrigate his deserts rather than pray for rain, can vaccinate his children rather than beg God to spare them from smallpox, can increase food production and regulate population rather than await manna from heaven."[21]

As such phenomena of our experience were explained, "God"

shrank with the narrowing gap of ignorance. Thus, scientific naturalism became "the strongest intellectual enemy of the church."[22] The Spirit of God is popularly understood to be acting providentially only when its effects cannot be understood naturalistically. A spokesman for the charismatic movement, for instance, complains of our being "blinded by a modern world view that intellectually and empirically views all that happens—or may happen—as belonging to the realm of natural forces."[23]

There are said to be not only natural forces evident in our lives, but also spiritual forces. Since God *intervenes* from time to time, the natural account is presumed incomplete, although we recognize that God does *use* natural laws to achieve his creative ends. Human history is perceived as a child's windup toy which is set running toward its appointed destination. Soon, however, it wanders off course, requiring a guiding hand to reach down and correct its aim. Only with the help of numerous interventions does the toy reach its master's goal. By this view nature is basically autonomous, but occasionally needs to be tinkered with by the divine mechanic. God is the spectator rather than the author of events in this world.

Biblical View: Unity of Divine and Natural

To this familiar dualism of God versus nature, the Scriptures speak a resounding NO! Dichotomizing events as either natural or supernatural, for example, viewing Scripture as either inspired *or* cultural, radically misconceives the relation of the Creator to his continuing creation. In biblical thought, nature does not function apart from God—it is sustained by his power and graced by his providence. "If God's activity were withdrawn, the object of his creation would no longer exist. The carpenter may presumably leave his table without imperiling its existence, but not so the God who participates in the life and being of his creatures. He is never merely the spectator of the world."[24] This conception of God's activity is expressed in the familiar Christian doctrine that God is immanent (indwelling) within his creation as well as transcending (exceeding, surpassing) it.

Christians who are worried about the success of scientific explanation fail to understand that a biblical view need not depend upon there being some gap or hole in the natural account of things to leave room for God's intervention. As Donald MacKay noted:

'Room' is not what we want for God's action; for nothing is held in being apart from his creative power. 'Natural laws' are neither necessary nor even available to Him as an instrument of creation; for He creates by a mere word, and what we call natural laws emerge only *post hoc* as features of and within the created order.[25]

We demean God if we believe his action is limited to extras introduced here and there. Is the Holy Spirit a *separate* psychological force, with observable effects distinct from those of nature, and could it therefore be included among a list of causal factors, as was the master's hand in our windup toy simile? Such a view diminishes our respect for the sovereign Lord of history. It makes no sense to think that God needs to "intervene" in order to accomplish his will, for all events of the natural world are already dependent on his activity.

This understanding of God's hidden action within the fabric of nature is illustrated in Michael Novak's comment on the congeniality of Thomas Aquinas and B. F. Skinner: "For Aquinas, grace operates (except in the rarest cases) through the ordinary contingencies and processes of nature. . . . The whole environment, the whole 'schedule of contingencies' that constitutes history, is graced."[26] This is not to deny that God could and does sometimes act in ways which we must consider supernatural. The biblical miracles and, especially, the incarnation and resurrection defy our categories of cause and effect.

To sum up, the biblical view of God and nature is that the universe is governed by God, who is revealed throughout creation and in the events of human history; he is active and ever-present. "For us there is one God, the Father, from whom are all things and for whom we exist, and one Lord, Jesus Christ, through whom are all things and through whom we exist."[27] Because the God of redemption is the God of creation, the various manifestations of the Word must recite a consistent story; God presumably does not contradict himself. True conflict between revelation in nature and in Scripture is impossible because both are authored by the same God.

Christian Response to Secular Scholarship

Believing God to be the author of all truth, from whatever source it comes, encourages the pursuit of truth on all fronts. Is this not part of what it means to worship God with our minds? Christians ought never to agree with Don Quixote that "facts are the enemy of the truth." And is this not why Christians can be enthusiastic about the vigorous pursuit of scholarship without having to create a special "Christian biology" or "Christian psychology"? We have no "Christian life" distinct from a "professional life" in science because our commitment to excellence in science is a part of an all-encompassing Christian commitment. "Christian science is *good* science. And good science is science that is faithful to the structure of reality."[28] Human conceptual systems are, to be sure, always imperfect models of objective reality, and they are, as we shall later see, inevitably influenced by implicit presuppositions that lie beneath them. Our commitment must thus be to exploring the reality beyond our systems, not to the systems themselves. Nevertheless, if John Calvin was right to assert that "in everything we deal with God," then there is no easy dichotomy of sacred and secular.

I shudder when advised that the task of the Christian psychologist is to *resist* advances in scientific explanation when they come from secular sources. Surely, such advice is foreign to biblical religion: John declared in his gospel that the Word is "the true light that enlightens every man," even those who do not recognize it.[29] If the Spirit of God is the only source of truth, then we will not despise the truth, wherever it is revealed, lest we offend the Spirit of God. For the Apostle Paul, God's nature has "been visible, ever since the world began, to the eye of reason in the things he has made."[30]

Paul reminded the Philippians that one's motive for preaching mattered little; what mattered was that the Truth be preached. Calvin advised much the same attitude toward secular scholars. We cannot read them, he wrote,

without great admiration. We marvel at them because we are compelled to recognize how preeminent they are. But shall we count anything praiseworthy or noble without recognizing at the same time that it comes from God? . . . Those men whom Scripture (I Cor. 2:14) calls "natural men" were, indeed, sharp and penetrating in their investigation of inferior things. Let us, accordingly, learn by their example how many gifts the Lord left to human nature even after it was despoiled of its true good. . . . If the Lord has willed that we be helped in physics, dialectic mathematics, and other like disciplines, by the work and ministry of the ungodly, let us use this assistance. For if we neglect God's gift freely offered in these arts, we ought to suffer just punishment for our sloths.[31]

Problem: When Naturalism Becomes Reductionism

Does rejecting the natural/supernatural dualism mean that Christians must simply conform to the assumptions of thoroughgoing naturalism? Are we thereby obliged to deny the uniqueness and dignity of the human person? An assumption common to a number of recent popular books—Jacques Monod's *Chance and*

Necessity, B, F. Skinner's *Beyond Freedom and Dignity,* Desmond Morris's *The Naked Ape,* Dean Woolridge's *Mechanical Man*—is that once a naturalistic account of the person is achieved, little more will remain to be said. "Man is a machine" implicitly becomes "man is *only* a machine." Critics who charge that this reductionism is dehumanizing are sometimes consoled that Skinner's views do not change reality, for no theory changes what it is a theory about. We are reminded that if Skinner is wrong and what he calls "the literatures of freedom and dignity" turn out to be correct, then his mechanistic analysis cannot possibly succeed, and the practical applications of his theory are doomed to failure. If we are free, we are, as Jean-Paul Sartre declared, not free to cease being free. So why fear the potential applications of a theory we believe to be untrue—unless we secretly suspect that it *is* true?

What this response fails to recognize is the enormously important fact that people *are* changed by what they believe to be true. Our basic assumptions regarding human behavior lay the foundation for our social and political values and for our conceptions of ourselves. This is why I have written this book integrating biblical and psychological images of the person. Our views of human nature lead to some very practical consequences that we need to explore. First, however, we must better understand why the naturalistic account of human behavior does not render other perspectives meaningless, why scientific explanation need not imply the reduction of human thought and action to "nothing but" biology and social conditioning.

LEVELS OF EXPLANATION

If we are to understand why scientific and religious explanations need not be considered mutually exclusive, we must recognize that there are a variety of possible ways by which one might explain a given event, all of which can be simultaneously true in their own terms. An exhaustive description at one level does not invalidate explanation at some other level. For example, there are many levels at which we could describe the action of the brain. We could describe its atomic and biochemical composition, the individual cells within it and how they interact, the evolutionary history of these neurons, the feelings and observable responses of the person, and so on. A statement like "She is angry" could be provided with a description at any one of these varying levels. Which one is relevant depends on the circumstances.

This argument can be portrayed graphically as a hierarchy of disciplines. (See Figure 1.) Each discipline incorporates knowl-

```
┌─────────────────────────────────────────────┐
│                                               │
│      HOLISTIC OR SYSTEMS EXPLANATIONS         │
│                 Theology                      │
│                                               │
│                    .                          │
│                                               │
│                    .                          │
│                                               │
│                    .                          │
│                                               │
│                 Sociology                     │
│             Social Psychology                 │
│                Psychology                     │
│                Physiology                     │
│               Microbiology                    │
│                Chemistry                      │
│                 Physics                       │
│                                               │
│                                               │
│       ELEMENTAL, UNIT EXPLANATIONS            │
│                                               │
└─────────────────────────────────────────────┘
```

Figure 1. Hierarchy of Disciplines.

edge from other, more elemental disciplines as phenomena are considered which transcend the more elemental understandings.[32]

It is interesting to note the way in which this hierarchy tends to be reflected in the course requirements of academic departments. Religion students are urged to take social science courses. Students in sociology or communications are often urged to study psychology, since psychology is to some extent incorporated into the higher level social sciences. Psychology faculty highly recommend that psychology students take biology, which is foundational to their chosen discipline. Biology majors all study chemistry, and chemistry students cannot escape without studying enough physics to comprehend the structure of the atoms chemistry manipulates.

Bear in mind that these levels of explanation are not given to us by nature. They are convenient categories defined by the questions and methods of the scholars in these fields. Furthermore, the boundaries between these levels of explanation are not sharply defined; a series of overlapping circles best describes the hierarchy. Psychology, for example, is concerned with three levels—physiology, conscious experience, and public behavior—and with their interrelationships.

Confusion results when any one of these levels is asserted to be primary, as in the needless debates over whether psychoses are biochemical abnormalities or socially induced. Since a given event can very often be described by simultaneous, correlated explanations at various levels, it makes no sense to say that one level is causing the other—to say, for example, if someone is angry, that the brain state is causing the anger or that the anger is causing the brain state.[33] The emotional and the physiological perspectives are simply two ways of looking at the same event.

Now for the important point: if we are to welcome scientific advances at the elemental levels without succumbing to reductionism, we must remember that explanation at an elemental level need not invalidate or diminish higher level explanations. Whole systems need also to be understood at the level of the whole. The point is cleverly illustrated by the British scientist and philosopher Donald MacKay.[34] Suppose some mathematicians are standing by their computer, awaiting the solution of an elegant equation. Some computer engineers wander in and explain the mathematical transformations at the level of computer electronics. Would we not think them fools should they then claim to have reduced mathematics to electronics and to have started work on a book translating mathematics into electronics, to be titled *Beyond Mathematics?*

In an era when Skinner's behaviorism is stirring up so much controversy, it is encouraging that within psychology there is now a growing recognition of the usefulness of the mentalistic ("cognitive") level of explaining behavior. It is increasingly evident, for example, that a person's behavior is much more likely to be affected by its consequences when the person is aware of what is being reinforced.[35]

We need also to be aware that the *meaning* of an event may transcend its reductionistic description. Another of MacKay's delightful analogies helps. We can understand the principles of a neon sign—how the filaments work, how the current goes through, how the atoms are broken down into electrons with positive ions going in opposite directions to maintain beautiful colors—perfectly well without realizing that what it says is "Joe's Bar and Grill." The meaning of the sign is not reducible to the physical chemistry of the tube. Likewise, the meaning of this sentence is not reducible to its letters, even though the letters make up 100 percent of its content. In the same sense we may affirm, at its own level, the completeness and accuracy of a naturalistic description of the person without retreating for a moment from a conviction that this person is also the noblest work of God's creation. There is meaning at the higher levels of understanding. But we must look there to find it; the meaning does not reside in the component parts.

Once we recognize the complementary nature of various levels of explanation, we are liberated from all the useless argument over whether human nature should be studied scientifically or introspectively and humanistically. It is not an either/or matter. Both methods are valuable for their own purposes. Although in this book particular attention is paid to the fruits of scientific research, I do not for a moment denigrate the rich insights of other approaches. Andrew Greeley has written, "Try as it might, psychology cannot explain the purpose of human existence, the meaning of human life, the ultimate destiny of the human person."[36] If at some time there is a preoccupation with science and a negation of higher level questions, then we may expect that eventually the human need to find meaning, purpose, and commitment will reassert itself.

Naturalistic and religious understandings of the person can complement one another, then, just as the sun's rising can be viewed both as a natural process and as the result of God saying each morning, "Sun, get up!" Indeed, we all accept the unity of religious and natural explanation when we thank both God and the farmer for the food on our table. Only a few days ago, I witnessed the birth of my third child. As my wife still lay on the delivery table I thanked her, thanked the doctor, and thanked God. Did the gratitude given my wife and her doctor subtract from my gratitude to God? Of course not. God was present and acting in this natural event, just as God acts through every part of our lives and environment.

If theological explanation of human behavior is generally not on the same plane as scientific explanation, then there is no longer a need to seek gaps in the scientific accounts. If God's action is properly seen as the ultimate cause—not merely as a particular cause, but as the ground of all events—then the Holy Spirit need not be injected into a psychological explanation of an event in order to understand it as God's redemptive work.

Those who feel threatened by advances in the behavioral sciences can therefore relax. Rather than hope and proclaim that the human sciences will never succeed, they can welcome scientific advances, recognizing that questions of religious meaning are higher level questions. Divine intention is, in one sense, superfluous to the scientific account of human behavior, just as human intention is superfluous to the physiological account of my hand movements. Yet psychology is not just something to do until the biologist comes, nor is religion merely something to occupy us until psychology arrives.

Scientists can say that religious speculation is irrelevant, that "we have no need of the God hypothesis." In a sense they are right. The religious understanding of nature is not intended to enter scientific description merely as an extra causal factor. It rather speaks to questions which science cannot answer: What is the source and destiny of nature? Who am I? Why am I here? What ought I to do? The language of psychology is appropriate, and *only* appropriate, to its own purposes. It is richer than physical explanation, but impoverished compared to religious understanding, for the Christian's experience makes sense at the deepest level only when it is understood as a dialogue with God. Consequently it is

no longer necessary to debate whether Christian conversion is a psychological or a theological experience. Christian conversion can be understood only when described as a psychological *and* a theological experience, as well as a biological, biochemical, and biophysical experience. It is no longer necessary to debate whether man is a machine or a person created by God. Man can be understood only when described as a machine and as a person created by God, created with real personality in the image of a personal God but functioning on the biological, biochemical, and biophysical levels according to the laws that govern the rest of nature as well.[37]

An important corollary is that a successful psychological account of someone's religious conversion or commitment need not undermine that person's conviction of its truth. Whether your beliefs are true or false is a separate question from why you happen to believe as you do.[38] If one person's atheism and another person's theism were both explained in terms of their family backgrounds and psychological make-ups, this explanation would imply nothing about the actual existence or nonexistence of God. It is a logical blunder for someone to say, "your belief is not true—you just believe it because . . ." A small child's beliefs that the tooth fairy exists and that Columbus sailed to America are both acquired by mere hearsay; knowing the sources of those beliefs tells us nothing about their truth. Psychological analyses of religious commitment (such as will be presented in Chapters 5 and 6) are therefore no substitute for the higher level religious meaning of that commitment. This point frequently escapes people, causing unnecessary hostility among Christians toward psychological explanation and unwarranted religious skepticism among psychologists. Once, after Archbishop William Temple gave an address at Oxford, a questioner opened the discussion with a challenge: "Well, of course, Archbishop, the point is that you believe what you believe because of the way you were brought up." To which the Archbishop reportedly replied: "That is as it may be. But the fact remains that you believe I believe what I believe because of the way I was brought up, because of the way you were brought up."[39]

Does the perspective of nature and supernature as a unity diminish our confidence in the power of prayer or in the reality of the Spirit of God? No, it simply reminds us that what is understood naturalistically can also be understood as the Spirit of God at work—God in the present tense. If anything, this should *strengthen* our concept of the Spirit, for it does not limit the Spirit to special acts only. If someone gives a satisfactory naturalistic explanation of an unusual happening, a spiritual event, or an outcome of prayer, does this threaten one's sense of divine providence at work? Not for Christians who see the presence of God in the whole of creation. Unlike the faith of those who assign the Spirit of God to the gaps in natural explanation, a true biblical faith will not be undercut by advances in the human sciences. Christians need not first persuade people to abandon naturalistic understandings before helping them to see that events may be simultaneously understood in religious terms. C. S. Lewis nicely illustrates the point:

In the play, *Hamlet*, Ophelia climbs out on a branch overhanging a river: the branch breaks, she falls in and drowns. What would you reply if anyone asked, 'Did Ophelia die because Shakespeare for poetic reasons wanted her to die at that moment—or because the branch broke?' I think one would have to say, 'For both reasons.' Every event in the play happens as a result of other events in the play, but also every event happens because the poet wants it to happen. All events in the play are Shakespearian events; similarly all events in the real world are providential events. All events in the play, however, come about (or ought to come about) by the dramatic logic of events. Similarly all events in the real world (except miracles) come about by natural causes. 'Providence' and Natural causation are not alternatives; both determine every event because both are one.[40]

Am I attacking a straw man? Most Christians, if they stopped to think about it, would agree that God acts within and through nature because, after all, nature is *his* creation. Still, when it comes right down to understanding and talking about human nature, many Christians evidence very much of a God-of-the-gaps religion. Since, by this view, that which is left for God to explain grows smaller and smaller as natural explanation expands, there emerges a great need to "protect" God by attacking science, by focusing attention on unusual or seemingly miraculous events, or by retreating into the mystical spirtuality of an otherworldly religion. These are not biblical responses, because in isolating God from natural processes, they deny the incarnational current that runs through the Bible. Carl and LaVonne Braaten have noted that the

Old Testament idea of the Spirit as the creative sources of bodily life means that we can speak of the Spirit in the common life of people in the world. We do not have to adopt a spiritual tone and dwell upon psychic phenomena privy to a handful of pious people. The Spirit is at work in nature and in history, in creation and in redemption, in the individual and in the group, in culture and in religion, in the nature and in the Church. For the Spirit is the source of life—all life.[41]

Evolution provides another illustration of how a phenomenon can be understood from *both* naturalistic and religious perspectives. That humanity has evolved by mechanisms of chance, as Jacques Monod argued, can be granted and yet understood from another perspective as Providential. William Pollard spoke eloquently to this point: "The Christian sees the chances and accidents of history as the very warp and woof of the fabric of providence which God is ever weaving." Providence is not an added force in nature "whose operation produces discernible and verifiable empirical consequences by means of which it can be objectively established."[42] It is not God's distortion of natural probability patterns through some extranatural spiritual force.

Scientific inquiry halts at the elementary barrier of chance and accident. "Chance" is not an explanation or cause of anything—it is simply a scientific end-of-the-road. Neither purpose nor purposelessness can be deduced from it. This allows Jacques Monod to speculate that we are "alone in the universe's unfeeling immensity." Yet the continuing openness of the maze through which history threads its course—the conviction that "destiny is written concurrently with the event, not prior to it," to use Monod's words—is just what is required for affirming God's immanence in history, the responsiveness of the chain of events to his hidden will. Which of these views is correct cannot be empirically determined, for science cannot penetrate the final mystery of existence.[43] Thus Rudolph Bultmann concludes:

In faith I realize that the scientific world-view does not comprehend the whole reality of the world and of human life, but faith does not offer another general world-view which corrects science in its statements on its own level. Rather, faith acknowledges that the world-view given by science is a necessary means for doing our work within the world. Indeed,

I need to see the worldly events as linked by cause and effect not only as a scientific observer, but also in my daily living. In doing so there remains no room for God's working. This is the paradox of faith, that faith "nevertheless" understands as God's action here and now an event which is completely intelligible in the natural or historical connection of events.[44]

CONCLUSION

I have argued that just as psychological understanding of a given event is not diminished by physiological explanation (for these are complementary, not competing perspectives), so also a Christian understanding of an event, say of conversion, is not diminished by psychological explanation. Any given reality can legitimately be viewed from multiple perspectives, each of which may be accurate at its own level yet incapable of serving the functions and purposes of other, complementary understandings. One level of explanation is not a substitute for the others. Realizing this can keep us out of the foolish trap of pitting God against his own creation.

Shall we therefore also conclude that science and religion are totally unrelated, that one takes up only where the other leaves off? If that is true, there is nothing more to write. Psychology and Christianity become insulated from each other, and Christian scholars become intellectually schizoid.

The argument does not go this far, for it also entails that there is an ultimate unity to the various levels of explanation. When a three-dimensional figure is projected on a two-dimensional plane, each of several two-dimensional descriptions may be accurate, yet none conveys the whole picture. Nevertheless, the three-dimensional picture is related to the various two-dimensional pictures, so if all pictures are true, there will be consistency among them. "All truth is one"—there is a fundamental continuity and harmony among all things true.

We should therefore find that some translation and bridge building from one level to another is possible, such as is now occurring at the fast moving frontier of biopsychology. Just as biopsychologists explore the connection between the brain and behavior without obliterating the distinction between neurology and psychology, so also we can relate the fruits of psychological research to biblical and theological concepts without forgetting their distinct functions. There will be obstacles in doing so—differences in purpose, in focus, in vocabulary, and in the criteria by which something is judged to be true. Nevertheless, although psychology and religion are not identical, they *do* have their meeting places, some of which will be explored in subsequent chapters. Theology and psychological science both make claims about human nature and both offer propositions concerning observable experience. Yet their integration is largely uncharted, partly because there are so few theologically interested research psychologists. An exciting new challenge therefore awaits those who, in search of a coherent world view, would probe both the essential unity and the apparent tension between religious and scientific perspectives of human nature.

NOTES

1. The Gallup Opinion Index, *Religion in America,* 1975, Report no. 114, American Institute of Public Opinion, 53 Bank St., Princeton, N.J. 08540.

2. Dean R. Hoge, *Commitment on Campus: Changes in Religion and Values over Five Decades* (Philadelphia: Westminster Press, 1974), p. 61.

3. The Gallup Opinion Index, *Religion in America,* 1976, Report no. 130, American Institute of Public Opinion, 53 Bank St., Princeton, N.J. 08540 ($15.00)

4. The Gallup Poll, in syndicated newspapers December 31, 1976; Hoge, *op. cit.* If there has been a religious renewal during the 1970s, it is not yet evident in surveys from college campuses. Students' self-described religious commitments were unchanged from 1969 to 1975 (see Martin Trow, *Aspects of American Higher Education, 1969–1975* [Carnegie Council on Policy Studies on High Education, 2150 Shattuck Ave., Berkeley, Calif., 1977, $2.00]).

5. J. Russell Nazzaro, "Identity Crisis in Psychology," *Change* 8, no. 2 (1976): 44–45.

6. L. Nyman, "Some Odds of Getting into Ph.D. Programs in Clinical and Counseling Psychology," *American Psychologist* 28 (1973): 934–35.

7. *APA Monitor,* January, 1976.

8. Dean M. Kelley, *Why Conservative Churches are Growing* (New York: Harper & Row, 1972).

9. The Gallup Opinion Index, *Religion in America, 1976.* These freshmen versus senior comparisons do not prove that college tends to erode religious commitment. For one thing, the freshmen and seniors were different people, not the same group tested at entrance and exit. It is thus possible that the 1975 seniors were just as irreligious when they entered college. To prove that college is detrimental to religion, it would also need to be shown that comparable changes in religious behavior do not occur among college-age people who are not attending college.

10. Kenneth A. Feldman and Theodore M. Newcomb, *The Impact of College on Students,* vols. 1,2 (San Francisco, Jossey-Bass, 1969).

11. Hoge, *op. cit.,* p. 70.

12. E. C. Lehman, Jr., "Academic Discipline and Faculty Religiosity in Secular and Church-Related Colleges," *Journal for the Scientific Study of Religion* 14 (1975): 205–20.

13. *Chronicle of Higher Education,* April 6, 1970. An earlier survey of

academicians indicated that one one-third of psychologists but more than half of political scientists were as much as "moderately religious"—despite the fact that in other background characteristics the psychologists and political scientists were quite similar (C. G. McClintock, C. B. Spaulding, and H. A. Turner, "Political Orientations of Academically Affiliated Psychologists," *American Psychologist* 20 [1965]: 211–21). In a recent survey of American Psycholgical Association members, 34 percent of the respondents denied the existence of God (C. Regan, H. N. Malony and B. Beit-Hallahmi, "Psychologists and Religion: Professional Factors Associated with Personal Belief" [Paper presented at the American Psychological Association Convention, 1976]). Public opinion surveys indicate that, by comparison, only 3 or 4 percent of Americans share that denial.

14. G. C. Berkouwer, *The Providence of God* (Grand Rapids: Eerdman's, 1952), p. 20.

15. Donald Campbell, "On the Conflicts Between Biological and Social Evolution and Between Psychology and Moral Tradition," *American Psychologist* 12 (1975): 1103–26.

16. Paul C. Vitz attacks humanistic psychology as the enemy of Christianity in *Psychology as Christianity* (Grand Rapids: Eerdmans, 1977).

17. Lynne White, Jr., "The Historical Roots of our Ecologic Crisis," *Science* 155 (1967): 1203–07.

18. Robert K. Merton, *Science, Technology and Society in Seventeenth-Century England* (New York: Fertig, 1970 [first published 1938]). Merton attributes the Puritan spur to science to the attitudes and values of the Puritan ethos as well as to its doctrine of God and nature.

19. R. Hooykaas, *Religion and the Rise of Modern Science* (Grand Rapids: Eerdmans, 1972), pp. 9, 29.

20. Kenneth R. Hardy, "Social Origins of American Scientists and Scholars," *Science* 185 (1974): 497–506. M. Elizabeth Tidball and Vera Kistiakowsky's "Baccalaureate Origins of American Scientists and Scholars" (*Science 193* [1976]: 646–52) indicates that among the top twenty five colleges and universities in the proportion of male graduates who obtained the Ph.D. between 1920 and 1969 (excluding the 1940s), eight were members of the Great Lakes Colleges Association, making this group of twelve midwestern small colleges proportionally the country's richest source of Ph.D. scholars and scientists. To give the reader a feel for these surprising findings, I point to my own institution, Hope College, which was in a virtual tie for twentieth place with Harvard and Wabash.

21. Roger L. Shinn, *New Directions in Theology Today*, vol. 6, (Philadelphia: Westminster Press, 1968), p. 54.

22. Paul Meehl et al., *What Then is Man?* (St. Louis: Concordia Publishing House, 1958), p. 173.

23. J. Rodman Williams, *The Era of the Spirit* (Plainfield, N.J.: Logos International, 1971).

24. L. Charles Birch, "Creation and the Creator," in *Science and Religion: New Perspectives on the Dialogue*, ed. Ian Barbour (New York: Harper & Row, 1968), p. 194.

25. Donald M. MacKay, "The Sovereignty of God in the Natural World," *Scottish Journal of Theology* 21 (1968): 13–26.

26. Michael Novak, "Is He Really a Grand Inquisitor?," in *Beyond the Punitive Society*, ed. Harvey Wheeler (San Francisco: W. H. Freeman, 1975), p. 235.

27. 1 Cor. 8:6, RSV.

28. Richard Bube, "Editorial," *Journal of the American Scientific Affiliation* 23, no. 1 (1971): 1–4.

29. John 1:9, RSV.

30. Rom. 1:20, NEB.

31. John Calvin, *Institutes of the Christian Religion*, II, II, 15–16 (John T. McNeill, ed., Ford L. Battles, trans.), Westminster, 1975, pp. 274–75. Christians who deny Calvin's contention that they have much to learn from secular scholarship are denying the doctrine of common grace.

32. Regarding the place of theology, "the queen of the sciences," in this hierarchy, Michael Polanyi comments: "A universe constructed as an ascending hierarchy of meaning . . . is very different from the picture of a chance collocation of atoms. . . . The vision of such a hierarchy inevitably sweeps on to envisage the meaning of the universe as a whole. Thus natural knowing expands continuously into knowledge of the supernatural" ("Faith and Reason," *Journal of Religion* 41 [1961]: 237–47).

33. Steven Rose, *The Conscious Brain* (New York: Alfred A. Knopf, 1973), pp. 18–24.

34. Donald MacKay, "Case Against Freedom," a debate with B. F. Skinner on *Firing Line*, October 17, 1971. (For transcript send 25¢ to P.O. Box 5966, Columbia, South Carolina 29205)

35. Albert Bandura now concludes that "since consequences affect behavior through the influence of thought, beliefs about schedules of reinforcement can exert greater influence on behavior than the reinforcement itself. . . . Incidence of behavior that has been positively reinforced does not increase if individuals believe, based on other information, that the same actions will not be rewarded on future occasions. . . . ("Self-Efficacy: Toward a Unifying Theory of Behavioral Chage," *Psychological Review* 84, [1977]: 192).

The need for holistic understanding is also exemplified at the level of social institutions. The conservative impulse to reform institutions by converting the individuals who comprise them is just as reductionistic as understanding the person only in terms of physical parts. It fails to recognize that·evil transcends individuals, that institutions and political systems can, in the Revelation image, become bestial and demonically corrupt well-meaning people.

36. Andrew M. Greeley, "Pop Psychology and the Gospel," *Theology Today* 23, (1976): 224–31.

37. Richard H. Bube, *The Human Quest* (Waco, Texas: Word Books, 1971), p. 35.

38. Except when your belief is about why you believe. If you believe that your beliefs are beyond natural explanation, then a satisfactory natural explanation *would* contradict that belief.

39. Malcolm Jeeves recounts this story in *Psychology and Christianity: The View Both Ways* (Downer's Grove, Illinois: InterVarsity Press, 1976), p. 133.

40. C. S. Lewis, *Miracles* (New York: Macmillan, 1947), pp. 213–14.

41. Carl and LaVonne Braaten, *The Living Temple* (New York: Harper & Row, 1976), p. 12.

42. William Pollard, *Chance and Providence* (New York: Harper, 1958), pp. 71, 78.

43. Daniel Callahan, "Faith and Reason and Survival," *Christianity and Crisis* 32 (1972): 175–78.

44. Rudolph Bultmann, *Jesus Christ and Mythology* (New York: Scribners, 1958), p. 65.

CHAPTER 2

Psychological Science and Human Values

Before relating recent psychological research to theology, we should first understand the extent to which the theories of both psychologists and theologians are controlled by their underlying assumptions and values. Religion and science are popularly thought to involve entirely different ways of thinking. Science is said to be objective. It proposes theories which are proved true or false in light of factual observations. Religion, by contrast, is seen as subjective. Some even argue that because religious beliefs cannot be falsified by objective evidence, they have no real meaning.

During the past fifteen years philosophers of science have convincingly shown that this old view of science is unrealistic.[1] The image of a purely objective science against which religion is found wanting has been rejected. Scientific theories are not, in fact, directly verified or falsified by clear, incontestable observations. The notion of "crucial experiments" which prove or disprove a theory is a myth. More frequently, a theory is modified to accommodate disconfirming results until, eventually, like too many straws piled on a camel's back, the cumulative effect prompts a new way of viewing reality.

Theories are resilient to disconfirming evidence because they are not simple, descriptive pictures of reality to begin with. They are products of our imagination, mental constructs which attempt to simplify and impose some coherence on the external world. In creating and testing these theoretical models we must begin with certain assumptions about the nature of reality, about what we will accept as relevant data, and about what constitutes an acceptable theory. These assumptions control the construction and rejection of theories. Yet they operate unconsciously because they are generally shared by the community of scientists at work in any given field. It is only when someone challenges these "control beliefs" that we step back and reflect seriously about them.

If this picture of science is correct, then it is only a short step to argue, as Nicholas Woltersdorff has done, that "the religious beliefs of the Christian scholar ought to function as *control* beliefs within his devising and weighing of theories."[2] His argument is not restricted to Christians—all people are urged to be true to themselves by seeking consistency and wholeness among their beliefs and commitments.

Historically, Woltersdorff contends, the control beliefs of the secular scientist have been unquestioned. Christians have sought to harmonize or adapt their beliefs to fit new theories, or interpreted the theories within a larger Christian context, or offered Christian applications of scientific theories. Better it would be, he argues, to relate science and Christian belief more fundamentally. This means that sometimes the discoveries of science will prompt revisions in the understanding of Christian belief. It certainly also means, Woltersdorff concludes, that Christian scholars should bring their beliefs to bear upon their research and see the world through the spectacles of informed Christian theology and philosophy.

I will demonstrate below the dynamics of control beliefs with some examples of psychologists' blindness to their own presuppositions. I hope to show that we psychologists are indeed influenced by our world views, and that, therefore, we had better think consciously about what presuppositions and values should shape our theory and research. First, however, a few words of qualification are in order.

DANGERS OF SUBORDINATING SCIENTIFIC THEORIES TO RELIGIOUS DOGMA

At first blush one shudders at recollections of submissions of scientific theories to religious tests. Is it not clear from history that Christian belief does not guarantee an inside track to objective truth? Would anyone care to provide evidence for a correlation between the depth of a scholar's Christian belief and the quality of his or her scientific work? And if there is such a correlation, is it because the Christian's beliefs have provided a reliable guide in scientific endeavors?[3]

The scientific merit of Christian beliefs seems, in fact, to be a presumption of many Christians. Consider the "Calvinistic philosophy" of Herman Dooyewerd: "The Bible is the final norm" for science. "All scientific thought which either denies or conflicts with God's Word is condemned." God's revelation in nature "can only be understood correctly in the light of the special revelation of

Scripture. Calvinistic philosophy wants to do just that. It is the *scientific investigation of the cosmic totality in complete submission to the Word of God*." [4]

This suggests that Christian beliefs are somehow immune to the distortions which infect scientific theory. But are they? The diversity of existing theologies and biblical interpretations indicate the finiteness of all such thought and the consequent danger of subjecting wholesale one's understanding of natural revelation, socially conditioned as this may also be, to any particular understanding of biblical revelation. The Christian's ultimate loyalty is to God and to humble pursuit of God's truth, not to any human conceptual system. Just as scientific models are human abstractions, not something handed to us by nature, so also our theologies and philosophies are human abstractions, not something written directly by God on tablets of stone. We must therefore be careful not to idolize any human abstraction as ultimate truth, even if it goes by the name of "Christian psychology" or "Calvinist philosophy." History records too many instances of Christendom's departure from truth to allow us to identify our own thinking with God's. Because *both* biblical and scientific data are part of divine revelation and because both are viewed through the spectacles of our implicit control beliefs, we should be wary of subjecting one to the other.

The subjection of science to control beliefs is not unique to Christians. Lysenko rejected modern genetics because it contradicted the Stalinist version of Marxism and therefore was presumed false. By 1948, when Lysenko had become the autocrat of Soviet biology and education, research in standard genetics was virtually outlawed. More recently, Ricardo Zuniga and others have called for the submission of social science to leftist ideology.[5]

To all such attempts at subordinating science to external authority we are eager to cry, No! To do science means to remain open to reality and not to force upon it prior conclusions from any source. When Kepler discovered that the orbit of the planet Mars departed from the dogma of uniform and circular heavenly motion, he struggled for several years and then "submitted to given facts rather than maintaining an age-old prejudice; in his mind a Christian empiricism gained the victory over platonic rationalism."[6]

Some people therefore say that the only established dogma in science is that scientists should not accept established dogma. This is a bit simplistic, as Woltersdorff, Thomas Kuhn, and others make evident. Scientists, successful scientists especially, operate from their basic assumptions, even if they are blind to their own metaphysics and values. Nevertheless, pursuit of the one Truth compels us to free science from the authoritarian constraints of any ideology. It also compels us to beware of reducing theological critique of science to what Charles Kraft calls the kind of ground-hogism practiced by many evangelical theologians and preachers who simply come out "whenever some important behavioral science issue surfaces to critique what they understand of the issue before retreating into the safety of the accustomed hole."[7]

The pitfalls of subjecting science to religious dogma flash as warning signals, admonishing us to give our allegiance to pursuit of the infinite Truth, not to human authority or to the world view of any culture, past or present. Christians take Scriptures to be the "rule of faith and life"; the creeds do not claim that the Bible provides the content of politics, economics, or science. On scientific matters biblical revelation is obviously incomplete. Is it not like a parent's explanation of reproduction to a child? The important things are told, but the details will be understood only as maturity increases. As Jesus told his disciples, there was much more to be revealed after he had left them. The wisdom of God revealed in the whole of creation is inexhaustible, making science an endless pursuit.

These cautions should not, however, obscure the philosophers' fundamental point—that scientists are deeply influenced by their own world views. Among social scientists, at least, there is an increasing awareness of the extent to which implicit assumptions determine our view of the world. To this we now return.

THE SOCIAL PSYCHOLOGY OF PSYCHOLOGICAL KNOWLEDGE

There is a growing awareness within the scientific community that the order we impute to nature is imposed upon it. Scientific concepts are creations of the mind, not inherent in the objective world. "There are *no bare uninterpreted data*. . . . Man supplies the categories of interpretation, right from the start."[8] In order to interpret what we observe, we create symbolic models to represent the unobservable. These theoretical models, such as the billiard-ball model of gas or a mathematical model of learning processes, are more than useful fictions, yet less than literal pictures of reality. Ian Barbour contends this is common to science and theology—both walk a path between pure fiction and literal truth. This is why we often discover, in both science and theology, that no single model is adequate to the task, forcing us to accept the paradoxes of complementary models—as in the wave and particle theories of microphysics or in the theologian's simultaneous affirmation of human freedom and divine sovereignty.

Figure 2. From *Psychology Today,* Third Edition. Copyright © 1975 by Random House, Inc. Reprinted by permission of CRM Books, a Division of Random House, Inc.

This subjectivity within the scientific enterprise opens the door to Woltersdorff's control beliefs. What scientist has not felt the emotions imputed by Michael Polanyi:

Viewed from the outside as we described him the scientist may appear as a mere truth-finding machine steered by intuitive sensitivity. But this view takes no account of the curious fact that he is himself the ultimate judge of what he accepts as true. . . . The scientist appears acting here as detective, policeman, judge and jury all rolled into one. He apprehends certain clues as suspect; formulates the charges and examines the evidence both for and against it, admitting or rejecting such parts of it as he thinks fit, and finally pronounces judgment. Far from being neutral at heart, he is himself passionately interested in the outcome of the procedure. . . . The scientist ought to be delighted when his theory, supported by a series of previous observations, appears to collapse in the light of his latest experiments. If he was wrong, then he has just escaped establishing falsehood and been given a timely warning to turn in a new direction. But that is not how he feels. He is dejected and confused, and can only think of possible ways of explaining away the obstructive observation.[9]

Here we can continue to draw a parallel between science and theology, for as Rudolph Bultmann declares, "the basic presupposition for every form of exegesis" is "that your own relation to the subject-matter prompts the question you bring to the text and elicits the answers you obtain from the text."[10] Both scientists and theologians begin from assumptions which shape their interpretation of the data. And both have tendencies to turn their models into absolutes, to miss the distinction between their models and the reality which they crudely describe.

What is true of scientist and theologian is also true of each of us: *our* beliefs and perceptions are controlled by our underlying assumptions. We impose order on what we observe, and the order we impose controls our interpretations. For instance, look at Figure 2. What do you see in it? Can you see a Dalmatian dog on the right sniffing the ground at the center of the picture? Until you were given this perceptual "set," you were probably blind to what those who have the set see. But once your mind has the set, it controls your interpretation of the picture—so much so that it becomes difficult *not* to see the dog. This is the way our minds work. While reading these words you have probably been unaware, until this moment, that you are looking at your nose. This illustrates a common phenomenon—the mind blocking from awareness something that is there, if only we were predisposed to perceive it. Our tendency to prejudge reality on the basis of our expectations is one of the most important facts about the human mind.

Another classic demonstration of how our presuppositions control our interpretations was provided by a Princeton-Dartmouth football game some years ago.[11] The game lived up to its billing as a grudge match; it turned out to be one of the roughest and dirtiest games in the history of either school. A Princeton All-American was gang-tackled, piled on, and finally forced out of the game with a broken nose. Fist fights erupted, and further injuries occurred on both sides.

Not long after the game, two psychologists, one from each school, showed films of the game to students on each campus. The students acted as objective scientists, noting each infraction as they watched and who was responsible for it. As you might suppose, there was a strong tendency at each school for the students to see their fellow students as the victims rather than the agents of illegal aggression. Princeton students, for example, saw twice as many Dartmouth violations as the Dartmouth students saw.

More recent experimental research confirms that people tend to use information which fits their intuitive suppositions and ignore information which does not.[12] C. S. Lewis recognized this phenomenon many years ago. "What we learn from experience," he said, "depends on the kind of philosophy we bring to experience."[13] In all areas of human thinking—whether reading Scripture, doing science, or interpreting historical events—our prior beliefs control the way we view and interpret information. This is not necessarily bad—it enabled the Hebrew people to see God's mercy and providence in their historical experience, and it enables a community of scientists to work from a shared perspective. But it is true, and knowing it is true can keep us from taking our scientific interpretations too seriously.

These contentions about science in general seem especially applicable to the social sciences. The human sciences inevitably unfold within a social-historical context of control beliefs and values.[14] For example, Freud and Skinner have operated from different assumptions as to what constitutes acceptable data and acceptable theory, just as our views of acupuncture, ESP, and flying saucers are influenced by our implicit control beliefs. Our observations are always theory-laden. There *is* an objective reality, but we are always viewing it through our own spectacles. This being the case, we had better identify the beliefs and values implicit in our theorizing. To exemplify my advice, I will examine my own discipline, asking how values control psychological thinking.

HIDDEN VALUES IN PSYCHOLOGY

Value considerations obviously bear upon our ethical standards in doing research and therapy in psychology and upon our selection of which investigations and applications are right and good. Less often recognized are the subtle ways in which value commitments masquerade as objective truth. The social sciences seem especially vulnerable to the expounding of values in the guise of fact. Unlike workers in the physical sciences, whose data are more value free, and in the humanities, which are knowingly explicit about values, psychologists, sociologists, and educational theorists often mistakenly see themselves as making objective, value-free conjectures about truth. Some concrete examples will illustrate the pervasiveness of hidden values in psychology.

Among clinicians, the penetrating analyses of Thomas Szasz are well known. *Mental illness* is actually defined, not in medical terms as are other illnesses, but in terms of deviant communication or behavior. Much as we like individualism as an abstract idea, we tend to dislike real individuals. For them, a psychiatric label can serve as a convenient semantic blackjack, as was vividly evident in *One Flew Over the Cuckoo's Nest*.

Hidden values have also been apparent in many real life situations. When publisher Ralph Ginsburg printed the diagnoses of liberal psychiatrists indicating that presidential aspirant Barry Goldwater exhibited paranoid tendencies, something more than a medical judgment about the Arizona Senator was being expressed. Fifteen years ago, who had heard of school children suffering "learning disabilities"? Now some people are suggesting that there are five million "learning disabled children" in our schools. Without disputing the fact that some children are handicapped by brain disorders, we may still wonder if the diagnostic label is not sometimes applied because it allows the school to blame a teaching failure on the child. Much of the current discussion of "gifted children" presumes that "giftedness" is an objective entity which a child has or does not. The arbitrariness of all such definitions escapes people.

Diagnostic labels are not just neutral descriptions of people. Once a person is assigned to a diagnostic category, the label can influence our perception and interpretation of the person's behavior. David Rosenhan and seven colleagues demonstrated this after gaining admission to twelve mental hospitals on the basis of the single complaint of hearing voices.[15] Apart from this complaint and giving false names and vocations, they scrupulously reported the truth of their life histories and emotional states. Once admitted, seven of them with the label "schizophrenic," they exhibited no further symptoms and, when questioned by staff, reported they were feeling fine. Nevertheless, they were confined an average of nineteen days and given twenty-one hundred tranquilizers before finally being released. Their normal behaviors, such as note taking, were often overlooked or misinterpreted to fit the staffs' preconceptions about these "patients." The psychological reports of their life histories were also clearly shaped by the diagnosis.

The extent to which medical language can be stretched to camouflage value judgments was evident when the Joint Commission on Mental Health of Children declared that "racism is the number one public health problem facing America today." Racism is an enormous problem, but it is surely not a *health* problem.

Or consider the flip side of the coin—defining what mental health is. We refer to people as mature or immature, as well-adjusted or poorly adjusted, as if these were statements of fact, when they are in reality disguised value judgments. Abraham Maslow, for example, is well known for his sensitive descriptions of the characteristics of "self-actualized" people. Seldom recognized is that since the initial selection of the self-actualized persons to be analyzed was done on a subjective basis by Maslow himself, the resulting description of the self-actualized personality is a statement of Maslow's personal values. I do not mean to demean his values, for his descriptions can be inspiring. I mean only to remind us that such descriptions are not inherent in nature; they are a creation of someone's mind. When Carl Rogers gives us his best professional definition of the "good life," we need to welcome this as a statement of his values—values which emerged from his observations of clients, to be sure—yet not as a scientific assessment which can be judged true or false.

Much of what we teach as humanistic psychology is loaded with implicit value judgments. I have found it helpful to identify these values and compare them with the more traditional values. (Any such delineation is something of a caricature, since there is, of course, a great diversity among both humanistic psychologists and "traditional Americans," and there is considerable overlap between the two categories.)

Humanistic Psychology Values		*Traditional American Values*
Open, honest expression of feelings; sensitivity to others	vs.	Self-control, right to privacy, unemotionalism
Egalitarian (e.g. use of first names)	vs.	Status oriented, respectful
Own feelings as criteria for what is good	vs.	External criteria for what is good
Life goal of fulfillment	vs.	Life goals more materialistic
Existential emphasis on the here and now	vs.	Pragmatic, future orientation
Capacity for joy	vs.	Endurance of stress

My purpose is neither to glorify nor vilify the values implicit in humanistic psychology, but simply to point them out. It clarifies our thinking to distinguish factual statements from statements of value.

If our definition of mental "health" and maturity comes from our values and not our science, then we may also be sure that advice on how to raise children will mix factual presumptions about the effects of different parenting styles with value presumptions about what ends are desirable. Although the appropriate task of the scientist is to specify the effects on children of differing parental behaviors, leaving it to parents to decide what outcomes they value, the typical child-rearing manual is written with little consciousness of implicit values. Consider so impartial a source as the United States Children's Bureau, whose pamphlet *Infant Care* has been distributed to millions of American mothers. Remember now, this is not the work of some fringe psychologist, but our government's statement to the mothers of America. First, from the 1938 edition:

Immediately after birth he will begin to form habits, which if they are the right kind will be useful to him all his life. Regularity from birth on is of first importance. Through training in regularity of feeding, sleeping, and elimination the tiny baby will receive his first lessons in character building. He should learn that hunger will be satisfied only so often, that when he is put into bed he must go to sleep, that crying will not result in his being picked up or played with whenever he likes. He will begin to learn that he is part of a world bigger than that of his own desires.

But the 1942 edition tells a different story:

Suppose a very young baby becomes hungry. He becomes vaguely conscious of discomfort, begins to wiggle and twist, and finally to cry. Soon after he is thoroughly aware of his discomfort his mother appears with a cheerful, quiet voice, a warm bosom, and firm arms. The baby responds by nuzzling about until he finds the nipple and sucks it, and then warm milk flows into his stomach. Not only the milk, but also the warmth, the sense of being held firmly, and probably even the sound of his mother's voice all help to give that baby a sense of comfort. Through many repetitions of this experience the baby responds with pleasure, not only to food but to friendly human contact. Such experiences help him become a likeable, friendly person.

   On the other hand, to take an extreme example, suppose another baby becomes hungry, and he wiggles, twists, and finally cries as did the first baby described. Instead of having his needs for food and affection satisfied soon, this baby is allowed to cry on and on, and finally a bottle is put into his mouth. . . . He may have so exhausted himself that he is too tired to obtain much pleasure from the food. . . . Eventually . . . the baby may develop an attitude of dislike toward the world and instead of responding in a friendly way he remains withdrawn, fearful and a little suspicious—an attitude that will make his ultimate adjustment to life difficult.

   The contrast between the rigid advice of the 1930s and the more permissive advice of the 1940s reflects not only our limited understanding of the effects of parenting on children, but also differences in the hidden values of their authors. The 1938 advice places a premium on respect for authority and some of the other more traditional values identified above. By 1942, attributes such as security, openness, and independence seem to have become the desired aims. Shortly thereafter, in 1946, Benjamin Spock joined the chorus with the first edition of *The Common Sense Book of Baby and Child Care,* a book which ultimately became the world's third leading best seller (surpassed only by the Bible and Mao's little red book). After research revealed that student activists of the late 1960s tended to come from relatively permissive and democratic homes, Spock reflected on the wisdom of his advice:

The modern crop of youths is not only reassuring, they're inspiring. Our only hope is their thoughtfulness, idealism and realism.

I admit there are problems. But when Norman Vincent Peale accuses me of helping raise spoiled children, I say nonsense. I didn't have that much influence. Besides, he's talking about activists who are against discrimination. Compared with the kids of the 1950s I think they're wonderful. I would be proud to say I helped encourage liberal parents to understand their kids.[16]

If psychological advice inevitably reflects someone's personal values, then the practical lesson is that consumers of psychology should try to discern those values before following the advice. In his latest edition, Benjamin Spock explicitly informs the reader at the outset of his personal goals for children. Many clinicians openly inform clients of their values or encourage clients to decide therapy goals for themselves. Other psychologists would do well to emulate these examples. "The professions' role in a free society," Eliot Freidson argues, "should be limited to contributing the technical information men need to make their own decisions on the basis of their own values. When he preempts the authority to direct, even constrains men's decisions on the basis of his own values, the professional is no longer an expert but rather a member of a new privileged class disguised as expert."[17]

These illustrations of hidden values have been drawn from personality theorizing and from clinical applications. The point can be made just as easily using scientific research in personality and social psychology. The very language in which we report our observations may reflect our judgment of a behavior. Take a person who does not admit to emotional difficulties on an objective personality instrument. Is this person "repressive" or "low anxiety," "defensive" and therefore motivated to give "socially desirable responses" or possessed of "strong ego strength" and "high self-esteem"? These various labels could all describe the same set of responses. The choice of label, therefore, depends on the implicit value judgment which the researcher unconsciously places upon the trait.

Consider the classic research done by American social psychologists on the "authoritarian personality." Roger Brown has noted a striking similarity between this "rigid" character type studied by Americans and the "stable" personality identified by psychologists in pre-Nazi Germany.[18] Shall we condemn this character type for its "ethnocentrism" (American label) or praise it for its strong "in-group loyalty" (German label)?

Social psychology also reflects the individualism of our culture in its description of responsiveness to social influence. It is no mere accident that our terms for this are "conformity," "submissiveness," "compliance," "suggestibility"—all conveying a sense of mindless, docile tractability. Might not a different people with contrasting control beliefs use terms like "corporate consciousness," "group unity," "social sensitivity," "cooperative team play," and "community identification" to describe the same events?

The tendency for our values to subtly influence our descriptive labels which in turn bias our interpretation of events is, to be sure, not unique to psychology. Whether someone engaged in guerilla warfare is labeled a "terrorist" or a "freedom fighter" depends on our sympathy with the cause. "Brainwashing" is social influence we do not approve of. "Perversions" are sex acts we do not practice. A persuasive message is "education" to those who believe it and "propaganda" to those who do not.

The controlling effect of values extends even beyond our choice of descriptive labels. Something more serious than labeling was involved when political motivations prompted a commitment to the idea that intelligence is entirely hereditary. The racist intentions of some pioneers of mental testing transformed IQ tests into a potent political weapon. The ready acceptance of invalid data suggesting varying intelligence in different national groups provided a handy rationale for quotas limiting the immigration of people who were not northern Europeans.

The recent revelation that Cyril Burt's classic evidence for the genetic determinants of intelligence was apparently fraudulent provided a real embarrassment to psychology.[19] Our embarrassment has stemmed not so much from this demonstration of the extremes to which a scientist can go to grind his own axe, for every profession is contaminated by a few dishonest scoundrels. It came rather from the length of time it took us to challenge his data, perhaps because professors were already disposed to believe that their genes made their children naturally bright. Not surprisingly, it was a scholar whose egalitarian values biased him toward refuting the assumption of heritable intelligence who first uncovered the obvious flaws in Burt's evidence.

Leonard Berkowitz has called attention to contrasting conclusions drawn by presidential commissions on violence and on obscenity and pornography, despite parallel findings.[20] The violence commission reasoned that because observing violence is shown to have at least a small, temporary effect on aggressive behavior, we should *tighten* restrictions on media violence. The obscenity commission concluded that because observing sexually explicit material is shown to have only a small, temporary effect on sexual behavior, we should *relax* censorship of such material. Here again, we see how the social sciences both lead and follow the ideas of their age. Of course, because *any* policy recommendation is a product of values as well as facts, Berkowitz's own concerns emerge from his values.

One of the more fascinating areas of recent research in developmental psychology is moral development. Lawrence Kohlberg and others have observed that moral thinking unfolds through a consistent series of stages, just as physical development occurs in a predictable sequence. Few people, however, ever reach the "highest" stage of moral development, the "post-conventional" level of self-chosen moral principles. Experiments have therefore been undertaken to ascertain how people may be stimulated to achieve higher levels of "maturity" in their moral thinking. Notice here a subtle shift from objective *de*scription of stages of moral thinking to *pre*scription of the post-conventional stage, which is essentially equivalent to the application of situation ethics. People have flocked to Kohlberg not only because he has renewed our appreciation for the importance of moral thought and has so effectively described its development, but also, I suspect, because his implicit moral philosophy fits so well with our liberal intellectual control beliefs. By seeming to provide a scientific basis for our own moral thinking, Kohlberg's scheme also provides a handy rationale for judging opposing moral philosophies as "immature." This becomes explicit in Kohlberg's contention that "the scientific theory as to why people factually do move upward from stage to stage, and why they factually *do* prefer a higher stage to a lower, is broadly the same as a moral theory as to why people *should* prefer a higher stage to a lower."[21]

But is it not the case that one could intellectually understand a post-conventional level of moral thinking and yet espouse a preceeding stage of moral thinking (e.g., a subjection-to-the-will-of-God morality), as do many sophisticated philosophers and theologians?[22] Joseph Adelson even suggests that the presumed universalism of the Kohlberg system "conceals an essentially ethnocentric bias, wherein the pinnacle of moral perfection amounts to little more than upper-middle-class American high-mindedness."[23] (The self-contained individualism of Kohlberg's moral ideal also further illustrates the individualistic bias of American psychology.)

Again, my purpose is not to quarrel with the implicit value judgments—in this case, Kohlberg's ethical system. In many of these cases I fully sympathize with the hidden values. I am simply trying to demonstrate that *there is no way to move from objective statements of fact to prescriptive statements of what ought to be without interposing one's values*—a point C. S. Lewis made so cogently in *The Abolition of Man*.[24]

A final illustration comes from experimental psychology. In psychology texts, it is often said that punishment is ineffective as a training method. Actually, learning psychologists have demonstrated that, under some conditions, strong punishment combined with reward for the desired response can be very effective. This fact does not, however, necessarily commend its use, since our value of loving kindness may compel us to use more humane techniques of control. Our valuing of loving kindness rightfully intervenes between our scientific description of the sometime effectiveness of punishment and our prescription of practical advice. This point is apparently missed by those who allow their devaluing of punishment to intrude upon their scientific statements of its actual effectiveness.

I have identified all these examples of hidden values in psychology to drive home the conclusion that psychologists are pervasively influenced by their own world views. They confuse their moral commitments with their knowledge. It is therefore of no small consequence that antipathy to religion and other aspects of cultural orthodoxy is widespread. Small wonder that Donald Campbell created a storm of controversy by arguing in his 1975 presidential address to the American Psychological Association that psychologists' tendency to celebrate individual self-gratification and to deprecate traditional restraints encourages us to discard the wisdom of social evolution. There is functional truth in moral, religious, and social traditions, he contends, and we ignore it at great peril.

If, as I assert, there is in psychology today a general background assumption that the human impulses provided by biological evolution are right and optimal, both individually and socially, and that repressive or inhibitory moral traditions are wrong, in my judgment this assumption may now be regarded as scientifically wrong. . . . Furthermore, in propagating such a background perspective in the teaching of perhaps 90% of college undergraduates (and increasing proportions of high school and elementary school pupils), psychology may be contributing to the undermining of the retention of what may be extremely valuable social-evolutionary inhibitory systems which we do not yet fully understand.[25]

Campbell has challenged the control beliefs implicit in much of psychology. Regardless of whether one agrees with what he proposes, the essential point must not be lost: because values inevitably influence social scientific description and application, we had best reflect on what our implicit values are and learn to be true to ourselves by seeking consistency and wholeness in all our beliefs and commitments.

Because value decisions should properly concern us all, scientists included, we must not abdicate them to the scientists alone. Questions of moral obligation, of purpose and direction, of ultimate meaning, are not directly addressed by a science of behavior. Some writers argue therefore that we should "humanize psychology" to include such questions. Although education in psychology should indeed clarify the assumptions and values which are fundamental to the discipline and should encourage students to be true to their own convictions, we need not make psychology into another competing humanities discipline. It is arrogant and foolish for psychologists to attempt to preempt the insights of religion, philosophy, literature, and the arts. Let the science of behavior be the science of behavior, contributing its insights to one level of discourse, yet humble and unpretentious enough to recognize that many of the deeply significant questions of life are *not* psychological questions and that we ought not talk of them as if they were.

SUMMING UP

Several conclusions have emerged from our consideration of the relationship between religious and scientific explanations of persons.

1. During the past twenty-five years young Americans have become increasingly fascinated with psychology and decreasingly committed to traditional religious orthodoxy and church attendance. It is tempting to speculate that the first trend has contributed to the second because it is also true that education in psychology tends to be associated with irreligiousness.

2. Contrary to popular opinion, biblical thought has, on the whole, historically been congenial to the scientific spirit, at least in the natural sciences. With the old science-religion skirmishes largely behind us in the biological and physical sciences, the newer human sciences are now the primary focus of science-

religion tension. Many people on both sides of the issue surmise an inherent competition between scientific and religious understandings of persons—as one wins the other loses. This distorts the biblical witness by separating God from his own creation, as in the idea that the Spirit of God acts only through divine interventions to fill the gaps in the natural explanation of events.

3. The alternative view is that God acts and reveals himself in every event of the creation, which he continually sustains and upholds. Various levels for comprehending this revelation—the biological, psychological, and religious, among them—are each appropriate and only appropriate to their own level. Thus, a Christian view of psychology will celebrate psychological research as it complements other levels of explanation and yet be sensitive to the inherent limitations of the discipline.

4. There is a fundamental unity to these different levels of explanation, and some of the most exciting scholarship today is at the meeting points of different disciplines. As yet, however, little attention has been given to the integration of theology with psychological research. A new adventure therefore awaits those who probe the integration of biblical and scientific insights regarding human behavior. As Henry Stob has written,

Biblical and natural revelation should never be disjoined; they were meant to interact. It is only from the perspective supplied by the Bible that we can rightly apprehend the message God conveys through the medium of nature and history. And it is only in the light of the experience acquired through our engagement with the space-time world that we are able to read and understand the Bible.[26]

5. Before pursuing the integration of theological and psychological perspectives on human nature, we should first recognize the extent to which the theorizing of both psychologists and theologians is subtly controlled by their underlying assumptions and values. Thus we should (a) be wary of subjecting science to any particular theology or subjecting theology to any current scientific theory; (b) strive to identify and achieve consistency among our beliefs and values, both scholarly and religious; and (c) scrutinize statements made in the name of psychology, including those which I will be making, in order to discern the beliefs and values which are assumed.

The remaining sections of this book relate psychological research and biblical thinking in four different areas. For each of these areas I have put the scientific conclusions and the related religious ideas into separate chapters. Three of the sections begin with a review of recent research and follow with relevant Christian concepts; one does the reverse. In every case the separation between my scientific and religious thinking is actually not so sharp as the chapter divisions might suggest. I have read the research literature while wearing Judeo-Christian spectacles and read biblical and theological scholarship with the mind-set of a research psychologist.

Why hide my own commitment, as do so many academic people? The truth is that if I had no personal interest in Christianity, I would never have gotten involved in this project. I do not apologize for this lack of neutrality because, as we have seen, neutrality seldom exists anyway. In being honest about where I am, my purpose is not to coerce you into agreement, but just the reverse—to stimulate you to reflect upon your own view of human nature and to draw from what follows that which is useful in doing so.

NOTES

1. The best known of these philosophers is Thomas Kuhn. See his *The Structure of Scientific Revolutions,* 2nd. ed. (Chicago Press, 1970).

2. Nicholas Woltersdorff, *Reason within the Bounds of Religion* (Grand Rapids: Eerdmans, 1976), p. 66. This material was first delivered as lectures to the Association of Reformed Colleges in 1974–75, two years before I lectured in the same series.

3. My colleague, James van Putten, raised the last two questions in response to Professor Woltersdorff's lectures.

4. J. M. Spier, *What is Calvinistic Philosophy?* (Grand Rapids: Eerdmans, 1953), pp. 21–22.

5. Ricardo B. Zuniga, "The Experimenting Society and Radical Social Reform: The Role of the Social Scientist in Chile's Unidad Popular Experience," *American Psychologist* 30 (1975): 99–115.

6. R. Hooykaas, Religion and the Rise of Modern Science (Grand Rapids: Eerdmans, 1972), p. 36. Hooykaas goes on to explain how the fathers of modern science considered their secularization of science to be its Christianization because "they had freed science from the human authority of theologians and philosophers and from the oppressive burden of its old idols, forms and ideas" (p. 50). Science becomes truly free when we put off rationalistic preconceptions and become as a little child, humbly open to wherever nature leads.

7. Charles H. Kraft, "Can Anthropoligical Insight Assist Evangelical Theology?" *Christian Scholar's Review* 7 (1977): 165–203, p. 181.

8. Ian Barbour, *Myths, Models and Paradigms* (New York: Harper & Row, 1974), p. 95.

9. Michael Polanyi, *Science, Faith and Society* (Oxford: Oxford University Press, 1964), pp. 38–39.

10. Rudolph Bultmann, *Jesus Christ and Mythology* (New York: Scribners, 1958), p. 51.

11. A. Hastorf and H. Cantril, "They Saw a Game: A Case Study," *Journal of Abnormal and Social Psychology* 49 (1954): 129–34.

12. Icek Ajzen, "Intuitive Theories of Events and the Effects of Base-Rate Information on Prediction," *Journal of Personality and Social Psychology* 35 (1977): 303–14.

13. C. S. Lewis, *Miracles* (New York: Macmillan, 1947), p. 11.

14. See Allan R. Buss, "The Emerging Field of the Sociology of Psychological Knowledge," *American Psychologist* 30 (1975): 988–1002.

15. David L. Rosenhan, "On Being Sane in Insane Places," *Science* 179 (1973): 250–58.

16. *Newsweek,* September 23, 1968, p. 71.

17. Eliot Freidson, *Profession of Medicine: A Study of the Sociology of Applied Knowledge* (New Yok: Dodd, Mead & Co., 1971), p. 382.

18. Roger Brown, *Social Psychology* (New York: Free Press, 1965).

19. See "IQ and Heredity: Suspicion of Fraud Beclouds Classic Experiment," *Science* 194 (1976): 916–19.

20. Leonard Berkowitz, "Sex and Violence: We Can't Have it Both Ways," *Psychology Today* 5, no. 7 (December, 1971): 14, 18, 20, 22, 23.

21. Lawrence Kohlberg, "From is to Ought: How to Commit the Naturalistic Fallacy and Get Away with It in the Study of Moral Development," in *Cognitive Development and Epistemology*, ed. Theodore Mischel (New York: Academic Press, 1971), p. 223.

22. William P. Alston, "Comment on Kohlberg's 'From Is to Ought,' " in Mischel, *op. cit.*, pp. 269–84.

23. Joseph Adelson, "Review of Moral Development," *Science* 190 (1975): 1288–89.

24. The attempt to move from descriptions of what *is* to prescription of what *ought* to be has been termed the *naturalistic fallacy.* I am arguing that we psychologists are often guilty of committing the naturalistic fallacy. Conclusions sometimes drawn from surveys of human sexual behaviors provide another example of this.

25. Donald Campbell, "On the Conflicts Between Biological and Social Evolution and Between Psychology and Moral Tradition," *American Psychologist* 30 (1975): 1103–26.

26. Henry Stob, "The Bible Alone?," *Reformed Journal* 27, no. 3 (1977): p. 2.

PART II

Mind and Body

One of the most exciting frontiers of current scientific inquiry is the biopsychological investigation of the relationship between mind and body. Seldom has a scientific field developed so rapidly. Although far from complete, today's biopsychology is dramatically advanced over what it was just twenty years ago. What do recent insights pertaining to the evolution of behavior, to the genetics of intelligence and other traits, to physical control of the mind and mind control of the body, and to the relation between brain state and consciousness contribute to our understanding of human nature? Chapter 3 concludes that the human image which emerges from modern research is one of unity between mind and body.

There is an enduring and still lively philosophical debate over how the mind-body relationship is best conceived. This is a highly sophisticated issue ("the ultimate of ultimate problems," said William James). My purpose is not to resolve the philosophical issues, but simply to relate the human image emerging from biopsychological research to the human image discerned by biblical scholars. Most of us are only dimly aware of our implicit views of the relation of mind and body. Our assumptions nevertheless have important practical implications, making reflection on this issue worthwhile.

Here is another arena in which we find the popular but fallacious natural/spiritual dichotomy discussed earlier. The majority of a national sample of United Presbyterian ruling elders recently *disagreed* that "the nature of man is unitary, not a dualism of body and soul." Chapter 4 shows how discoveries in biopsychology raise to new levels of credibility an ancient but underappreciated aspect of Christian thought—the holistic view of human nature assumed by the Hebrew people. The Old and New Testaments view human nature as a psycho-physical unity, an image which is reinforced by the radical New Testament assumption of the resurrection of the whole person—body included. This biblical holism contrasts sharply with the popular assumption that mind and body are separate, as suggested, for example, by the pagan doctrine of the immortal soul. The idea that our human essence is disembodied spirit or mind is nearly as foreign to the Scriptures as to current scientific thought.

CHAPTER 3

The Unity of Mind and Body

BIOPSYCHOLOGY: THE BIOLOGY OF HUMAN BEHAVIOR

The most mysterious, intriguing area of our universe lies not in the farthest reaches of outer space, but in the inner space of the human skull. The 3½ pounds of pinkish-grey jelly which we carry around in our heads is the subject of a new scientific explosion. Psychologists, neurophysiologists, brain surgeons, evolutionary biologists, and even computer scientists are analyzing the brain in a massive interdisciplinary attempt to unlock its secrets.

The difficulty of this enterprise mirrors the bewildering intricacies of the human brain. The brain is so complex that it can hardly grasp its own complexity. Ten billion nerve cells are joined by one hundred times that many connections; some nerve cells are connected with 60 thousand others. As many as 100 thousand nerve cells may be included in transmitting the information involved in as simple an act as stepping back to avoid a passing car. The overwhelming complexity of our brains is one reason why perfect predictability of human behavior will forever remain a practical impossibility.

The brain's complexity results not only from the thousand billion interconnections among its nerve cells but also from the intricate complexity of every one of those cells. Each individual nerve cell contains the language of life: millions of RNA molecules which carry genetic instructions from the DNA molecules. These genetic instructions contain information equivalent to thousands of printed books packed into the size of a millionth of a pinhead. We begin our scrutiny of the biology of human action at this elemental level by considering the contribution of these biochemical codes to the evolution of our behavior.

Genetic Foundations of Behavior

The emergence of behavior. Since this is a book about human beings and their behavior it is appropriate that we first consider the genetic basis of our human nature. Nearly every cell of the body contains in its nucleus the genetic master code for the entire body. It is as if every room in the gigantic Sears Tower in Chicago had a bookcase containing the architect's plans for the entire building. The architect's plans run to forty-six volumes in human-kind—twenty-three volumes from one's mother and twenty-three volumes from one's father. These volumes, called chromosomes, are visible under a microscope as long threads. The genes, which are the pages of these chromosome volumes, are strung out along them. All told, there are many thousands of pages which have intricately cooperated in the manufacture of our bodies. Each gene page is formed of complex DNA molecules which are, in turn, composed of smaller nucleotide molecules.

In sexual reproduction the genes are reshuffled into new combinations. Every sperm and egg cell contains twenty-three chromosomes, each composed of a unique combination of the gene pages from the father and mother chromosome volumes. These two sets of chromosomes combine at conception to form a new genetic master copy which, in turn, divides into two cells, then four, then eight, and so forth, each with its own copy of the master code.

These genes, writes Richard Dawkins, "created us, body and mind; and their existence is the ultimate rationale for our existence. . . . We are their survival machines. . . . The currency used in the casino of evolution is survival, strictly gene survival."[1] A chicken, it seems, is only an egg's way of making another egg.[2]

For millions of years, each new organism, each new gene set, has competed with others for survival. The net result is that almost any characteristic of an organism can be analyzed for its survival value. Polar-bear genes program a thick coat of warm, camouflaging snow-white hair; this is why they emerged and persist in the Arctic gene pool.

For the psychologist, one fascinating area of current inquiry concerns the evolution of social behavior. Complex social behaviors have been influenced by natural selection and can therefore be analyzed for their adaptive significance. A prominent new theme in this literature of sociobiology will be of special interest to anyone who has struggled to better understand the doctrine of original sin, both as a theological abstraction and as a historical reality. Biological evolution, the argument goes, has selected tendencies·which advance the selfish individual at the expense of the group welfare.

Donald Campbell summarizes how this might happen:

Let us suppose that mutations have produced a heterogeneity within a social group so that there are some individuals with genes predisposing a self-sacrificial altruism which furthers group survival and others with genes predisposing a self-saving selfishness, such as cowardice in battle, theft, cheating, dishonesty in the service of self-interest, etc. Let us suppose that, due to the presence of the altruistic genes in some individuals, the group as a whole survives better. This increases the average reproductive opportunity of both the altruistic and the selfish among the group members. The net gain for the altruistic is reduced to some degree because of the costs of risks they incur. The net gain for the selfish has no such subtraction. Thus, while all gain, the selfish gain more, and their genes will gradually become more frequent as a result. There is no way in which the altruistic genetic tendencies could increase, to say nothing of becoming predominant, relative to the selfish if there is a self-sacrificial component to the altruism.[3]

Campbell does not shy away from understanding this biological selfishness of genetic competition as "original sin."[4]

Garrett Hardin embodied the same calculus of self-interest in his classic essay on the tragedy of the commons.[5] Consider one hundred farmers, each of whom uses the same meadow to feed one cow. With one hundred cows in residence, the common feeding ground is being used to capacity. But any one farmer may reason: "If I put a second cow in the pasture, I'll receive a 100 percent increase in my output, minus the mere 1 percent increase in the overcrowding of the meadow." His cost-benefit analysis is correct, so he adds his second cow. But so do each of his neighbors. The tragedy of the commons is the inevitable result.

There are many parallels to this story in real life. Environmental pollution is the sum of many small pollutions, each of which benefits the individual polluters much more than they could benefit themselves (and the environment) by stopping only their small contribution to the pollution. So we freely litter our dormitory hallways and public places but keep our personal spaces clean. The same dynamic explains why we are so willing to deplete our many natural resources to our collective detriment. Once again, the immediate benefit to an individual outweighs the cost, which is distributed among all.

Social psychologists have embodied this moral dilemma in laboratory games which pit the pursuit of immediate self-interest against the common good. The irony of these games, also some-times the irony of life itself, is that when everyone rationally pursues immediate self-interest it is to their collective detriment. Selfish behavior by all leads to benefits for none; selfless cooperation by all leads to profits shared by all.

Nevertheless, the dominant behavior among college students playing these games is the pursuit of immediate self-interest. Cooperative behavior is usually quickly eliminated because selfish behavior so easily takes advantage of it. The result is great frustration, clearly demonstrating that "the wages of sin is death," that the blind pursuit of self-interest is mutually destructive.[6] Yet it is short-term self-interest which generally motivates us. B. F. Skinner's reinforcement psychology, built on self-serving tendencies intrinsic to human nature, has been successful for just this reason. In this respect, Skinner is closer to the realism of biblical religion than are the romantic optimists among humanistic psychologists. For economists, also, it is axiomatic that people act out of self-interest; they seek to maximize their subjective satisfaction.

The dominance of human selfishness is evident in other experimental situations as well. Research on the "group polarization phenomenon," for instance, reveals that group interaction tends to amplify the dominant tendencies of individual group members. The phenomenon is sufficiently well documented that we can interpret the behavior changes of individuals in a group context as clues to their dominant personal motives. It is of particular interest that when group members are given a choice between behaving selfishly or with self-sacrificial altruism, it is selfishness rather than altruism that tends to be amplified by group discussion.[7] This seems to support Reinhold Niebuhr's idea that the "inferiority of the morality of groups" stems from "the revelation of a collective egoism, compounded of the egoistic impulses of individuals, which achieve a more vivid expression and a more cumulative effect when they are united in a common impulse than when they express themselves separately and discretely."[8]

This brief digression into social psychology anticipates later chapters which will further confirm that the principle of biological selfishness makes good social psychological sense. There is, then, ample evidence of the primacy of self-interest and of our ability to hide it behind our sense of superiority, or under the veneer of social graces, "moral principles," and religion. If we fully appreciate this insight of both science and Scripture—that the "natural man" is fundamentally selfish, and that the wages of this sin is our own impoverishment—we will be more likely to earnestly seek some redemption from it.

Now back to the genetic story. The genetic selfishness of natural selection should prompt at least three types of altruism. The first is altruism which benefits the group without any risk of self-sacrifice. When a wolf pack hunts elk this cooperative behavior entails mutual gain without cost. Animals will cooperate in a group if they gain more survival benefit than they contribute. Humans often behave in ways which seem altruistic but which are really calculated to elicit reciprocation or social approval.

There also exist selection pressures which favor self-sacrificial altruism toward one's offspring and kin. Parents who protect their offspring, even at risk to themselves, will be more likely to pass on their genes than will those who save themselves instead. Other relatives share genes in proportion to the closeness of their relation. It has been suggested that altruism will therefore generally correspond to relatedness—second cousins, for example, share one-sixteenth as much gene commonality as one's brothers and sisters. The selfish gene principle also implies that parents will care more about their grandchildren than about their son-in-law or daughter-in-law. Their genetic future resides in their children and grandchildren; the in-laws are genetic rivals.

A third type of biologically disposed altruism should occur when there exists no genetic competition among the cooperating animals, as in the amazing case of the social insects. Soldier and worker ants, bees, and termites do not have offspring. Self-sacrificial behavior therefore advances the gene transmission of their colonies, and thus these insects give dramatic examples of kamikaze suicide and division of labor in support of the colony.

By now, some readers are surely saying that this story of genetically disposed selfishness is far too grim. There are many human examples of heroic altruism, and nearly everyone exhibits some measure of goodhearted generosity.

Fortunately, there is more to the story. We are not simply the products of our genes. Our genes predispose us to be responsive to other people and to retain traits and rules of behavior which are learned early in life. Once the brain developed to a point where language and memory were possible, elaborate cultures could then evolve. Consider the historical development of fashions, beliefs, and customs. Celibacy also is obviously of no service to gene perpetuation; its origin lies outside of population genetics. Or consider language—Chaucer is separated from a modern Britisher by just twenty generations, but the two would converse with great difficulty. Our genes, then, have endowed us with a great capacity for various types of learning. We must therefore be wary of attempts to reduce complex social behaviors to genes.

Dawkins, Campbell, and others argue that among the products of social evolution is social learning which balances the biological priority on selfishness with concern for the welfare of the community. Many of the commandments inculcate "tendencies that are in direct opposition to the 'temptations' which for the most part represent dispositional tendencies produced by biological evolution." Unfortunately, continues Campbell, the modern cultural view of human nature as benign has strengthened the desire to throw off repressive restraints. "Part of our problem may be due to a loss of a precious part of tradition which was carried by religious symbols, a loss which social scientists, psychologists especially, have stupidly, shortsightedly, and unscientifically furthered."[9]

Dawkins concludes similarly: "Let us try to *teach* generosity and altruism, because we are born selfish. Let us understand what our own selfish genes are up to, because we may then at least have the chance to upset their designs, something which no other species has ever aspired to."[10]

Our social policies do even better than this. They *insist* on sharing. Taxation and public welfare systems are rooted in a realistic distrust of the magnitude of voluntary generosity. No one who would completely do away with this system takes original sin seriously. The primacy of selfishness provides the driving force behind the great success of modern capitalism, but it also reminds us of the need for its control. Do the proponents of unrestrained capitalism (who would give free reign to greed) and of socialism (who seem unprepared to harness the power of self-interest) fail to take original sin seriously? If, as Campbell believes, intrinsic selfishness needs to be balanced by restraints, this surely has implications for economics as well as psychology.

Campbell comes close to reasserting the Platonic dualism of nature (biological selfishness) as evil versus human reason (cultural restraint) as good. As will be emphasized in later chapters, and Campbell would surely agree, this is not the whole story—human reason and human culture are subject to corruption. Moreover, our biological impulses are essential to our individual health and vigor and are therefore a good as well as a potential evil. One can acknowledge the Christian view of the essential goodness of the creation by affirming that the whole creation—biological self-interest *plus* its cultural-religious restraint—is good and that what is bad (original sin) is the unrestrained self-interest manifested by human pride.

Heredity and individual differences. No discussion of the genetic foundations of behavior is complete without acknowledging the heritability of human traits and abilities. Biologists tell us that natural selection depends upon genetically produced diversity. But how much genetic contribution is there to the diversity among human behavior traits?

A new area of psychology, behavior genetics, is devoted to the study of heritability. Psychologists working in this area do not study the extent to which a given trait is due to genes or environment but the extent to which observed *differences* among people are due to genes or environment. Many types of evidence converge in pointing to a substantial hereditary contribution to personality and intelligence.

Through the study of identical twins, we can compare test scores obtained by people with identical genetic make-up. Their scores are very close, reliably closer than those obtained by fraternal twins who have the same degree of genetic similarity as non-twin brothers and sisters.[11] But identical twins also share a very similar environment. Does this perhaps account for their similar traits? Some twins have been separated shortly after birth and raised separately. Yet being reared apart does not destroy the similarity typically so evident between identical twins. The importance of heredity for intelligence is also documented by the finding that the IQ scores of adopted children are much more similar to those of their biological parents than to those of their adoptive parents.[12]

Since it is clear that heredity contributes to individual differences in intelligence and since different racial groups differ in average IQ test scores, some have concluded that the racial differences may be inherently biological. However, there are good reasons to presume that, although individual differences have a substantial genetic component, racial group differences, which are far smaller than the range of individual differences, are environmental.

Further confirmation of the genetic contribution to the diversity of personalities and abilities comes from animal breeding studies. By selective breeding, it has been possible to develop rats which learn a maze very rapidly or very slowly, and rabbits which exhibit a fierce, aggressive emotionality or a very placid nature. We have all seen the results of animal breeding in the high-strung temperaments of race horses. Animal babies and human babies, too, bring their temperaments with them into the world.[13]

Behavior genetics has made a special contribution to our understanding of certain emotional disorders. Schizophrenia, the most prevalent and serious form of mental disorder, has a strong genetic component. If one member of an identical twin pair is diagnosed schizophrenic, chances are better than 50 percent that the other twin will be similarly diagnosed. Moreover, most of those other twins not carrying the diagnosis will exhibit some schizophrenia-like abnormalities. The likelihood of other relatives of schizophrenics becoming schizophrenic themselves increases with the closeness of the relationship.[14] The relative success of drug treatment of schizophrenia is also consistent with the genetic hypothesis since biochemical abnormalities are likely to be expressions of genetic abnormalities.[15]

Despite the abundant evidence for genetic contributions to individual differences, researchers are generally unwilling to assign percentage weights to the hereditary and environmental influences upon any given trait. For one thing, the relative importance of heredity and environment depends on the amount of variation in each. Environment, for example, will appear more important if you compare people from extremely different environments than if you compare people who have grown up in similar circumstances. Furthermore, the influences of heredity and environment are not separate; they interact in complex ways. What individuals encounter in the environment often depends on what they bring to the situation. Foster parents, for example, adapt their child-handling techniques to the peculiar attributes of succeeding foster children. This illustrates why a correlation between child-rearing technique and child characteristics is not clear evidence for the effectiveness of a particular mode of parenting. It could just as easily be the effect of the child on the parent or of the shared heredity between parent and child.

Nevertheless, it is clear that the genetic contribution to the diversity of our personal traits is substantial. Furthermore, there is now a growing scientific awareness of the possibility of engineering the mind by manipulating the body's genetic structure. This confirms our growing sense of the unity of mind and body.

Is there a practical lesson here for us all? Are we not better off accepting, rather than judging, attributes such as emotionality where the genetic influence is clear? Attempts to change such traits through mere will power or exhortation are likely to be quite frustrating. Genetically influenced traits are not unmodifiable, but we might better focus our efforts where modification is easier. Reinhold Niebuhr's famous prayer expresses this notion well: "O God, give us serenity to accept what cannot be changed, courage to change what should be changed, and wisdom to distinguish the one from the other."

The Brain and Behavior

Studying the brain is like looking at a building called "Post Office" and trying to figure out what it's for. You can get some idea by watching people come and go from the outside. You can get an even better idea if you examine its operation more closely from the inside. The new brain research, which has so quickly rendered yesterday's textbooks obsolete, is made possible by new techniques for manipulating the brain and recording its activity. It is now possible, by inserting extremely fine wires into the brain, to record electrical activity, to electrically stimulate or destroy specific areas of the brain, or to deliver minute quantities of chemicals to precise spots. A quick glimpse at some of the results will demonstrate that manipulating the brain also manipulates mind and motives.

At the lowest brain level, in the stem where the spinal cord merges with the brain, is an arousal system which controls sleep and alertness. (See Figure 3.) Stimulate this region in a sleeping cat and the animal will suddenly awaken. (Would you like your alarm clock hooked to your arousal system?) Sever this area and the cat lapses into a lethargic state from which it never awakens. Upon instruction from higher brain regions, this center also filters out many sensory inputs, allowing only some to get through to the brain. If a cat is attending closely to a mouse in a jar, this center suppresses auditory information (just as it did the sound of my wife's voice as I wrote this paragraph).

The core of the brain contains fascinating clusters of nerve cells

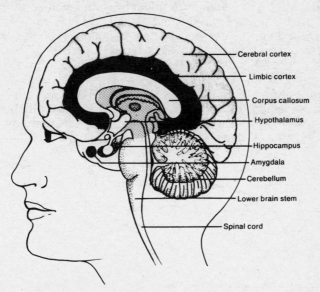

Figure 3. Medial View of the Brain. From *The Brain Changers: Scientists and the New Mind Control,* copyright © 1973 by Maya Pines. Reproduced by permission of Harcourt Brace Jovanovich, Inc.

in the limbic system. One part of this, the hypothalamus, performs many of the brain's housekeeping duties. Manipulations of the hypothalamus reveal that here is located the thermostat, which regulates body temperature, the "appestat," which tells us when we are hungry or thirsty, and the controls for our entire hormonal system, including sexual motivation. For example, chemical or electrical stimulation of one part of the hypothalamus will cause a satiated rat to exhibit all the signs of gnawing hunger. Destroying this tiny area has the opposite effect; the rat will stop eating and starve. Stimulating a nearby area of the hypothalamus causes hungry rats to stop eating; destroying this area produces such overeating that the rat may grow to the size of a football before finally eating itself to death. Thus hunger is regulated by two areas, one stimulating hunger and the other inhibiting it. This illustrates how the brain uses controls which are complementary and balanced against each other.

When rats are themselves allowed to trigger stimulation of yet another bundle of fibers in their hypothalamus by pressing a lever, they will do so two thousand times an hour until they finally drop from exhaustion. They will surmount almost any hurdle to get to the bar, even an electric grid that stops a starving rat from reaching food. The animal's behavior suggests this might be a pleasure zone that is touched and, sure enough, stimulation of the same portion of the human brain produces feelings of physical pleasure.

Electrical tampering with another complex structure in the brain core, the amygdala, can elicit powerful emotion. The controversial neuroscientist José Delgado has provided dramatic demonstrations of artificial stimulation provoking otherwise docile animals into rage, or raging animals into submission.[16] In his most publicized demonstration, Delgado climbed into a bull ring and used a remote radio transmitter to electrically switch off angry behavior, turning a charging bull into a Ferdinand. But it is too simplistic to presume that there exist specific brain structures which correspond to complex social behaviors.[17] Aggression, for instance, is actually mediated by several different brain regions. The flexibility of the brain further defies the idea that specific brain areas have rigidly fixed functions. When one brain area is damaged, often other areas will eventually take over some of the functions of the damaged area.

The brain feature which distinguishes human beings from other animals is not the structures in the core of the "old brain," but the rich contours of the brain surface, the cerebral cortex. Different areas of the cortex serve different functions, as brain damage and brief electrical stimulation of different points on the brain surface

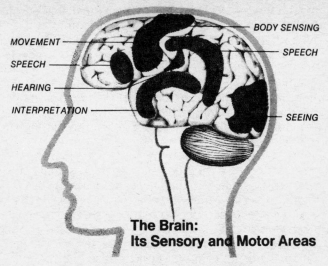

MOVEMENT

SPEECH

HEARING

INTERPRETATION

BODY SENSING

SPEECH

SEEING

**The Brain:
Its Sensory and Motor Areas**

Figure 4. From *Newsweek* / Ib Ohlsson.

clearly demonstrates. (See Figure 4.) Once Delgado used electrical stimulation to force a patient undergoing brain surgery to close his fist every time the current was delivered. When asked to voluntarily keep his hand open, the patient could not do it. "I guess, Doctor," he noted, "that your electricity is stronger than my will."[18]

Some of the most exciting brain research concerns questions about how the brain receives, processes, and stores information. Visual information has been brilliantly traced from the electrochemical reactions in the eye's retinal cells to the cortex area in the back of the head, where this information is reassembled by the brain into a visual perception. It is becoming evident that the brain is not merely, as once thought, a passive switchboard which connects a stimulus with a response.

What brain processes enable us to learn and remember? One approach to understanding the mechanics of human thinking is to create models or computer simulations of human intelligence. These have met with extraordinary success. A machine can learn, can apply general strategies to solve problems flexibly, can play chess with expert proficiency, and can process information with incredible sophistication. All of this defies our image of machines as necessarily rigid and repetitive. The limits of artificial intelligence have hardly been approached, but already it is apparent that many of the complex thinking processes which formerly were thought unique to the human organism can, in fact, be simulated.

One eminent scholar in this area concludes that this encourages the view that mind itself is also a product of nature.[19]

Other scholars remind us that the machine model is far from adequate because the human brain greatly outstrips any conceivable computer in its complexity, flexibility, and self-activating capacities. Take memory, for example. In a computer each bit of information is stored in a single electronic "cell." Human memory is, by some incredible process, diffused over large areas of the cortex. Although electrical stimulation of a specific point in the human cortex during brain surgery will sometimes evoke a vivid but long forgotten experience, this does not mean that the memory of it was somehow located in that specific cell. The point stimulated seems rather to have been an outcropping of the memory. Destroying various regions of the cortex disrupts our capacity to think and form new memories, but it does not destroy specific memories.

This has prompted the search for an explanation of memory which accounts for its "delocalized" character. Since memories survive brain damage, coma, electroconvulsive shock and other events which disrupt the brain's electrical activity, some researchers have set out on a search for a chemical basis to memory. This is an extraordinarily difficult task, and, despite some sensational claims, it has yet to be accomplished. But progress is being made. If rats are given electric shock or certain drugs immediately after learning a new skill, memory of the skill is lost. If these interventions are delayed an hour or more the memory is retained. Human beings typically cannot remember the moments preceding electroshock therapy or a head injury. These traumas presumably interfere with the chemical coding or "fixing" of the experience, since they do not disrupt older memories.

The physical basis of mind is further evident in the intimate link between the complexity of the brain cortex and the capacity to think and use language. The child's brain contains all its nerve cells at birth. As the interconnections among these nerve cells develop, so also do the child's mental capacities. The same correspondence between brain structure and mind is evident when we look up and down the hierarchy of animal life. Lower mammals, like rats, have a smooth cortex with much less surface area than our own. More similar to ourselves are the great apes, including the chimpanzee. It has generally been thought that the creative use of language is a unique, defining characteristic of humanity. Might it be, however, that chimpanzees could also be shown to be capable of language if only we could find a way to communicate with them? In the late 1960s the first reports emerged of chimpanzees being taught to communicate using the hand signals of the deaf. The most celebrated of these chimps, Washoe, learned with this method to ask for food, toys, and human companionship.

More recently, Duane Rumbaugh, working at the Yerkes Regional Primate Research Center in Atlanta, assembled a team of psycholinguists, computer scientists, and psychologists to create a computer system by which a chimpanzee could communicate with people. Hearing Rumbaugh describe the results of this project is an awesome experience. By punching at a panel of multicolored push buttons, Lana, the first chimpanzee in the project, is able to "talk" to people outside her room. The computerized language machine translates her punchings into English, and it stands always ready to answer Lana's requests for food, drink and entertainment—provided her requests are made in grammatically correct form. After many months of learning her new language, Lana became capable of carrying on conversations such as the following:

Lana: "Please Tim put juice in machine."
Tim: "Juice in machine."
Lana: "No juice in machine."
(Tim finds the machine empty and refills it.)
Tim: "Juice in machine."
Lana: "Yes. Please machine give juice."
(The computer delivers juice and Lana drinks.)
Lana: "Please Tim move into room."
Tim: "Yes."
(Tim enters and is pulled by Lana to her keyboard.)
Lana: "? Tim tickle Lana."
(Tim starts toward the "No" key but Lana grabs his hand and forces it toward "Yes." After he pushes it Lana bounds about the room until Tim catches her for a robust session of tickling.)[20]

Most amazing is Lana's ability to recombine symbols to form new concepts. When a researcher came to the lab with an orange one day, Lana wanted it, but had no word for orange. But she knew her colors and the word for apple, so she improvised: "? Tim give apple which-is orange-color." Nuts she has called "rock berries," and ducks, "water birds." She also spontaneously creates grammatically correct sentences by recombining parts of stock sentences. The limits of chimpanzee vocabulary are not yet defined, but Rumbaugh believes that five hundred or even one thousand words are not beyond possibility.

Chimpanzees are *not* human. Their thinking and language capabilities are vastly inferior to our own. What is significant for our present discussion, however, is that chimpanzees, whose brain complexity is intermediate between a dog's brain and our own, have mental abilities which are correspondingly intermediate. This confirms the dependence of mind on brain.

Another window on the mind is provided by brain destruction. Strokes, tumors, accidents, diseases, and surgical removal of parts of the brain have highly selective effects. From observations of brain-damaged patients it has been known for more than a century that the physical symmetry of the two halves ("hemispheres") of our brains is *not* mirrored by symmetry of their functions. Destruction of the left hemisphere typically destroys language and logical thought but leaves musical and artistic talents intact. The reverse generally occurs when the right hemisphere is destroyed.[21]

During the last fifteen years, the specialized functions of the two brain halves have been explored in some of the most fascinating brain research ever performed. In normal people the brain's two hemispheres, looking something like the two halves of a walnut, are joined by a large bundle of fibers known as the "corpus callosum." The corpus callosum enables the two halves of the brain to communicate with one another. Occasionally, this communication goes haywire. A neural storm starts up in one hemisphere and then reverberates between the two hemispheres, causing epilepsy. In some severe cases this was relieved by severing the corpus callosum. This produced a "split brain" and cut off the reverberation. Incredibly, the patients awakened with no obvious deficits except for a "splitting" headache. Their personalities and intellects remain intact. You could converse with a split-brain person and never suspect that the largest bundle of fibers in the brain had been severed.

Closer scrutiny of split-brain humans and monkeys, revealed some amazing subtle effects. Shortly after one of these operations, it was noted that when the patient brushed against something with his left side he was unaware that he had done so, and that when an object was placed in his left hand he denied its presence. Since the two halves of the brain are cross wired, each controlling and receiving information from the other side of the body, it was evident that this patient's right hemisphere was incapable of reporting these events.

The independence of the split brain halves—the existence of two separate minds in one head—has subsequently been explored in many experiments.[22] Our eyes are "wired" to our brains in such a way that the left half of our visual field is perceived only by our right hemisphere and the right visual field by the left hemisphere. By asking the patient to fix attention on a designated point and then briefly flashing information in the left or right visual field, an experimenter can easily communicate solely with the right or left hemisphere.

See if you can guess the results of a simple experiment using this procedure with a split-brain patient. When the word HEART is flashed across the visual field as H E · A R T, what word will the patient report seeing? Remember that the left side of the visual field transmits information through both eyes to the right hemisphere only, as Figure 5 illustrates.

The patients *says* that he saw the word *art*. Asked to identify with his *left* hand, which of two words he has seen, HE or ART, he *points* to HE. Note that when a verbal response is requested, the left hemisphere responds with what *it* sees, but when the other hemisphere is given opportunity to express itself nonverbally, it understands the instruction and does so. This is also evident when a picture of a spoon is flashed to the right hemisphere. The patient cannot say what he saw. His left hand can, however, select a spoon from a number of objects behind a screen. This demonstrates the perceptual abilities of the right hemisphere. In fact, the right hemisphere is better than the left at reproducing drawings. This specialization is also evident in the brains of normal individ-

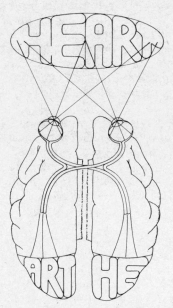

Figure 5. From *The Psychology of Consciousness,* Second Edition, copyright © 1977 by Robert E. Ornstein. Reproduced by permission of Harcourt Brace Jovanovich, Inc.

uals. When the right hemisphere is occupied with a perceptual task, the left hemisphere's brain waves are those associated with relaxed states. This is reversed when the person is engaged in a language task.

Cut off from normal communication with one another, the two hemispheres have sometimes learned ingenious means for communicating. In one experiment, a red or green light was flashed to the right hemisphere, and the patient was asked to guess verbally which color it was. At first he exhibited chance accuracy, but then, mysteriously, he started getting better. The experimenters soon caught on to the patient's strategy. When the patient's left hemisphere started to speak a wrong answer, the right hemisphere, which had seen the light, would hear this and cause a frown or shake of the head. The left hemisphere soon learned to trust this inarticulate intuition and would correct itself: "Oh no, I meant red."

Sometimes the two hemispheres war against each other. Sperry has a dramatic film in which a person's left hand (right hemisphere) easily rearranges some blocks to match a drawing. When the right hand (left hemisphere) is asked to perform the same perceptual task, it makes many errors, much to the frustration of the right hemisphere, which is observing all this. The left hand finally interrupts the bumbling right hand, precipitating a small skirmish. In the case of monkeys, the two split hemispheres have been taught opposite answers to the same task. The left hand "knows" the answer is A, and the right hand "knows" it is B. As you might imagine, a real mix-up occurs when the two are allowed to answer simultaneously.

It is not unheard of for one hand to button a shirt while the other hand unbuttons it. One man actually attacked his wife with his left hand while trying to rescue her from the attack with his right hand. The extent to which the left hand is literally unaware of what the right hand is doing can be illustrated by imagining a split-brain patient enjoying the old game of rocks, paper, and scissors—played between the two hands. (Question: for which hand would the patient root?)

The importance of this research is not only that it reveals the communication function of the corpus callosum and demonstrates that dividing the brain seems to divide the self, but also that it provides new information concerning the different functions of the two hemispheres. Unlike the symmetrical halves of the cat brain, which are like two identical computers side by side, the two halves of the human brain are not redundant. Part of the richness of being human emanates from the complementary special functions performed by our right and left hemispheres.

For more than 90 percent of right-handers and the majority of left-handers, language resides primarily in the left hemisphere, as in the examples above. (This asymmetry of brain function is for some reason stronger in males than in females, for whom the two sides tend to be not quite so dissimilar.*) About one-third of left-handers, however, have the opposite cerebral organization—language function is located primarily in the right hemisphere. By some peculiar design of nature, this third generally write in the noninverted position that is characteristic of right-handed people.[23] Left-handed people who write using the hooked position generally have brains which are organized the same as the typical right-handed person.

Although there appears to be a genetic blueprint for each person's brain organization, the specialties of each half-brain are not fully developed until later childhood. This accounts for the fact that very young children who suffer the destruction or surgical removal of their left hamisphere will still develop language.

The general superiority of the left hemisphere in language and logic has led many to label this the "major" or "dominant" hemisphere. The value judgment is hardly surprising since it is the left hemisphere which does this verbal labeling. Recently, some writers have reacted in the opposite direction.[24] They celebrate the supposed creative, sensuous, intuitive, artistic capacities of the right hemisphere and they praise cultures which develop these human qualities. Western education is criticized for one-sidedly emphasizing and testing the propositional, logical, sequential, rational attributes of the left hemisphere. (See Figure 6.)

The distinction between left and right hemisphere functions roughly corresponds to the distinction between Greek thought (emphasizing rationally deduced propositions) and Hebrew thought (emphasizing less analytical modes of knowing). The development of personal wholeness involves *both* modes of thought.[25] Emil Brunner has made a parallel observation:

Theo-*logy* has to do with the Logos and therefore is only qualified to deal with matters that are in some sense logical, not with the dynamic in its a-logical characteristics. . . . Theology, through its unconscious intellec-

---

*This biological sex difference may be a source of some psychological differences between the sexes. One speculation is that the more specialized hemispheres of the average male brain facilitate specialized competencies, and that the less specialized female brain facilitates the integration of verbal and nonverbal competencies.

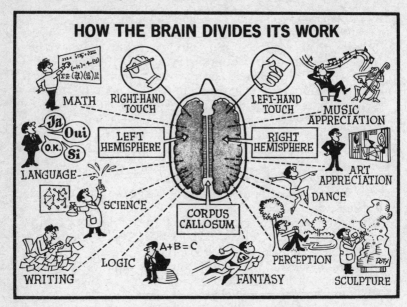

Figure 6. From *Newsweek* / Roy Doty.

tualism, has often proved a significant restrictive influence, stifling the operations of the Holy Ghost, or at least their full creative manifestations.[26]

The left-right distinction is easily overblown. Recent work indicates that the right hemisphere has greater speech comprehension abilities than previously thought; its limited speech production abilities had just made it difficult to discover this. Although quite dumb, and incapable of phonetically analyzing words (e.g., recognizing rhyming words), the right hemisphere is not deaf. The asymmetry in our brain's function is, nonetheless, sufficiently beyond dispute that we may deduce some practical advice: if a head-on collision is imminent, right-handed musicians, craftsmen, and studio artists should turn their heads to the right, exposing only the left hemisphere. Analytic philosophers, lawyers, scientists, and engineers should look left. Poets had better wear crash helmets.

Much more could be written concerning the biology of human behavior. But I trust this overview is sufficient to paint a picture of the intimate, mysterious union of mind and body. The evolutionary emergence of mind within the physical organism, the genetic foundations of our individual differences, and the correspondence between our brain states and our emotions, thoughts, and actions, all point to the same conclusion: mind and body are a unity.

THE MIND-BODY PROBLEM

Our task in this and the next chapter is to relate the human image emerging from biopsychological research with the human image of biblical anthropology. Doing this does not require delving deeply into complex philosophical discussions of mind and body. Neither recent research nor the Scriptures directly imply any systematic philosophy of the mind-body relation. Scientists and biblical scholars, all of whom know their literature well, have adopted varying philosophical positions on the issue.

Some general conclusions about the mind-body relation are nevertheless unavoidable; they are implicit in the rest of the discussion. My general contention is that both scientists and biblical scholars are increasingly inclined toward *holistic* and away from *dualistic* and *reductionistic* images of human nature. A brief review of these three contrasting views will prepare us for the arguments of the next chapter.

Dualism

People are accustomed to thinking of mind and body as distinct entities, as separate and yet as interacting with one another. My body is "this old house of mine" in which the essential me lives for but a short while. I command its actions, yet I am limited by its capabilities.

Numerous metaphors have expressed this dualism. The ancients saw mind and body as rider and horse. Augustine likened mind and body to a carpenter and his hammer. Descartes declared that "I am . . . lodged in my body as a pilot in a vessel."[27] Mind is seen as a distinct entity, existing independently of the body, although closely conjoined to it.

Although ancient, this view is not without modern proponents. Wilder Penfield, the famous neurosurgeon, writes that "the mind makes its impact upon the brain through the highest brain-mechanism. The mind must act upon it. The mind must also be acted upon by the highest brain-mechanism. . . . The mind seems to act independently of the brain in the same sense that a programmer acts independently of his computer."[28] The brain is a computer, Penfield analogizes, and computers cannot program themselves.

The presumption that our minds are separate from our brains

requires some mode of interaction, some way by which the nonmaterial mind could get ahold of the material brain. With the computer programer and the computer the mode of interaction is perfectly clear. But by what process could mind conceivably interact with the physical brain? Descartes thought it occurred through the pineal gland. We now know that Descartes was wrong. Are there other possibilities?

John Eccles has for many years been arguing a modern version of Descartes's theory, based on an analogy with physical systems (such as a pinball machine) in which an infinitesimal difference in initial conditions is amplified into major differences.[29] An impulse traveling along a nerve cell in the brain must cross a "synaptic gap" in order to trigger the next nerve cells in the sequence. Some impulses make it across while others fail. Since this firing across neural connections involves uncertainty, this is a point at which mind could impose itself on the machinery of the brain, throwing a single switch here and there and thereby directing the neural avalanche which follows. Eccles's attempt to place mind and free will in the synaptic gap is reminiscent of the "god-of-the-gaps"; it is a small view of mind and a mechanistic perspective on the body.

A recent defense of dualism by a philosopher of religion, Paul Badham, acknowledges a means by which dualism could be shown to be false. If minds are separate entities which reside in bodies and which at death become disembodied, then surely mind must be indivisible. Thus, writes Badham, "If it could be established that each half of a divided brain possessed its own consciousness, then I would regard dualism as disproved."[30] This is precisely what most split-brain researchers believe has been achieved. Joseph Bogen observed that splitting the brain produces "two minds in one person."[31] Roger Sperry echoes, "The surgery has left each of these people with two separate minds; that is, with two separate spheres of consciousness."[32] Eccles tries to salvage his dualistic hypothesis by declaring there is still only one mind—it resides in the verbal, left hemisphere.[33]

Badham also proposes the evidence by which dualism could be supported: ESP (extra-sensory perception). Parapsychological phenomena, if they exist, would indeed seem to demonstrate mental capacities which go beyond the capacities of the brain. If, for example, minds could be shown to leap free of the brain and communicate directly with one another, then the mind-brain unity would be refuted.[34] Some dualistic thinkers therefore eagerly welcome evidence for telepathy in hopes of weakening the case for mind-brain unity.

The evidence for ESP is of two varieties. First are those many accounts of extraordinary happenings described in popular books and magazines and demonstrated by entertainers such as Uri Geller. These accounts are generally unconvincing, even to professed parapsychologists. They are subject to selective reporting and distorted memories. Almost every important event has been prophesied—but so has its opposite. Which prophecies do you suppose are most often remembered and reported? Even outright fakery occurs. Uri Geller has been caught cheating and his psychic feats demystified by psychologists and magicians who have duplicated his acts.[35] Magicians know they can fool people so they take it for granted that a good "psychic" could even fool scientists.

Parapsychologists have therefore attempted to put ESP on more solid ground by seeking to demonstrate it in controlled laboratory experiments. These generally have subjects make guesses on tasks where their accuracy may be compared to a known chance rate of right answers. Despite the enormous public interest in these experiments, research psychologists generally remain as much unconvinced as most magicians are of purported stage demonstrations of ESP. There are several reasons for this skepticism.

First, when significant results are claimed, they are usually of very small magnitude—about a 5 percent improvement on the chance rate. This is nothing like the claims made for ESP in popular publications. If anything like the purported powers of mind over matter or of prophesy exist in even a few individuals, gambling casinos would long ago have gone bankrupt. ESP effects are so minimal under controlled conditions that we may reasonably presume them to be the result of subtle biases or of the natural tendency to publish only newsworthy results. The pressure for positive results in parapsychological laboratories is sufficiently great that the research director of a well-known laboratory recently was forced to resign after being caught tinkering with the apparatus to improve scores.

Second, the phenomenon is slippery and undependable. "Sensitive" subjects tend to "lose" their ESP. The tighter the experimental controls, the less likely one is to observe an ESP effect.[36] Moreover, skeptical scientists have generally not been able to replicate the claims of parapsychological laboratories. In other sciences, such unreliability is generally assumed to disconfirm a theory.

Third, the idea of ESP contradicts what we know of the dependence of mind on brain. All the biopsychological evidence of this chapter is evidence against the idea that mind could operate apart from the brain. In view of the lack of reliable, convincing evidence for ESP one has to stretch to believe it. If ESP exists, why do so few people display it and why do the "gifted" people display it so minimally and undependably? If thoughts are controlled by another person miles away, why not by all the thousands of people living within that radius?

The laws of chance tell us to expect some incredible coincidences. Since these rare, chance events are disproportionately noticed and publicized we tend to overestimate and overinterpret their occurrence. Let's pretend that the 2,000 students here at Hope College come together for an all-campus coin tossing contest.[37] The task is to flip heads. On the first toss, 1,000 students flip heads and advance to the second round. As you might expect, about 500 of these progress to a third round, 250 to a fourth, 125 to a fifth, 62 to a sixth, 31 to a seventh, 15 to an eighth, 8 to a ninth, and 4 amazing individuals, having flipped heads nine times in a row with great displays of concentration and effort, advance to the tenth round.   ·

By now the crowd of losers is watching in awe-struck silence as these expert coin-tossers display their amazing ability. The finalists are the object of much celebration and adulation. A journal article is begun, documenting their mysterious ability. As the contest continues over dozens more trials a few gifted individuals among the original 2,000, some having re-emerged from the initial losers division, display an average tossing ability at least five percent better than the expected fifty percent. A panel of impartial scientists is brought in to investigate the amazing ability of these gifted individuals. Sadly, all but one or two fail to replicate their achievements before this new audience and even the persistently gifted one or two eventually lose touch with their coin-tossing gift. But, of course!, their ardent followers surmise, successful coin tossing is a highly sensitive skill. The tense, threatening atmosphere created by the formal test situation has disrupted this sensitive gift.

Still, millions of people believe they have at some time experienced ESP. If this belief is false, then we must account for the strength of their convictions. Chapter 7 will present new evidence which explains why we so easily come to believe things that are not true. For the present, we may conclude that belief in ESP is, at best, a shaky foundation on which to establish the dualism of mind and body.

Reductionism

The mounting evidence against popular versions of dualism has prompted some radical alternatives. If there is only one substance to our reality, we may presume this ultimate basic "stuff" to be either mind (idealism) or matter (materialism). These alternatives are captured in this little conversation:

What's mind? No matter.
What's matter? Never mind.

Although reductionism can go either direction, the challenge to dualism comes mainly from the materialists, who argue that mind is reducible to the physical operations of the body. According to this view, mind is a pseudophenomenon which does not really cause anything; it simply rides piggyback on the brain. This materialism underlies the position of the radical behaviorists in psychology who would have us dispense with all mentalistic explanation.

However, neither a materialist philosophy nor a dualist philosophy follows directly from the facts. Those who most loudly expound one or the other philosophy do so partly because of their control beliefs. Materialistic philosophy seems especially congenial to the assumptions of agnostic or atheist scientists. Likewise, those such as Eccles and Penfield who expound the autonomy of mind seemingly do so more on the basis of their religious conceptions (e.g., belief in an immortal human essence) than on the basis of facts. My yearning for a third alternative to these two extremes is, of course, also rooted in some controlling assumptions.

Holism

There is a third approach which respects the integrity of both physical and mental explanations without presuming these refer to separate events. By this holistic view, there are two ways of talking about a single event: brain-talk and mind-talk. Their relation is something like the relation of a computer's electrical impulses to the computer program, or of the electrical events in a telephone line to what the speaker is saying.[38] To rest content with the physical description would be to miss the telephone message; to stop with the brain story would be to miss the meaning of being human.

Science contains other instances of complementary perspectives on one reality. "The questions as to whether the reality 'man' is mind or body," wrote William Pollard, "is remarkably reminiscent of the question whether the reality 'light' is wave or particle."[39] Although I may sometimes wonder whether my mind controls my body more than my body controls my mind, this is really an inappropriate question. Mind and body refer to the *same* events, much as do wave and particle theories of light. We are neither merely machines, as the materialists suggest, nor ghosts in machines, as the dualists suggest; we are a unity of mind and body.[40]

The complementary character of physical and mental explanations is evident in psychosomatic medicine. The numerous examples of physical effects on mind and personality are complemented by equally numerous examples of the effect of emotional states on general health. The new research on "biofeedback" has shown that people can learn to voluntarily exert some control over what were previously thought to be uncontrollable bodily states— brain waves, heart rate, blood pressure, and skin temperature. There is nothing terribly mysterious about all this; many of the effects of biofeedback and transcendental meditation are easily reproduced by other relaxation exercises. But this research does provide further evidence for the unity of mind and body; altering either mind or body alters its complement (a fact which many dualists could easily accomodate).

This is not to say that because mental and physical explanations refer to the same events, one can therefore be substituted for the other. The physical brain manifests nonphysical properties such as self-consciousness. A complete description of the neural circuitry involved when you are stuck by a pin would fail to capture your private experience of pain.[41] Each explanatory level is appropriate for its own purposes. Psychology therefore works at several levels simultaneously. Whole systems need to be explained at the level of the whole as well as at the level of their parts. A symphony is built of music from the individual instruments; describing the individual instruments cannot do justice to the whole symphonic experience, yet nothing extra is added to the instruments to produce the symphony. Subatomic particles are not stable, material substances, yet out of their complex interaction something different emerges— the stable, solid chair on which you are now sitting. The whole person is also more than the sum of his or her parts. This is not because some mystical extra has been added, but because qualities have emerged which are not discernible in the isolated parts of the body. Memories, ideas, and social behaviors have no specific location; they result from the diffuse coordination of many brain elements.

Many scientists, such as Barry Commoner, Michael Polanyi, and Roger Sperry, have noted that living systems form hierarchies.[42] Each level relies on and harnesses the principles of the levels below it, even while it transcends and directs the more elemental levels. Whole systems are composed of nothing more than the interacting subsystems, yet they have properties not inherent in the individual subsystems. In this view, mind does not intervene or violate biophysical laws, as Eccles would have it. Rather, it emerges out of them. Sperry elaborates this argument:

Compared to the elemental physiological and molecular properties the conscious properties of the brain process are more molar and holistic in nature. . . . Just as the holistic properties of the organism have causal effects that determine the course and fate of its constituent cells and molecules, so in the same way . . . the present proposal may be said to place mind over matter, but not as any disembodied or supernatural agent. . . . The present hypothesis represents a midway compromise between older extremes of mentalism on the one hand and materialism on the other. The present is mentalistic in accepting the existence of potent mental forces that transcend the material elements in cerebral function. It is materialistic in denying that these mental forces can exist apart from the brain process of which they are a direct property.[43]

The increasing appreciation for the significance of conscious mind is evident not only in biopsychology but in personality and social psychology research as well. In subsequent chapters some of this new research will be introduced.

Does the emerging picture of mind-brain unity diminish our esteem for the image bearer of God? No mystical entity seems required to account for our human spirit. Still, it is just as misleading to say our emergent consciousness is "nothing but" the stuff of which it is composed as to say that a work of art is "nothing but" the strokes of a brush, or a Shakespearean play "nothing but" its individual words.[44] That God apparently chose to create human qualities like self-awareness, rational farsightedness, aesthetic sensitivity, and God-consciousness through the interaction of material elements need not destroy our reverence and awe for either God or humanity.

NOTES

1. Richard Dawkins, *The Selfish Gene,* New York: Oxford University Press, 1976), pp. 21, 59. This fascinating book is also the source of the architectural metaphor.

2. Credit Samuel Butler for this aphorism.

3. Donald T. Campbell, "The Conflict Between Social and Biological Evolution and the Concept of Original Sin," *Zygon* 10 (1975): 234–49. Campbell developed this argument most fully in his presidential address to the American Psychological Association ("On the Conflicts Between Biological and Social Evolution and Between Psychology and Moral Tradition," *American Psychologist* 30 (1975): 1103–26). This is a modern sci-

entific version of some ancient biological theories of original sin. These date back at least to the early Christian theologian Tertullian, (160–230 A.D.).

4. Theologians often conceptualize original sin in terms of human pride and alienation from God. Selfishness is seen as an inevitable result of pride, but not as the only result. Sin, they say, is the idolatry of making anything other than God—a political ideology, sensual pleasure, personal success—an object of our ultimate loyalty. The Kamikazi pilots' devotion to the Emperor was apparently idolatrous, but not selfish—unless, of course, one defines selfishness after the fact in terms of whatever act occurs. "It is wrong to describe all of our action as 'selfish,'" writes Richard Mouw; "but because we are willing to trust in anything but the Creator, our attitudes can be rightly viewed as stemming from 'selfish pride'" (*Politics and the Biblical Drama* [Grand Rapids: Eerdmans, 1976], p. 45).

A distinction is sometimes drawn between self-interest and selfishness. Granted, there are some cooperative acts which are promoted by self-interest. When a basketball player passes up a clear shot at the basket in order to pass to a teammate who has a better shot, shall we say that this action is in his self-interest but is not selfish? If this is all that is meant by the distinction, anyone could surely agree, but might then be inclined to doubt whether this distinction will carry much freight.

5. Garrett Hardin, "The Tragedy of the Commons," *Science* 162 (1968): 1243–48.

6. Rom. 6:23, RSV.

7 See Helmut Lamm and David G. Myers, "Group-Induced Polarization of Attitudes and Behavior," in *Advances in Experimental Social Psychology*, vol. 11, ed. L. Berkowitz (New York: Academic Press, forthcoming).

8. Reinhold Niebuhr, *Moral Man and Immoral Society* (New York: Scribner's, 1932), p. xii.

9. Campbell, *op. cit.*, p. 243.

10. Dawkins, *op. cit.*, p. 3.

11. For a review and some new evidence see John C. Loehlin and Robert C. Nichols, *Heredity, Environment, and Personality: A Study of 850 Sets of Twins* (Austin: University of Texas Press, 1976).

12. Harry Munsinger, "The Adopted Child's IQ: A Critical Review," *Psychological Bulletin* 82 (1975): 623–59.

13. Alexander Thomas, Stella Chess, and Herbert G. Birch, "The Origin of Personality," *Scientific American* 223, no. 2 (August, 1970): pp. 102–9.

14 Leonard L. Heston, "The Genetics of Schizophrenia and Schizoid Disease," *Science* 167 (1970): 249–56.

15. Seymour S. Kety, "It's Not All in Your Head," *Saturday Review*, February 21, 1976, pp. 28–32.

16. José M. R. Delgado, *Physical Control of the Mind: Toward a Psychocivilized Society* (New York: Harper & Row, 1969).

17. Elliot S. Valenstein, *Brain Control* (New York: John Wiley & Sons, 1973).

18. Delgado, *op. cit.*, p.114.

19. Herbert A. Simon, "What Computers Mean for Man and Society," *Science* 195 (1977): 1186–91.

20. A technical report of this project appears in Duane Rumbaugh, ed., *Language Learning by a Chimpanzee: The Lana Project* (New York: Academic Press, 1977). A simpler summary appeared as "The Ape That 'Talks' with People," *Reader's Digest*, October, 1975, 94–98.

21. For an account of early medical observations which pointed to the asymmetry of brain function see Joseph E. Bogen, "The Other Side of the Brain: An Appositional Mind," *Bulletin of the Los Angeles Neurological Societies* 34 (1969): 135–62. New evidence indicates there is also some observable asymmetry in the physical structure of the two hemispheres (A. M. Galaburda, M. LeMay, T. L. Kemper, N. Geschwind, "Right-Left Asymmetries in the Brain," *Science* 199 (1978): 852–56.

22. I have drawn some of my descriptions of split brain experiments from Michael Gazzaniga's, "The Split Brain in Man," *Scientific American* 217, no. 2 (1967): 24–29.

23. Jere Levy and Marylou Reid, "Variations in Writing Posture and Cerebral Organization," *Science* 194 (1976): 337–39.

24. Most notably, Robert E. Ornstein, *The Psychology of Consciousness* (New York: Harcourt Brace Jovanovich, 1977). See also Thomas R. Blackburn, "Sensuous-Intellectual Complementarity in Science," *Science* 172 (1971): 1003–7.

25. James Ashbrook has used the asymmetrical brain model to suggest how mature faith demands balance. See James B. Ashbrook and Paul W. Walaskay, *Christianity for Pious Skeptics* (Nashville: Abingdon, 1977).

26. Emil Brunner, *The Misunderstanding of the Church* (Philadelphia: Westminster Press, 1953), pp. 48–49.

27. René Descartes, *The Meditations and Selections from the Principles of René Descartes* (LaSalle, Ill.: Open Court Publishing, 1948), p. 94.

28. Wilder Penfield, *The Mystery of the Mind* (Princeton: Princeton University Press, 1975), p. 79.

29. See, for example, John C. Eccles, "Hypothesis Relating to the Brain-Mind Problem," *Nature*, July 14, 1951, pp. 53–57; and his "The Brain-Mind Problem as a Frontier of Science" (Paper presented at the 1975 Nobel Conference, Gustavus Adolphus College, October, 1975).

30. Paul Badham, *Christian Beliefs About Life After Death* (New York: Barnes & Noble, 1976), p. 111.

31. Bogen, *op. cit.*, p. 117.

32. Roger W. Sperry, "Problems Outstanding in the Evolution of Brain Function" (James Arthur Lecture, American Museum of Natural History, New York, 1964), as cited by Ornstein, *op. cit.*, p. 29.

33. For more discussion of this issue see Roland Puccetti, "Brain Bisection and Personal Identity," *British Journal for the Philosophy of Science* 24 (1973): 339–55; and Larry W. DeWitt, "Consciousness, Mind, and Self: The Implications of the Split-Brain Studies," *British Journal for the Philosophy of Science* 26 (1975): 41–47.

34. Unless one views ESP as an occasional miraculous event which tells us no more about human nature than Peter's walking on water tells us about the laws of physics.

35. Jules Asher, "Geller Demystified," *APA Monitor*, February, 1975, pp. 4–5.

36. For a fascinating chronicle of this, see Martin Gardner's "Concerning an Effort to Demonstrate Extrasensory Perception by Machine," *Scientific American* 223, no. 4 (1975): 114–18.

37. This coin tossing illustration is adapted from Burton G. Malkiel, *A Random Walk Down Wallstreet* (New York: W. W. Norton, 1975).

38. Donald MacKay develops more of these analogies in many of his writings, including *Freedom of Action in a Mechanistic Universe* (Cambridge: Cambridge University Press, 1967).

39. William Pollard, *Chance and Providence* (New York: Harper & Row, 1958), p. 149.

40. Webster's New Collegiate Dictionary (1959) defines *unity* as the state of being one, singleness, a systematic whole. Although I have not argued for any specific philosophical theory of mind-body relation, my position does deny any philosophy which presumes that mind could exist separate from body.

Holism is also a slippery term; it is sometimes used by people who mean something quite different than a unity of mind and body. Mind and body may be viewed like different states which form a single country. It does not take much reflection to realize that this type of mind-body analogy is still dualistic; the different states are *separate* entities which together and in their interaction define the whole.

41. This is all that some who call themselves dualists want to argue—that although private experience may be a manifestation of the body, it cannot be reduced to physical description. This is not the meaning of dualism which these chapters attack.

42. Barry Commoner, "Do Life Processes Transcend Physics and Chemistry?" *Zygon* 3 (1968): 442–72; Michael Polanyi, "Life's Irreducible Structure," *Science* 160 (1968): 1308–12.

43. Roger W. Sperry, "A Modified Concept of Consciousness," *Psychological Review* 76 (1969): 532–36.

44. These analogies are incomplete. Unlike the mental phenomena of the whole brain, the symphony, the painting, and the Shakespearean play do not have a reciprocal influence upon their elements.

CHAPTER 4

Platonic Dualism or Hebraic Holism?*

What is our essential nature—two separate realities, physical and spiritual, or only one? On few issues do the beliefs of Christian lay people diverge so sharply from those of pastors, biblical scholars, and theologians. In one recent survey most Presbyterian lay leaders disagreed with the statement "The nature of man is unitary, not a dualism of body and soul"; the overwhelming majority of their pastors *agreed* with it.[1] Among biblical scholars there is a growing consensus that the Scriptures present human nature not as two distinct substances but as one whole entity.

Although the aim of the Bible is to tell us the story of God's saving activity, not to give us lessons in science and philosophy, its language does convey some assumptions about our human nature. Close scrutiny of the Old Testament Hebrew and New Testament Greek terminology has revealed a distinctly holistic picture. The meanings given to various words change slightly over time, yet it is remarkable that in this library of sixty-six books, written over at least twelve hundred years, in two languages, and under varying historical circumstances, a consistent understanding of human nature emerges.

OLD TESTAMENT ANTHROPOLOGY

What scientists have come to understand about the physical basis of mind and emotion was assumed in Old Testament

---

* Chapters such as this one which deal mostly with biblical theology will lean heavily on the work of respected biblical scholars and theologians. Any psychologist, starting from scratch, could find some texts here and there to support a particular contention, but I know no psychologist who is competent to examine all relevant biblical texts in their original languages. Fortunately, scholarship is a community enterprise and we can benefit from the insights of those who have devoted their lives to faithfully exploring the whole of Scripture.

thought. In Hebrew psychology, beings think with their hearts, feel with their bowels, and their flesh longs for God. One's physical being is the root of one's whole being. "The body is the predominant partner in the Hebrew idea of personality," Walther Eichrodt has written. "For the Hebrew, 'psychical' includes much that we should call simply physiological; they simply did not distinguish the two."[2] Woman was thought to be created not from man's "soul" but from his body—"Bone of my bone and flesh of my flesh."[3]

This holistic picture is clearly evident in the meanings of three important Hebrew words: *nephesh, ruach,* and *leb.* Since the usual rendering of these terms as "soul," "spirit," and "heart" is a source of some misunderstandings about the biblical idea of human nature, it will pay us to become acquainted with them.

The 755 occurrences of *nephesh* have different shades of meaning in different texts. "First and foremost the word means life . . . *life bound up with a body.*"[4] God formed man, breathed life into him, "and man became a living *nephesh.*"[5] That our *nephesh,* our whole being, terminates at death and that animals as well as humans are said to have *nephesh* makes it clear that its translation as "soul," which we usually understand to be an immortal, nonmaterial essence, is most unfortunate. As one Old Testament scholar concludes, "The unhappy rendering of the term by 'soul' opened the door from the start to the Greek beliefs concerning the soul. . . . The vital force connoted by [*nephesh*] has no independent numinous character, but is the gift of the Creator to the creature. It remains susceptible to the grip of death."[6]

There is, of course, a different meaning of our word *soul* which does no violence to Hebrew thought. When we say "there wasn't a soul in the room," we do not mean that there were no ghostly spirits to be seen, but only that no *person* was present. If we declare to someone, "I love you from the depths of my soul," we mean with our whole being, from the center of our self. Often, though, we confuse names with things. Because we speak of the "soul" we come to think it really exists as a separate entity. Nothing could be farther from what the Hebrews meant by *nephesh.* "The Bible is not suggesting that man has a soul as an invisible extra *thing* plugged into a bodily compartment. . . ."[7] We do not have *nephesh* (a soul); we *are nephesh* (living, breathing souls).[8]

The 378 occurrences of *ruach* assume diverse meanings. They denote wind, the spirit of God, the energy of life, and, later in the Old Testament, human life, with all its phenomena of consciousness. Thus, *nephesh* and *ruach,* "soul" and "spirit," eventually denote the same thing, although *ruach* involves a more religious point of view, stressing divine influence. "There is no trichotomy in Hebrew psychology," wrote H. Wheeler Robinson, "no triple division of human personality into 'body, soul, and spirit'."[9] Walther Eichrodt echoes this conclusion. *Nephesh* and *ruach* "always represent the whole life of the person from a particular point of view. A trichotomistic human psychology is therefore as little to be based on the Old Testament concepts as a dualistic one."[10]

The unity of mind and body in Hebrew thought is further evident in the extent to which reason and emotions are linked to specific body organs. Psychological functions are attributed to the eye, ear, mouth, flesh, bones, belly, breast, loins, and thighs. The most important organ of all is the heart (*leb*), which is mentioned 851 times in the Old Testament. This term is used variously to denote the whole personality, the emotional side of conscious life, or, most often, the intellect and will. The heart thus embraces a range of physical, emotional, rational, and volitional functions; it is the center of life which is called to hear the Word of God.

The belief that mental and spiritual qualities are manifested by specific body organs further demonstrates that

for the Hebrew, man is a unity, and that that unity is the body as a complex of parts, drawing their life and activity from a breath-soul, which has no existence apart from the body. . . . As Hebrew myth and legend often enshrine permanent truths about God, so the Hebrew ideas about man seem to have anticipated by intuition some of our modern science.[11]

NEW TESTAMENT ANTHROPOLOGY

The New Testament was written after Alexander the Great imposed the Greek language on the Jews. The expression of Hebrew faith in Greek words had significant consequences. As Thorleif Boman has noted, Jesus and the Apostles spoke Aramaic and lived in the Old Testament world of images. Soon after Jesus' death the early Christian community was severed from its motherland and the words of Jesus were preserved only in Greek—a language embodying different images and modes of thought. The dogma of the Christian Church was thereafter considerably influenced by Greek language and thought patterns.[12]

Platonic concepts carried by Greek language have penetrated through to modern times, coloring our interpretation of the New Testament. They lead us sometimes to read meanings that were not intended. When we read Paul's wish that "your spirit and soul and body be kept sound," we readily infer that Paul presumed three separate parts of human nature.[13] New Testament scholars assure us that this is not the case. The admonitions to "love the Lord your God with all your heart and with all your soul and with all your strength and with all your mind," to worship God in "spirit and truth," and to "present your bodies as a living sacrifice," are couched in differing images, but their meaning is the same.[14] They are simply different ways of expressing one fundamental injunction: commit your whole person to God.

An analysis of the words for persons in New Testament Greek reveals the same thing that was noted in the Old Testament: several interchangeable terms which refer to the whole person. Each of these terms describes the person from a different perspective. When Paul tells the Corinthians that he is present in spirit though absent in body, does this mean his spirit is in Corinth while his body exists spiritless elsewhere? This is obviously just a way of saying, "Although I'm not physically present, I'm thinking of you." Sometimes, as we saw in the last paragraph, more than one of these terms is used to add rhetorical emphasis, just as we often use redundant terms to emphasize an important point.

The Greek *psyche* parallels the Hebrew *nephesh* and is sometimes translated as "soul." The meaning of "soul" is often unambiguous. When Joseph brought his father Jacob and seventy-five "souls" into Egypt (Acts 7:14), he did not leave their bodies in Canaan. The rich farmer dreams of harvests so great that he can say to his *psyche*, "Soul, you have ample goods laid up for many years; take your ease, eat, drink, and be merry."[15]

What kind of soul is it that can eat, drink and be merry? A soul is a self, a person. In Rom. 2:9 every "human being" who does evil and suffers for it is a *psyche* and in Rom. 13:1 every "person" to be subjected to persons who govern is likewise a *psyche*. The whole man sins and the whole man is called to responsible citizenship. Paul, true to his Hebrew heritage, here thinks of man as a unity. . . . The Biblical teaching is not that one has a soul but that he is a soul.[16]

Other terms also describe persons from particular perspectives. *Pneuma* (spirit) characterizes the person in relationship with God and *sarx* (flesh) refers to the whole person alienated from God and fellow humans. The "works of the flesh" include jealousy, envy, and selfishness.[17] Since spirituality means relationship to God, not an entity within us, some scholars suggest doing away with words which shape a false understanding of spirit. Bruce Reichenbach put it this way:

To effect this important correction of our misuse of "soul" it might be healthy, at least for a while, to allow the term to drop from our religious vocabulary until such time as it can be reintroduced divorced from any reified content. Such an approach, far from destroying faith in the spiritual aspect of man, will aid in clarifying precisely wherein the spiritual lies, i.e., that it lies not in the possession of an entity, but in the style of life one leads insofar as it manifests a relation to God and to one's fellow man.[18]

The New Testament conception of spirit and body is further revealed in the word *soma,* meaning "body." Even for Paul, who was probably the most influenced by Greek thought of all biblical writers, "The only human existence that there is—even in the sphere of the Spirit—is somatic existence."[19] The variety of Paul's uses of *soma* indicates that it denotes the whole person. Never is a corpse called *soma.* "Thus," writes Rudolph Bultmann," Paul did not dualistically distinguish between man's self (his 'soul') and his bodily *soma* as if the latter were an inappropriate shell, a prison, to the former; nor does his hope expect a release of the self from its bodily prison but expects instead the 'bodily' resurrection. . . ."[20] When he teaches that husbands should love their wives as their own bodies, he means as their own selves. John A. T. Robinson summarizes Paul's view of the body:

The concept of the body forms the keystone of Paul's theology. In its closely interconnected meanings, the word [*soma*] knits together all his great themes. It is from the body of sin and death that we are delivered; it is through the body of Christ on the Cross that we are saved; it is into His body the Church that we are incorporated; it is by His body in the Eucharist that this Community is sustained; it is in our body that its new life has to be manifested; it is to a resurrection of this body to the likeness of His glorious body that we are destined. Here, with the exception of the doctrine of God, are represented all the main tenants of the Christian Faith—the doctrines of Man, Sin, the Incarnation and Atonement, the Church, the Sacraments, Santification, and Eschatology. To trace the subtle links and interaction between the different senses of this word [*soma*] is to grasp the thread that leads through the maze of Pauline thought.[21]

In summary, it is clear that the New Testament anthropology confirms the Old Testament witness that "man is a living unity."[22] This conclusion is reinforced by comparing the Platonic idea of immortal soul with the biblical teaching of the resurrected body.

IMMORTALITY OF THE SOUL OR RESURRECTION OF THE BODY?

If we were to ask an ordinary Christian today . . . what he conceives to be the New Testament teaching concerning the fate of man after death, with few exceptions we should get the answer: "The immortality of the soul." Yet this widely accepted idea is one of the greatest misunderstandings of Christianity.[23]

So begins Oscar Cullmann's classic 1958 essay, *Immortality of the Soul or Resurrection of the Dead?* Twenty years later the "misunderstanding" persists. Lay people still place their hope in the immortal soul, even while a growing chorus of biblical scholars and theologians are saying, mostly among themselves, that this is pagan doctrine. One children's book which found its way into our home explains the popular doctrine of the soul this way: "Maybe you have been to a funeral. You've seen the dead body. That's buried in the ground. But the inside part of you, the part that thinks and feels, that's the part that lives forever. This is the part of us that would go to hell."

To most of us, it is something of a shock to learn that the distinction between immortal soul and earthly body originates, not in the Bible, but in primitive thought, such as in the Greek pagan religion of the sixth century B.C. The idea came via the Pythagoreans and via Orphism, which, in turn, drew its inspiration from the Thracian worship of Dionysus. The Thracian cult held torchlight festivals filled with frantic music and dancing, culminating in a sacred frenzy through which worshipers achieved a sense of "spirituality" that broke free of the body's barriers. "In this 'sacred madness,'" reports Frank Stagg,

the "soul" seemed to leave the body to enter into union with the god. . . . From this sense of a soul freed from the body during the ecstatic experience came the further idea of a continuing, independent existence of the soul after death of the body, i.e., the idea of a divine and immortal soul.[24]

Plato, more than any other of the Greek thinkers, was responsible for refining and popularizing the idea of an immortal soul. In describing the death of Socrates in *Phaedo,* Plato has Socrates chronicle the arguments for immortality and for the duality of soul and body. In the end, Socrates lives his own teaching by drinking the hemlock with the calm conviction that his immortal soul will now find release from the prison house of his body. Bear in mind, Plato wrote several hundred years before the New Testament era.

Oscar Cullmann dramatizes the radical difference between Greek dualism and Christian holism by contrasting Socrates' and Jesus' approaches to death.

Like Jesus, Socrates has his disciples about him on the day of his death; but he discourses serenely with them on immortality. Jesus, a few hours before his death, trembles and begs his disciples not to leave him alone. . . . There is Socrates, calmly and composedly speaking of the immortality of the soul; here Jesus, weeping and crying. And then the death-scene itself. With sublime calm Socrates drinks the hemlock; but Jesus . . . cries: "My God, my God, why hast thou forsaken me?"[25]

For Socrates, death is welcome liberation. More than that, it is fundamentally *not dying*. No revolutionary event occurs; the soul lives on. For Jesus, death is no friend. It is nothingness, abandonment by God. It is, in Paul's words, "the last enemy."[26]

The human yearning for immortality, for invulnerability to death, is deeply embedded in us all. An awareness of the inevitability of death nevertheless breaks into our consciousness now and then. Each year at graduation I am shaken by the reality that we come together, we are intimate friends for a while, we go our own ways, and then we all die. Hours after celebrating the birth of my innocent, beautiful newborn daughter I wept in the sad realization that she, too, would soon grow old and die. I know just how the author of Ecclesiastes must have felt: "Generations come and generations go, but the world stays just the same."[27] "Indeed," wrote the Psalmist, "every living man is no more than a puff of wind."[28]

Surely the Scriptures are right: death is the ultimate enemy of all that is good in life. We all live under the "supreme penalty," the sentence of death. Unlike the Platonists, Christians do not believe that the divine attribute of immortality is intrinsic to human nature. But Christianity is not without its hope. It asserts that our lives possess value and hope, not because this is merited by our nature, but because God loves us. Christians believe that God values the lives he has created and that he will recreate them for eternity, *giving* us on that "great gettin-up morning" what we do not otherwise have—immortality. This resurrection hope is not something less than immortality of the soul, it is something more—the reconstitution of the whole person without imperfection. It is a hope grounded in God's initiative, not in our natural state. This is the hope Christians proclaim when saying the Apostle's Creed: "I believe in the resurrection of the body and the life everlasting."

C. S. Lewis has pointed out that belief in the immortal soul undercuts the significance of Christ's resurrection.[29] If human nature has always included an immortal soul, then Christ's achievement in rising from the dead was not the first defeat of death. But Christians believe that it was the first defeat, that God "alone has immortality," that Christ's resurrection forced open a door that had been locked since the death of the first person.[30] Lewis portrays his Christian belief concerning death and resurrection in the first of his *Chronicles of Narnia*. When the wicked witch turns creatures into stone statues, they cease to exist as conscious beings. But the ultimate victory belongs to the great lion Aslan. After sacrificing his life, Aslan breaks the bonds of death and returns to give new life to the statues. "Bless me!" declares the giant Rumblebuffin, "I must have been asleep."

The sharp contrast between this Christian view and the Greeks' belief in immortality was dramatically evident in Paul's visit to Athens—there was no laughter or mockery of Paul until he spoke of the resurrection. Let no one say that my faith is only in what can be empirically observed or rationally comprehended. That God will reconstitute the dead is as rationally incredible to us today as it was to the Greeks to whom Paul spoke.

Theologians have enjoyed discussing the nature of the resurrected body.[31] Surely, some say, resurrection cannot mean the literal reconstitution of the same body, because some of the elements of our bodies were previously a part of someone else's body. (Friends in physics and chemistry tell me that the next glass of water you drink may contain some atoms that were once in Moses' body.) Others argue that the recreated body will be identical to our present body, thus recreating the same mind and personality within it. Still others remind us of the new spiritual nature of the body to come. Of the details of this mystery we need not concern ourselves—this is a book about human nature, not about eschatology. The important point at present is that the Scriptural image of the afterlife is not that of an ethereal, disembodied soul, but of a renewed mind-body unit. Throughout the Bible, mind and spirit are seen as manifested by the body and inconceivable without it. To talk of the continuation of mind or soul after the death of the body is like talking of the continuation of running after the amputation of one's legs. For Plato or for Hinduism, on the other hand, mind predates the body and survives its death.

Scripture does not portray humans as disembodied spirits. At the transfiguration, Moses and Elijah appear as recognizable persons. Lazarus and Abraham are pictured in bodily form. The resurrection and ascension present no dichotomy between spiritual and material; the disciples were exposed to a living mind-body who appeared, ate food, and could be touched. I do not mean to push these examples too far; the spiritual body is portrayed differently than our present material body. But neither for this life nor for the life to come does Scripture give us a picture of mind and spirit separate from body. It therefore seems that, regardless of the actual nature of eternal life, this unified image is the human image with which we should live.

If the difference between the Greek assumption of immortality and the biblical assumption of bodily resurrection is so clear-cut, then we may wonder how the doctrine of immortal soul managed to infiltrate later Christian thought. Werner Jaeger has noted:

The most important fact in the history of Christian doctrine was that the father of Christian theology, Origen, was a Platonic philosopher at the school of Alexandria. He built into Christian doctrine the whole cosmic drama of the soul, which he took from Plato, and although later Christian fathers decided that he took over too much, that which they kept was still the essence of Plato's philosophy of the soul.[32]

St. Augustine referred to Plato as "the most pure and bright in all of philosphy." St. Augustine's own conversion involved a drastic turn from sensuality to asceticism, from the evil of the material body to the good of the spiritual soul.

John Calvin, who was much influenced by both Plato and Augustine, declared that Plato alone "rightly affirmed" the "immortal substance" of the soul, and that "there lies hidden in man something separate from body. . . . That man consists of a soul and a body ought to be beyond controversy. Now I understand by the term 'soul' an immortal yet created essence, which is his nobler part."[33]

Many of the old creeds reflect this blend of beliefs in a immortal soul and resurrection. The Athanasian Creed declares that "all men shall rise again," and then adds, almost as an afterthought, "with their bodies." The Heidelberg Catechism and the Westminster Confession both proclaim that at the resurrection our undying souls shall finally be reunited with our bodies. (See Figure 7 for one artist's rendition of this reunion.)

Is there more to be said for the body-soul dualism than my summary of recent biblical scholarship indicates? Not all biblical scholars and theologians agree with the holistic image. There are, to be sure, a few passages that seem troublesome at first glance. The best known of these is Jesus' admonition to "not fear those who kill the body but cannot kill the soul." But we must read on: "rather fear him who can destroy both soul and body."[34] What kind of soul is this if it can be killed? It is certainly not Plato's immortal soul. In the light of the many other passages declaring the reality of death and eventual resurrection, Jesus' statement seems to mean that we need not fear those who cannot take away the life principle. In other words, "Fear God, who is able to give you over completely to death; to wit, when he does not resurrect you to life."[35]

Figure 7. "The Reunion of the Soul and the Body." From *The Grave*, by Robert Blair. This engraving by L. Schiavonetti from William Blake's design. Courtesy Methuen & Co.

Appeals for the reality of an immortal soul come as strongly today from outside the church as from within it. The American Society for Psychical Research conducts studies on the existence of the soul. An Arizona miner, James Kidd, left his will to fund research intended to prove scientifically the existence of a soul which leaves the body at death. Hypnotists claim to have taken people back to earlier incarnations several centuries before.

These claims from the world of the occult illustrate Helmut Thielicke's argument that faith in the so-called immortality of the soul is no faith at all. It is rather a highly questionable assumption, which can be made even by a complete heathen and worldling. One can make it without caring two pins for God. One can still make it, even if one considers the resurrection of the Lord a highly superfluous spectacle of pious fantasy. . . . There is no such thing as immortality; God *gives* immortality.[36]

More thought-provoking on the immortality of the soul are reports by Elisabeth Kübler-Ross and by Raymond Moody about people who have been declared clinically dead and then revived.[37] Advances in high-speed rescue and resuscitation techniques are yielding a growing number of such cases, although since there is no exact moment of death, its definition is always somewhat arbitrary. A number of these people who have been revived claim to have had out-of-body experiences in which they watched the resuscitation attempts as though spectators. They claim to have seen deceased relatives, to have travelled down a tunnel and encountered a mysterious but loving being of light and to have experienced warmth, peace, even elation, before reuniting with their bodies.

Because these reports are all positive (no one has claimed a glimpse of hell), they have been understandably devoured by a public which yearns to be assured of blissful immortality.* Assuming the reports are truthful (they have not been systematically gathered and classified), what shall we make of them?[38] Do they confirm Plato's doctrine of the immortal soul (to which Moody refers approvingly)? The impossibility of any type of scientific experimentation on this phenomenon leaves it open to speculation. And anyone's speculation is sure to be shaped by the intrusion of existing beliefs.

Although the biblical claims for the spiritual body and the sleep state which precedes it are sufficiently ambiguous that they allow the possibility of the near-death experience, all that I have written of in this and the preceding chapter inclines me to skepticism. There are also other grounds for doubting the significance of these reports. The mind is quite capable of extraordinary experiences in

---

* We humans have a hard time accepting the limitations of our humanity. Believers in ESP hope to establish our potential for omniscience—reading others' minds and knowing the future. Immortalists likewise assume that we enjoy the imperishability of divinity. Although humanity is always tempted to arrogate to itself the attributes of God, the Christian faith proclaims this illusion unnecessary—it is okay to be merely human, because God accepts us as we are and promises to give us new life. We can therefore humbly accept our limitations without having to see ourselves as little gods.

situations other than near-death. Hallucinatory and anesthetic drugs can produce altered states of consciousness which seem vividly real, although in truth they are pure fantasy. Diminished sensory input to the brain—as occurs in experiments on sensory deprivation, and, perhaps, during the near-death experience as well—also induces the brain to manufacture hallucinations and out-of-body experiences. Strange manipulations of the body can produce strange manipulations of the mind, some of which have undeniable mystical significance for the people who experience them. If different people experience these altered states under similar circumstances, there will often be some similarities in their reports. Time perception is often greatly distorted. People faced with a sudden threat of death will sometimes report vivid, time-distorted experiences—while falling, for example. Complex mental events will transpire in seconds, just as apparently occurs in the near-death experiences.

The similarity of hallucinations from one person to another has been documented by Ronald Siegel and his colleagues.[39] Hundreds of people have experienced experimentally-induced hallucinations, often under the influence of drugs, and their reports examined for commonalities. The results are strikingly reminiscent of the near-death experiences reported by Moody. Under the influence of hallucinogenic drugs a number of subjects saw "a bright light in the center of the field of vision. . . . The location of this point of light created a tunnel-like perspective," as illustrated in Figure 8.

Other commonalities also duplicate the near-death reports. Vivid childhood memories often flashed past. Many of these images were mental reconstructions. The subjects would see themselves in a scene; obviously, these scenes were partially fictitious since in reality people do not look at themselves. The images became vividly real and would sometimes flash by at the rate of 10 per second. Moreover, the subjects frequently experienced themselves dissociated from their bodies.

The context in which the hallucination is experienced affects its content. If the drug is taken outdoors, people often "see" outdoor images, even if they are wearing blinders. One experiment found that people given an hallucinogenic drug in the context of a Good Friday service underwent a religious experience.[40]

Regardless of how the hallucinations are induced—whether by drugs, sensory deprivation, or whatever—it is presumed that what people are experiencing originates within their own brains. Various theories have been proposed to explain the physiological process involved. One theory is that when normal input from the

WHITE LIGHT seen during the early stages of intoxication with a hallucinogenic drug is portrayed. The visual imagery is reported to explode from the center to the periphery. Pattern appears initially in black and white, but bright colors may develop as the experience progresses.

Figure 8. Illustration © 1975 by Ronald K. Siegel, Ph.D. Used with permission.

outside world is suppressed the interior activity of the brain takes precedence. Louis West analogizes the process to a person gazing out a window at sunset. As the outside light dims, the fire in the fireplace behind the person comes to be reflected off the window, creating images which look as if they were coming from outside the window. The person's perception of a fire outside is a mirage, a reflected image.

Later chapters will present several examples of people inventing and believing ideas which serve a purpose for them, although patently false. Generally, the invented idea seems reasonable in view of the situation and the person's prior beliefs. I would thus predict that if near-death reports become available from different cultures, we will see that their content is somewhat culture-bound, not culture-free, as an immortal soul theory seemingly predicts.[41] It will always be difficult to gather these data because very few people are resuscitated from clinical death and most of these do not recall any mystical experience.[42] Indeed, the fact that most do not poses a problem for any attempt to infer universal truth from the experiences of the few. Surely, no one would want to argue that only some bodies possess immortal souls.

In summary, the near-death reports so closely exemplify the typical hallucinogenic pattern—the commonalities across people, the light, the tunnel, the memory flashbacks, the out-of-body experiences—and the mystical death-related content is so easily predictable from the context in which the experience occurs, that we are probably wise to take these reports as simply further testimony to the enormous creative capacities of the human mind. Although we should always be open to new discoveries and ideas—exploring human nature is a never-ending process—there is no compelling reason to give up the holistic image implied by both scientific research and recent biblical scholarship. In the *Interpreter's Dictionary of the Bible,* N. W. Porteous advises that "we are not to conclude that man is compounded of two separate entities, body and soul—the view characteristic of Orphism and Platonism."[43] The biblical idea of human nature is instead, to use H. Wheeler Robinson's oft-quoted phrase, that of "an animated body, and not an incarnated soul."[44] We may therefore conclude that *the holistic image implied by the resurrection doctrine is deeply consistent with the holistic anthropology of the Old and New Testaments— and with the emerging scientific picture as well.*

PRACTICAL IMPLICATIONS

More often than we realize, our personal attitudes and acts are rooted in doctrines of which we are only dimly aware. While one's unspoken image of human nature is only a single aspect of one's whole faith commitment, it is not without its practical effects. Consider the consequences of the dualistic and holistic assumptions. If the soul is believed to be the real self and the body its house, then what attitudes follow? Listen to Socrates:

> Do we believe death to be anything?
> We do, replied Simmias.
> And do we not believe it to be the separation of the soul from the body?
> Does not death mean that the body comes to exist by itself, separated

from the soul, and that the soul exists by herself, separated from the body? What is death but that?

It is that, he said.

Now consider, my good friend, if you and I are agreed on another point which I think will help us to understand the question better. Do you think that a philosopher will care very much about what are called pleasures, such as the pleasures of eating and drinking?

Certainly not, Socrates, said Simmias.

Or about the pleasures of sexual passion?

Indeed, no.

And, do you think that he holds the remaining cares of the body in high esteem? Will he think much of getting fine clothes, and sandals, and other bodily adornments, or will he despise them, except so far as he is absolutely forced to meddle with them?

The real philosopher, I think, will despise them, he replied.

In short, said he, you think that his studies are not concerned with the body? He stands aloof from it as far as he can, and turns toward the soul?

I do.

Well then, in these matters, first, it is clear that the philosopher releases his soul from communion with the body, so far as he can, beyond all other men?

It is.[45]

The body, Socrates goes on to explain, "fills us with passions, and desires, and fears, and all manner of phantoms, and much foolishness."[46] Mind and soul are good, the material world is bad.

The idea is still around. Television enacts ritual war on the evil body, observes Michael Novak: scrub, rinse, deodorize, sanitize. "To be Americanized, a man must retreat into his head, his body always under the sway and pressure of mind, proudly stiff and decorous and controlled."[47]

The soul (good) versus body (evil) dualism first made its way into Christianity as the gnostic heresy of the second century. Salvation became the release of the spirit through ascetic denial of the evil body and mystical rites aimed at gaining *gnosis,* saving knowledge. Today's refinement of this heresy suggests that salvation is purely a mental, verbal act, not the commitment of one's whole being. Evangelism becomes saving immortal souls rather than proclaiming the good news to the whole person. One's "Christian life" becomes distinct from the material activities of secular existence. Since life is merely the obstacle course to the pearly gates of the soul's liberation, poverty and oppression can be tolerated.

Niebuhr contrasts this dualism with biblical holism: "The monism of the Biblical view . . . is ultimately derived from the Biblical view of God as the creator and of the Biblical faith in the goodness of creation."[48] Our present bodily lives are valued aspects of God's creation. No wonder Christianity has played such a key role in the establishment of hospitals around the world. Elton Trueblood has noted that religions which minimize the importance of bodies offer little rational support for modern medicine. "Christianity, by contrast, is concerned with bodies as an integral part of its faith. The Christian who has any true understanding of his position, cares greatly about what happens to bodies. He knows that the Word became flesh (John 1:14)."[49]

Breaking down the cleavage between soul and body also reconciles the cleavage between the personal and social gospel. If matter and spirit are separate, then we may despise the material dimension, neglect it, abuse it, pollute it. But if the holistic human image is correct, then we can see why "Jesus was concerned with the whole man, as were the great prophets of Israel before him. Jesus fed the hungry, healed the sick, forgave sinners, accepted the rejects of society, and responded to human need at every level and expression."[50] Surely, if he were here today, he would be concerned with world hunger.

Our view of mind, spirit, and body has implications for our relationship with our *own* bodies as well as with the rest of creation. If it is true that without our bodies we are, quite literally, no-bodies, then the way we regard our own bodies assumes vital importance.

Accepting ourselves must include accepting our bodies. Many of us regard our bodies as something of an embarrassment. We are too fat or too short or too bald, and certainly we would not want our defects to be seen naked.

Loving ourselves must include being good to our bodies. I am pleased that at my college Physical Education is one of the stronger departments and that it is educating and motivating our whole campus community toward lifelong physical fitness and nutritional responsibility. We do not worship the body, but we believe that what we do to our bodies we do to ourselves. When the body is fit and its muscles relaxed, the *person* is healthy and relaxed. This holism also shapes the Christian view of sex. Sexual union reaches to the core of one's being because "our body is not something we have, separate from our person, but what we are."[51]

Knowing ourselves must include listening to our bodies. Our bodies respond with integrity, and we would do well to be sensitive to what they are saying. Although when painfully "in touch with our bodies," we might sometimes wish we could switch bodies with someone else, or wish at least for separate vacations for ourselves and our bodies, the truth is that we do not *have* bodies, we *are* our bodies. On this important concept scientific research and biblical scholarship seem to be approaching a consensus.

NOTES

1. Presbyterian Panel, "The November, 1973 Questionnaire," Research Division of the Support Agency, United Presbyterian Church, U.S.A., 475 Riverside Drive, New York, 1974.

2. Walther Eichrodt, *Theology of the Old Testament*, vol. 2 (Philadelphia: Westminster Press, 1967), p. 139.

3. Gen. 2:23 RSV.

4. H. Wheeler Robinson, "Hebrew Psychology," in *The People and the Book*, ed. A. S. Peake (New York: Oxford University Press, 1925), p. 360.

5. Gen. 2:7 RSV.

6. Eichrodt, *op. cit.*, pp. 134, 140.

7. Donald M. MacKay, "Man as a Mechanism," in *Christianity in a Mechanistic Universe*, ed. D. M. McKay (Downer's Grove, Ill.: InterVarsity Press, 1965), p. 53.

8. Hans Walter Wolff, *Anthropology of the Old Testament* (London: SCM Press, 1974), p. 10. If this is true, then the argument over when a fetus gains its soul becomes gratuitous.

9. Robinson, *op. cit.*, p. 362.

10. Eichrodt, *op. cit.*, p. 148.

11. Robinson, *op. cit.*, pp. 366, 382.

12. Thorleif Boman, *Hebrew Thought Compared with Greek* (New York: Norton, 1960).

13. I Thess. 5:23 RSV.

14. Luke 10:27 RSV (Jesus is here restating Old Testament teaching ([see Deut. 6:5 RSV]); John 4:24 RSV; and Rom. 12:1 RSV.

15. Luke 12:19.

16. Frank Stagg, *Polarities of Man's Existence in Biblical Perspective* (Philadelphia: Westminster Press, 1973), pp. 49–50.

17. Gal. 5:19.

18. Bruce Reichenbach, "Life After Death: Possible or Impossible?," *Christian Scholar's Review* 3 (1974); 232–44.

19. Rudolph Bultmann, *Theology of the New Testament* (New York: Scribner's, 1951), p. 192.

20. *Ibid.*, p. 17.

21. John A. T. Robinson, *The Body: A Study in Pauline Theology* London: SCM Press, 1957), p. 9.

22. Bultmann, *op. cit.*, p. 209. There are, to be sure, some biblical scholars who do not draw the Hebrew-Greek contrast as sharply as my sources have done.

23. Oscar Cullman, *Immortality of the Soul or Resurrection of the Dead? The Witness of the New Testament* (New York: Macmillan, 1958).

24. Stagg, *op. cit.*, p. 62.

25. Cullman, *op. cit.*, pp. 16–17.

26. I Cor. 15:26 RSV.

27. Eccles. 1:4, Good News.

28. Psalms 39:5, Good News.

29. C. S. Lewis, *Miracles* (New York: Macmillan, 1947), p. 173.

30. I Timothy 6:16 RSV.

31. For an interesting exchange on this issue, see Reichenbach, *op. cit.;* William Hasker, "Resurrection and Mind-Body Identity: Can There be Eternal Life Without a Soul?," *Christian Scholar's Review* 4, (1975); 319–25; and Bruce Reichenbach, "Re-Creationism and Personal Identity," *Christian Scholar's Review* 4 (1975); 321–30.

32. Werner Jaeger, "The Greek Ideas of Immortality," *Harvard Theological Review* 52 (1959); 146.

33. John Calvin, Institutes of the Christian Religion, I, XV, 6, 2 (John T. McNeill, ed., Ford L. Battles, trans.), Westminster, 1975, pp. 192, 185, 184. Not all of the early Protestants thought this way. William Tyndale and John Milton were among those who rejected the idea of human immortality. (See Norman T. Burns, *Christian Mortalism from Tyndale to Milton* [Boston: Harvard University Press, 1972]).

34. Matthew 10:28 RSV.

35. John A. T. Robinson, *op. cit.,* p.27.

36. Helmut Thielicke, *How the World Began* (Philadelphia: Fortress Press, 1961), pp. 248–49.

37. Raymond A. Moody, Jr., *Life After Life* (New York: Bantam Books, 1975); and *Reflections on Life After Life* (New York: Bantam Books, 1977).

38. Ronald K. Siegel, "Hallucinations," *Scientific American,* October, 1977: 132–40.

39. This experiment by W. N. Pahnke is discussed by John Bowker, *The Sense of God* (Oxford: Clarendon Press, 1973), p. 151.

40. Moody's reports apparently arise mostly from people who volunteered cases which fit his description. This self-selection procedure is obviously vulnerable to bias.

41. I know of no hard evidence on this, although one brief report supports this hunch (see Daniel Goleman, "Back From the Brink," *Psychology Today* 10, no. 11 [April, 1977]: pp. 56–59).

42. Robert Kastenbaum, editor of a leading journal on death and dying, notes that although there are bushels of journeys into the life-death border territory of which people remember nothing, the media do not feast on these (see his "Temptations From the Ever After," *Human Behavior,* September, 1977, pp. 28–33).

43. *Interpreter's Dictionary of the Bible,* III (Nashville: Abingdon, 1962), p. 244.

44. H. Wheeler Robinson, *op. cit.,* p. 362.

45. Plato, *op. cit.,* p. 9.

46. *Ibid.,* p. 11.

47. Michael Novak, "The Experience of Nothingness," Introduction to Helmut Thielicke, *Nihilism* (New York: Shocken, 1969).

48. Reinhold Niebuhr, *The Nature and Destiny of Man,* vol. 1 (New York: Scribner's 1964), p. 13.

49. Elton Trueblood, *Quarterly Yoke Letter* 16, no. 4 (1975).

50. Stagg, *op. cit.,* p. 59.

51. John A. T. Robinson, *op. cit.,* p. 27.

PART III

Behavior and Belief

What is the relation between thought and action, character and conduct, word and deed, faith and works—between that constellation of attitudes and beliefs which we call the "inner life" and a person's overt behavior? This enduring question cuts across theology and educational and moral philosophy and has also been a recent preoccupation of social psychology. The prevailing assumption has been that personal intention determines a person's public behavior. So if you want to change the way people act, you had best change their hearts and minds. This is the implicit theory that lies behind most teaching, preaching, counseling, child rearing, and various persuasive appeals. If social psychology has taught us anything during the last twenty years, it is that the reverse is equally true: we are as likely to act ourselves into a way of thinking as to think ourselves into action.

Chapter 5 assembles the evidence for this important generalization—from social psychological experiments and from real life observations of human change—and some suggested explanations are indicated for this effect of behavior on belief. Chapter 6 relates this recent attitude research to the development of religious faith and identifies practical implications for church life and Christian nurture. We will see that the new understandings of social psychology affirm and enliven some ancient biblical truths.

CHAPTER 5

Action and Attitude*

Attitude is the most widely used concept in social psychology. For most social psychologists, *attitude* is a package term that refers to our thoughts, feelings, and actions. Thus, action is thought of as part of attitude. If, for example, a person *believes* that a particular ethnic group is lazy and aggressive, he or she will probably *dislike* such people and may therefore *act* in a discriminatory manner. But in practice we distinguish attitude from action. Attitude usually refers to what is inside us, especially to the intensity and direction of our feelings about something or someone. This is the sense in which I use the term in asking, what is the relationship between what a person *does* (on the outside) and what the person *is* (on the inside)?

DO ATTITUDES PREDICT BEHAVIOR?

Conventional wisdom, as already noted, emphasizes the effect of our beliefs and attitudes on our actions. Although the thrust of this chapter is that beliefs and attitudes also follow actions, I am not denying this conventional wisdom. If I believed there were no consequences to achieving intellectually enlightened beliefs and attitudes, there would be little point to my teaching or, for that matter, to my writing these words. (Consider the irony were I to suggest that spoken and written words are usually forgotten or, at best, impotent, and that you will find it useful never to forget this!) A concern for truth is rooted in the conviction that ideas and doctrinal propositions make some difference. Indeed, I am interested in the internal consequences of action because beliefs and attitudes *are* a

*I gratefully acknowledge the National Science Foundation's support for the preparation of this chapter (Grant SER75–21247—"Behavior and Belief: An Integration and Application of Social Psychology").

source of subsequent action, as well as being intrinsically important. We all know in our hearts that our intentions do influence
our actions—which is one reason why it is said that a man's best
friend is his dogma.

Nevertheless, as will be emphasized in ensuing chapters, internal dispositions are turning out to be less predictive of behavior
than people have generally supposed. Allan Wicker, after reviewing several dozen studies covering a wide range of people, attitudes, and behaviors, concluded that seldom does a measurement
of some general attitude predict more than 10 percent of the observed variation in overt behavior.[1] Attitude toward cheating, for
instance, bears little relation to actual cheating. The reported attitude of members toward their churches has only a modest relationship with church attendance. Self-described racial attitudes
have little correspondence with actual interracial behavior, and so
on.

It is therefore hardly susprising that attempts to change people's
behavior by changing their attitudes often fall flat. Information
about the dangers of smoking has only modestly affected the behavior of those who already smoke. Increased public awareness of
the desensitizing and brutalizing effects of a prolonged diet of television violence has caused most Americans to *say* they want less
violent programing—but they still watch it as much as ever. Appeals to drive safely have far less effect on accident rates than environmental changes like lower speed limits and divided high-
ways.[2] T. S. Eliot said it well in *The Hollow Men:*

> Between the idea
> And the reality
> Between the motion
> And the act
> Falls the shadow.

Why this disparity between attitudes and behavior? Is common
sense all that wrong? Recent analysis of the attitude-behavior controversy helps clarify the conditions under which attitudes *will*
predict behavior. The modest relation between what people say
and what they do is more understandable when we realize that
both attitude expressions and overt behavior are determined by
several factors, as seen in Figure 9.

People's *expressed* attitudes may imperfectly reflect their actual
attitudes for a variety of reasons, including the nature of the questions asked and the conditions under which the responses are
elicited. This was neatly demonstrated in 1964 when the United

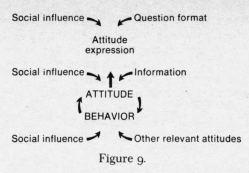

Figure 9.

States House of Representatives overwhelmingly passed a salary increase for itself in an off-the-record vote and moments later overwhelmingly defeated the same bill on a roll-call vote. Potential public criticism obviously made the overt expression a distortion of the true congressional sentiment. A person's behavior is also subject to other influences besides attitudes. As will be stressed in Chapter 10, social influences on people are enormous, as Peter knew well after his denial of Jesus.

When these other influences are minimized or when the person's behavior is averaged across many situations, an attitude can actually predict behavior fairly well. George Gallup effectively predicts voter behavior because his attitudinal measure is specific to the behavior in question, and because the anonymity of the voting booth minimizes other social influences. A recent survey of 640 white residents of the Detroit area ascertained their attitudes toward open housing.[3] Three months later, when each of those polled was asked to sign petitions concerning open housing, 80 percent responded in accord with their prior attitude statements. Here again, the attitude expression was specific to the behavior in question, and the attitude response and the action were elicited under similar social circumstances.[4]

Since it is evident that the relationship between attitude expressions and actions can range from no relationship to a substantial one, depending on the conditions under which the relationship is studied, we may conclude that attitudes are important as *one* determinant of behavior. Now the real fun begins as we turn our attention to the less commonsensical idea that behavior determines attitudes. If it be true that people *will* sometimes stand up for what they believe, it is equally true that people will believe in what they stand up for. The unity of thought and action is seen as much in the extent to which thought is the offspring of action as in the reverse. Much of the research which documents this conclusion is inspired by social psychological theories. But instead of looking at the theories first, I think it will be more interesting to turn things around and first marshall the evidence for the effects of behavior on attitude, for this principle synthesizes and makes intelligible a wide range of seemingly unrelated phenomena. As I present this litany of evidence, I invite you to play theorist and speculate *why* action affects attitude and then to compare your abstractions with the theoretical explanations which social psychologists have proposed.

THE CONTRIBUTION OF ACTION TO BELIEFS AND ATTITUDES

How do we learn to bicycle, type, play a musical instrument, or swim? Each of these skills is primarily acquired by *doing* them. We can read books on bicycling, but we cannot *know* bicycling until we perform the actions. The effect of action on knowing is easily recognized in these instances. But is the effect limited to knowing physical skills? Consider the following:

> A person is hypnotized and told to perform an act later and to forget being told to do so. At the prescribed time the act is committed as specified. But if asked why, the person volunteers an ingenious explanation for the action. The act produces the idea.

> A man has electrodes temporarily implanted in a brain region which controls head motion. When the electrode is stimulated by remote control, the patient always turns his head. Unaware of the remote stimulation, the patient thinks his evoked activity is spontaneous. When questioned, he always offers a reasonable explanation for it: "I am looking for my slipper," "I heard a noise," "I am restless," or "I was looking under the bed." [5]

> A split-brain patient is induced to blush by briefly presenting a picture of a nude to the nonverbal right side of her brain. When asked why she is blushing, she invents—and apparently believes—a plausible explanation. Another split-brain patient has the word *smile* flashed to the right hemisphere. He obliges and forces a smile. Asked why, he explains that the experiment is very funny.

> People (and animals) exposed to a perceptual illusion through distorting lenses or a misshaped room find that intellectual knowledge of reality does not correct the illusion. Activite experience is necessary for the development of correct perceptual knowledge.

These illustrations hint that the effects of action on knowing are not limited to physical skills. Indeed, the mental aftereffects of behavior are evident in such a rich variety of experimental and social situations that we can only sample from the smorgasbord. I trust that these examples will, nonetheless, sufficiently document how powerful a force this self-persuasion process is in shaping people's beliefs and attitudes.

Role Playing

The concept of *role* is borrowed from the theatre and, as in the theatre, refers to prescribed actions—actions expected of those who occupy a particular social position. When stepping into a new social role we may therefore feel somewhat inauthentic. But our sense of phoniness generally does not long endure. Roger Brown expressed this well:

In the playing of roles in society I think we function . . . first with conscious technique, later living the part. Try to remember a time when you had newly assumed some role that made a sharp break with your previous life. The first days of the freshman year in college or the first days in the Army will serve. At such times one is keenly alert to a new set of prescriptions and one tries to learn them and to satisfy them. The talk of college students or soldiers, their routines, their tastes and values are alien at first. You can still distinguish between that which is really you and that which you have undertaken to become. There is a feeling of "walking through the part," but this usually passes and one beomes a student or a soldier. . . . Important roles leave a residue in the personality, indeed personality is largely an integration of all the roles that have been played.[6]

There is evidence to confirm these speculations about the effects of role acting. Young women smokers engaged in playing the emotional role of lung cancer victim as part of an experiment subsequently reduced their smoking more than those merely given factual information about the dangers of smoking.[7] In another study, researchers observed industrial workers who were promoted to shop steward (a union position) or foreman (a company position). The new positions demanded new behavior of the men and new attitudes soon developed. The foremen became more sympathetic to the management and the stewards to the union.[8]

This study hints at the tremendous importance of one's choice of vocational role. It affects not only what job you do, but also the attitudes and values you are likely to develop. Idealistic new teachers, police officers, soldiers, and managers soon internalize their roles, with significant effects on their attitudes and personalities. The marines "make a man out of you"—not by intellectual indoctrination, but by active practice of the new role requirements. A recent study of sixteen hundred young men revealed that the status of their occupations had a direct effect on their self-esteem; those who obtained higher status jobs developed higher self-esteem.[9]

The effect of behavior on attitude is evident even in the theatre, where role playing is more artificial. Self-conscious play acting may diminish as the actor becomes absorbed into the role and experiences genuine emotion. Fantasy takes on the trappings of reality as each person acts within the rules of an imaginary reality.

The Foot-in-the-Door-Phenomenon

We can all recall times when, after agreeing to help out with a project or to hold an organizational office, we ended up far more involved than we ever intended to be and vowing that *next* year we would remember to refuse burdensome demands. How does this process happen? A number of experiments indicate that if you want people to do a big favor for you, a good technique is to get them to do a small favor first. In the best-known demonstration of this principle, California housewives who had been asked to sign a safe-driving petition were more likely to comply later with a bigger request to place a large, ugly "Drive Carefully" sign on their front lawns than were women who had not first been approached for the small favor.[10] Several features of this experiment are common to nearly all the situations in which a behavior commitment is internalized. The petition signature was an *irrevocable, public* action which was *chosen*, not coerced by threat or bribe. We will see again and again that when people bind themselves to public behaviors *and* perceive these acts to be their own doing, they come to believe more strongly in their action.

Note also that this experiment demonstrates the reciprocal influence of action and attitude. The small favor had an internal consequence which was demonstrated by the subsequent behavior (agreeing with the large request). This spiraling relation of action and attitude is evident in many other situations as well. In the best-known experiments in social psychology, Stanley Milgram induced adult males to deliver what were supposedly traumatizing electric shocks to an innocent victim in an adjacent room.[11] The participants were recruited by newspaper advertisements to assist in a learning experiment. In their role as "teacher" they were to inform the "learner" of wrong answers by flicking a switch on an elaborate shock panel with voltages ranging from 15 to 450 volts. The teacher was instructed to start with the lowest voltage and to increase the shock level one step each time the learner gave a wrong answer. The "shocking" result was that 65 percent of the teachers fully complied with the experimenter's commands right up to 450 volts—even after the learner pounded on the wall and then fell silent, in one experiment, and feigned agonized screams and shrieks of protest in another.

Although the majority of these men underwent severe emotional conflict while obeying the experimenter's commands, they were unable to free themselves from the role to which they had been assigned. How did they become so entrapped? Surely, if someone asked you to shock someone else for bad responses and if, upon delivering the first shock, you heard screams of protest, complaints of a heart disturbance, and then no responses at all, you would disengage yourself from the situation. But this is not what Milgram's subjects experienced. Their first commitment was a mild one—fifteen volts—and it elicited no protest. By the time seventy-five volts had been administered and the supposed victim first indicated discomfort, the teacher had already chosen to comply with the role demands on five occasions. Thus on the next trial he was asked to commit an action which was only slightly more extreme than what he had already bound himself to. His external behavior and his internal disposition were feeding on each other in a spiraling escalation. This is one way in which ordinary people can become unwitting agents of evil.

This entrapment process occurs in other real life situations as well. Salespeople and seducers make use of it. Our innocuous initial commitment—returning a card for more information and a free gift, agreeing to attend a meeting just to hear about a particular need—leads to great involvement. The day after I wrote these last words a life insurance salesman came to my office and offered to do an impressive family financial analysis for me. After finishing his presentation, he did not ask whether I wished to buy anything or even whether I wished to engage their free service. His question was rather a small foot-in-the-door, carefully calculated to elicit my agreement: did I think people would find this sort of information helpful?

Entrapping situations are not always so innocuous. If in the Netherlands during World War II the Nazis had immediately started arresting Dutch Jews and deporting them to concentration camps and gas chambers, they would probably have encountered even stiffer resistance from the Dutch people. But their technique was far subtler:

First of all, they required the Jews to wear yellow stars of David (a bit silly, but nothing to get upset about); then the Jews were forbidden to use public parks; then they were restricted in their employment; then they

were forbidden to live in certain areas; then they were forced to move into
a restricted ghetto area; then that area was sealed off with barbed wire
and gun emplacements. After waiting an appropriate length of time, the
Nazis spirited the first Dutch Jews to "work camps" in Germany. Each
step seemed less severe, once there had been compliance with the previous step.[12]

This same process of step-by-step commitment, of spiraling action and attitude, contributed to the escalation of the Vietnam war.
Analysts of the Pentagon Papers have noted that once difficult
decisions were made and defended, our leaders seemed blind to information which was incompatible with their acts. There was retention of ideas in harmony with the action, but selective inattention to information that undermined administration assumptions.
As Ralph White put it, "There was a tendency, when actions were
out of line with ideas, for decision-makers to align their ideas with
their actions."[13] Each turn of the screw created a new position to
be defended.

Effects of Moral and Immoral Acts

This last example suggests the interesting possibility that acts
which are morally discrepant from one's existing values may set in
motion a process of self-justification which leads ultimately to sincere belief in the act. Thomas Jefferson recognized this possibility
in 1785:

He who permits himself to tell a lie once finds it much easier to do it a
second and third time, till at length it becomes habitual; he tells lies
without attending to it, and truths without the world's believing him. This
falsehood of the tongue leads to that of the heart, and in time depraves all
its good dispositions.

Experiments bear out this point. People induced to give verbal or
written witness to something about which they have real doubts
will generally begin to believe what they are saying, *provided* they
were not excessively bribed or coerced into doing so. This is a well-
known phenomenon in social psychology, and we shall return to it
later when discussing possible theoretical explanations for the effect of action on attitude.

Harming an innocent victim also leads to an interesting side effect: the aggressor will often derogate the victim, especially when
the victim does not have a chance to reestablish equity by retaliat-
ing.[14] In one experiment, subjects watched another student being
interviewed and then told the student that he seemed shallow, un-

trustworthy, and dull. After saying these hurtful things, they evidenced increased dislike for the victim, especially if they had been gently coaxed rather than arbitrarily coerced into making these statements and if they expected no chance to retract them. Other studies make the same point: people induced to deliver electric shocks to other people tend to derogate their victims after causing them pain. In all these studies, too, people were most likely to convince themselves of their action if they had not been coerced, that is, if their act resulted from a conscious decision.

Once again, the laboratory studies point to and help us understand some tragic real life parallels. People who are cruel toward real victims do not come out unscathed. In times of war soldiers will generally derogate their victims, as in the dehumanizing references to Vietnamese people as "gooks." This is yet another instance of the spiraling effects of action and attitude: committing atrocities makes it easier to commit them again. The same point holds for prejudice in general. The social structure generates attitudes appropriate to it. If a dominant group holds another in slavery, slaves are likely to be perceived as having those traits which justify continuing the exploitation. Just as the aggressor derogates the victim in laboratory experiments, so also do oppressors denigrate their victims in real life.

These observations can help us understand why evil runs deeper than conscious decisions to engage in it. Evil acts not only reflect the self, they shape the self. Situations which elicit evil acts corrode the moral sensitivity of the actor. If, indeed, our motives are corrupted by immoral action, then evil power must be something more pervasive than evil intentions.[15] Consider the following interview with a man who was just a small cog in the Nazi machine.

Q. Did you kill people in the camp? A. Yes.
Q. Did you poison them with gas? A. Yes.
Q. Did you bury them alive? A. It sometimes happened. . . .
Q. Did you personally help kill people? A. Absolutely not, I was only paymaster in the camp.
Q. What did you think of what was going on? A. It was bad at first but we got used to it.
Q. Do you know the Russians will hang you?
A. (Bursting into tears) Why should they?
What have I done? [16]

Fortunately, the principle cuts in the other direction as well. Moral action has positive effects on the actor. Experiments demonstrate that when children are induced to resist temptation, they will internalize their conscientious behavior if the deterrent, though sufficient to elicit the desired behavior, is yet mild enough to leave them with a sense of choice. In one dramatic experiment, elementary school children were introduced to an extremely attractive battery-controlled robot, but instructed not to play with it while the experimenter was out of the room.[17] The experimenter used a severe threat with some children and a mild threat with the remainder, although either was sufficient to deter the child. Several weeks later, a different researcher, with no apparent connection to the earlier events, left each child to play in the same room with the same toys. Fourteen of the eighteen children who were given the severe threat now freely played with the robot; but two-thirds of those given the mild deterrent still *resisted* playing with the robot. Having previously made a conscious choice to not play with the toy, they apparently internalized their avoidance of the toy and this new attitude controlled their subsequent action.

Freud recognized this point years ago: "Every renunciation then becomes a dynamic fount of conscience; every fresh abandonment of gratification increases its severity and intolerance . . ."[18] John Dewey put it a bit more sympathetically: "Only the man whose habits are already good can know what the good is."[19]

All this suggests that the ancient discipline of doing penance may have had something to commend it—not for any manipulative effect on God, for his grace is already ours to enjoy—but because one antidote for the corrupting effects of evil action is repentant action. As James Burtchaell has written,

People have somehow got it into their heads that the evil in their lives will evaporate at their wish. But we are born in selfishness and nurture the infection within us by years and years of action for our own convenience. The way to purge the evil of years of action is by action.[20]

The effect of moral action on moral thinking is apparent in one other set of experiments. These demonstrate that children who are actively engaged in enforcing rules or in teaching moral norms to younger children subsequently follow the moral code better than children who are not given the opportunity to be teachers or enforcers. This indicates that the exercise of discipline has an effect on the disciplinarian as well as on the target, suggesting that opportunities for responsibility, such as first-born children often have, may be one way to enhance self-control.[21] Jean Piaget has likewise suggested that spontaneous rule enforcement during informal children's play contributes to the development of mature moral judgments.[22]

Interracial Behavior and Racial Attitudes

If moral action is conducive to moral attitudes, might not the elicitation of more positive interracial behavior lead to improved racial attitudes? Such was the testimony of Kenneth Clark, cited by the Supreme Court in its historic 1954 school desegregation decision. The argument ran something like this: if we wait for the heart to change—through preaching and teaching—we will wait a long time for racial justice. But if we go at it the other way around and legislate moral action, we can, under the appropriate conditions, indirectly affect heartfelt attitudes. Although this idea ran counter to the popular notion that "you can't legislate morality"— which in a sense is right, as you cannot *directly* legislate moral attitudes—the evidence suggests that in fact, substantial cognitive change has followed on the heels of desegregation:

> Since the Supreme Court decision, the percentage of white Americans favoring integrated schools has approximately doubled.
>
> In ten years after the Civil Rights Act of 1964 the percentage of white Americans who described their neighborhoods, friends, co-workers, or fellow students as all-white declined about 20 percent for each of these measures—a significant increase in interracial behavior. During the same period, the percentage of white Americans who said that blacks should be allowed to live in any neighborhood increased from 65 percent to 87 percent.
>
> More uniform national standards against discrimination have been followed by decreasing differences in racial attitudes among people of differing religion, class and geographic region. As we have come to act more alike, we have come to think more alike.

This evidence does not prove the point, for there are other possible ways of accounting for the changed attitudes, but it is at least consistent with the assumption that attitudes follow behavior.

In much of the research described it is clear that the attitudinal consequences of behavior are not uniform under all conditions. Behavior which is induced but not forced and which is committed publicly and irrevocably will have the greatest attitudinal aftereffects. Theorists have therefore speculated that maximum impact on racial attitudes will occur when there is a substantial amount of interracial behavior, when the person feels some sense of choice in the matter, and when authorities and laws make plain that the behavior change is inevitable and irrevocable. The practical problem has been how to offer people some sense of choice for behavior which is decreed. The threat to personal freedom presented by court-ordered busing has elicited a strong reaction, as when residents of Lamar, South Carolina, responded to forced busing by overturning school buses—with children inside. Yet it is amazing how, given time and conditions which promote cooperation, hostilities can soften. Once in a desegregated environment, most whites choose to behave at least politely toward blacks and their attitudes begin to fall in line with their positive behavior. This has been demonstrated over and over again, although it is also true that conditions which foster competition and negative interracial behavior increase prejudice.

The contention that positive interpersonal behavior fosters liking is supported by control experiments. Doing a favor for an experimenter or another subject leads to increased liking for that person. Helping people, even less competent people, increases attraction toward those helped.[23] (This is the reverse of the experiments which demonstrate that causing harm to another leads a person to derogate the victim.)

This notion was put to practical use by Benjamin Franklin in 1737 when, as the thirty-one-year-old clerk of the Pennsylvania General Assembly, he was disturbed by opposition from another important legislator. Franklin set out to win him over:

I did not . . . aim at gaining his favour by paying any servile respect to him but, after some time, took this other method. Having heard that he had in his library a certain very scarce and curious book I wrote a note to him expressing my desire of perusing that book and requesting he would do me the favour of lending it to me for a few days. He sent it immediately and I return'd it in about a week, expressing strongly my sense of the favour. When we next met in the House he spoke to me (which he had never done before), and with great civility; and he ever after manifested a readiness to serve me on all occasions, so that we became great friends and our friendship continued to his death. This is another instance of the truth of an old maxim I had learned, which says, "He that has once done you a kindness will be more ready to do you another than he whom you yourself have obliged."[24]

Social Movements

The effect of a society's racial behavior on its racial attitudes suggests the possibility, and the danger, of employing the same idea for political socialization on a mass scale. This was clearly evident in Nazi Germany, where participating in mass meetings, wearing uniforms, demonstrating, and, especially, the enforced public greeting "Heil Hitler" established for many a profound inconsistency between behavior and belief. Historian Richard Grunberger reports that

The 'German greeting' was a powerful conditioning device. Having once decided to intone it as an outward token of conformity, many experienced schizophrenic discomfort at the contradiction between their words and their feelings. Prevented from saying what they believed they tried to establish their psychic equilibrium by consciously making themselves believe what they said.[25]

The communist system in China employs similar techniques. Ritualistic denouncements of imperialism and praise for Chairman Mao are obviously intended to produce committed Maoists.

The practice, however, is not limited to totalitarian regimes. Our own political rituals—the daily flag salute by school children, the singing of the national anthem—build private conformity to patriotism through public conformity. I can recall my own fears of the Russians after participating in numerous air raid drills in my elementary school not far from the Boeing Company in Seattle. Several observers have noted that the civil rights marches and demonstrations of the 1960s were as important for what they contributed to the identity and commitment of the demonstrators as for their direct effects on legislation. It took an *idea* whose time had come to initiate these actions, yet the public action helped precipitate a more radical commitment to the cause. The President's Commission on Campus Unrest observed this same dynamic in the escalation of the radical student movement.

The direct functional cause of campus unrest has been the free existential act of commitment which each member of the student movement has made to a particular political vision, to the practice of expressing that vision publicly, and to particular acts of protest. To say this is to state more than a simple deductive truth, for the choice of an activist mode of expressing political opinion has important consequences for the development of that opinion itself. . . . As he acts in behalf of his vision, and especially as he does so in the face of opposition, his sense of commitment often grows.[26]

Ritual, Myth, and Identity

This social psychological discussion of the interplay between behavior and belief brings us close to what anthropologists and scholars in the humanities have understood as the reciprocal union of ritual with myth and identity.[27] Ritual repetitive behaviors both reflect and convey aspects of human experience which are otherwise difficult to fully communicate. Political rituals, like inaugurations, and social rituals, like weddings and funerals, express deep meaning. The anti-war rituals of the late 1960s took what the participants already knew in their heads and drove it into their souls.

Ritual also helps establish continuity between past and present. "When Israel ate the Passover," noted Gerhard von Rad, "she was manifestly doing more than merely remembering the Exodus: She was entering into the saving event of the Exodus itself and participating in it in a quite 'actual' way"[28] Erik Erikson even argues that personality evolves through ritual behaviors appropriate to each stage of child development.[29]

Brainwashing

In the public's mind the most dramatic instance of human change is suggested by the term *brainwashing*. Actually, the Chinese "thought control" program to which American POW's were subjected during the Korean War was not nearly as irresistible as this term suggests. Still, it was disconcerting that several hundred POW's cooperated with their captors and that twenty-one chose to remain behind after repatriation to America become possible. Edgar Schein interviewed many of these men in transit home and recorded that their captors' methods had included a

pacing of demands. In the various kinds of responses that were demanded of the prisoners, the Chinese always started with trivial, innocuous ones and, as the habit of responding became established, gradually worked up to more important ones. Thus after a prisoner had once been 'trained' to speak or write out trivia, statements on more important issues were demanded of him. This was particularly effective in eliciting confessions, self-criticism, and information during interrogation.

Closely connected with the principle of pacing was the principle of constant *participation* from the prisoner. It was never enough for the prisoner to listen and absorb; some kind of verbal or written response was always demanded. Thus if a man would not give original material in question-and-answer sessions, he was asked to copy something. Likewise, group discussions, autobiographical statements, self-criticisms, and public confessions were all demanded as active participation by the prisoner.[30]

This is an obvious application of the foot-in-the-door technique: compliance with a small request was followed by a larger request. Once you give in a little, the next act seems more palatable. It is also interesting that the compliance was generally not elicited under threat of torture, but rather through use of inducements and rewards which evidently left the men with some sense of responsibility for their behavior. Finally, by isolating the men emotionally from each other—through removal of leaders and through the use of informants—the Chinese effectively inhibited the men from supporting one another by giving witness to their democratic ideals.

We may never know exactly what happened to Patricia Hearst, but it is certainly possible that her thought reform occurred under similar conditions. Her statements of public confession and her forced cooperation were not unlike those of the Korean POW's. If, fearing the SLA and the civil authorities, she furthermore made a conscious decision not to escape when she might have, the mechanism would have been set in motion for her internalization of these induced actions.

These instances of attitude manipulation provoke us to wonder how people might be made resistant to unwanted persuasion. William McGuire has conducted a systematic research program on just this question.[31] McGuire reasoned that people might be inoculated against persuasion much as they are inoculated against a virus. To protect against smallpox, we can subject ourselves to a weakened form of the virus, thus stimulating our body's defenses in preparation for a virulent smallpox virus. Might it work the same way with attitudes? Take people who have been raised in a "germ-free ideological environment"—who hold some unquestioned belief—and stimulate their mental defenses by subjecting them to a small dose of belief-threatening material. This is what McGuire did by taking some cultural truisms like "It's a good idea to brush your teeth after every meal if at all possible" and showing that people were vulnerable to massive, credible assault on these truisms. If, however, prior to having their belief attacked, they were "immunized" by first receiving a small challenge to their belief *and* if they *actively* wrote an essay in refutation of this mild attack, then they were better able to resist the subsequent powerful attack.

This finding has several interesting implications. First, it suggests that the best way to build resistance to brainwashing may not be, as some Senators thought after the Korean War, to introduce more courses on patriotism and Americanism. Teachers might be better advised, suggested McGuire, to challenge somewhat the concepts and principles of democracy, forcing the individual to develop defenses. Christian educators should for the same reason be wary of creating a "germ-free ideological environment" in their churches and schools. The image of the unchallenged Sunday School faith being overwhelmed when the small town lad goes to the big university is all too familiar. Daniel Batson recently observed that teenage churchgoers who rejected a belief-threatening message actually intensified their belief commitment.[32] An attack refuted is more likely to solidify than to undermine one's position. Christian educators concerned about nurturing a faith which will endure assault are therefore best advised to introduce belief-threatening material within a supportive context for examining it. (This is precisely the intent of Part IV below, Superstition and Prayer.)

The second implication is that an ineffective persuasive appeal can be worse (from the standpoint of the persuader) than none at all, because it acts as an attitudinal inoculation. This was evident in one experiment in which high school students were invited to write essays advocating a strict dress code.[33] Since this contradicted their own position and the essays were to be published, they all chose *not* to write the essay, even those who were offered $1.50 to do so. The interesting finding was that the students who turned down the $1.50 became even more extreme and confident in their anti-dress code opinions. Having made an overt commitment against the dress code, they became even more resistant to it, just as one who has rejected appeals to quit smoking may become immune to further appeals. Thus it seems that ineffective evangelism, by stimulating the person's defenses, may be counter-productive—worse than no evangelism at all. Though even an ineffective attempt may make the evangelist feel better, it can also serve as an inoculating agent, "hardening the heart" against subsequent appeals.[34] This is not an argument against evangelism per se, for nothing ventured is nothing gained. But we should recognize that a price is being paid for simplistic evangelistic methods which elicit rejection by 99 percent of the recipients.

Action Therapies

Our last example comes from the professionals whose goal it is to offer effective, practical strategies for helping people change. It is discouraging to note that therapeutic interventions have developed in relative isolation from the basic experimental research on human change. Yet this makes all the more noteworthy the fact that many of the proliferating new psychotherapies share as a common denominator an emphasis on the client's chosen actions. In contrast to the older insight therapies like psychoanalysis, which basically engage the client above the neck, the newer therapies are united in assuming that intellectualized insight is not enough. Reality therapy induces people to act more responsibly.

Behavior therapists attempt to shape or induce behavior and, if they care about internal dispositions at all, assume that these will come along.

Other therapies also encourage the person to try out and practice new behaviors. In Recovery Training, Abraham Low instructs patients to "do the thing you fear to do" by using will-training to "command the muscles" to carry out action. Assertion training employs the same step-by-step procedure we have seen so effective in changing attitudes: the individual begins by practicing small assertions and by role playing in a supportive context. Rational-emotive therapy assumes that we generate our own emotions; its clients are given "homework" assignments to act in new ways that will generate new emotions. Encounter groups also subtly induce participants to behave in novel ways in front of the group: expressing anger, crying, acting with high self-esteem, expressing positive feelings. An anthropologist's analysis of an Esalen encounter/gestalt workshop concludes similarly in pointing to the importance of "ritual process"—a "simplified, standardized behavior which effectively manipulates human emotion toward some purpose."[35]

Regardless of the methods involved, treatments which elicit actual performance achieve results consistently superior to those based on symbolic forms of the same methods (e.g., verbal persuasion).[36] The experimental investigations described earlier suggest that lasting change is most likely to result from these procedures if the person is encouraged to "own responsibility" for the actions rather than to attribute responsibility to the pressure of the group.

There is a practical moral here for us all. If we want to change ourselves in some important way, we had best not depend exclusively on introspection and intellectual insight. Sometimes we need to get up and act, despite the fact that we, like Moses and Jonah and other biblical heroes, do not feel like acting. Even an ardent rationalist and humanist like Jacques Barzun recognizes this in advising aspiring writers to engage in the act of writing even if passive contemplation has left them feeling uncertain about their ideas:

You may ask what will set the caldron of ideas bubbling. *Wanting to tell is the answer.* . . . If you are too modest about yourself or too plain indifferent about the possible reader and yet are required to write, then you have to pretend. Make believe that you want to bring somebody around to your opinion; in other words, adopt a thesis and start expounding it. . . . With a slight effort of the kind at the start—a challenge to utterance—you will find your pretense disappearing and a real concern creeping in. The subject will have taken hold of you as it does in the work of all habitual writers.[37]

Such is my experience even as I write these words for you. My self-doubts are receding as my excitement over these ideas grows!

THEORETICAL EXPLANATION

We have seen that several independent streams of observation—laboratory experiments, social history, and therapeutic interventions—merge to form one river: the effect of overt action on internal disposition. This conclusion is more clearly established than its explanation. But do these diverse observations contain any clues as to why action affects attitude? Every research pyschologist plays detective, trying to solve the mysteries of the data. Two categories of theoretical explanation have been suggested. Both have been inspired by some of these experiments and an inspiration for others. Let's now go backstage and take a brief look at these ideas.

Self-Justification

One possible explanation is that we are motivated to find rationalizations for our behavior, especially when it departs from our self-concept. This is the implication of the best-known theory of attitude-action consistency: cognitive dissonance theory.[38] The theory is very simple, but its range of application has been enormous. It assumes that internal dissonance results when two cognitions are psychologically inconsistent—when they do not seem to fit together—and that people make cognitive adjustments to reduce this state of tension, just as we act to reduce other states of tension such as hunger. This is reminiscent of biblical statements like "No one can serve two masters" and "A double-minded man is unstable in all his ways."[39] For example, people who held President Nixon in high esteem and who then read key excerpts from the Watergate tapes were likely made uncomfortable by their awareness of inconsistency between their high opinion of the man and their low opinion of his behavior. This dissonance could be reduced by lowering their opinion of the President or by condoning his actions, or both.

Most of the applications of dissonance theory pertain to discrepancies between our behavior and our attitudes. Because we are aware of both, there is pressure for change if one does not follow from the other. So if you can persuade someone to adopt a new attitude, behavior should adjust accordingly—that's common sense. Or if you can induce a person to behave differently, dissonance may be reduced by attitude change—that's the interesting self-persuasion effect which we have been reviewing.

The theory of cognitive dissonance is noted for several nonobvious predictions, the most striking of which is that the less inducement used to gain compliance—the less money you offer someone, for example—the *more* attitude change results. We have already noted this phenomenon in several experiments. The dissonance theory explanation is that when people are coerced into doing something with a big bribe or threat they consider their action fully justified by the external constraints. Little dissonance thus results and no internal explanation is needed. Whereas if an action—such as resistance to temptation—is induced using only a mild deterrent, then people struggle a bit. Since their compliance is inadequately justified by the barely sufficient inducement, they are motived to marshall additional justifications from within. This is not to say we are consciously aware of this process. When experimenters have asked people why they acted or chose as they did, they typically deny any influence of the very experimental procedures which *have* influenced them.

It is important to note here that cognitive dissonance theory is concerned with what is done to induce a desired action, *not* with the relative effectiveness of small or big rewards and punishments administered *after* the act. It aims, for example, to have the child say, "I am behaving well because I chose to do so," rather than "I am behaving well because my parents make me behave." Given some sense of choice and responsibility for an action, people are likely to internalize it, to believe in what they have done.

Some practical implications follow. My college required chapel attendance for many years. By the late 1960s this coercion no longer seemed to be eliciting much internalization, so we made chapel voluntary. Although chapel attendance dropped, religious interest on campus has not noticeably suffered from this decision. Participatory business management and democratic campus governance are additional illustrations of practical attempts to give people a sense of responsibility for the rules under which they behave and hence lead them to further internalize their behavior. These humanizing implications of dissonance theory have led some to view it as an integration of humanistic and scientific perspectives. Authoritarian management by bribes and threats will be effective, the theory predicts, only so long as the authority is present; internalization of the behavior is not likely to occur when there is little sense of choice. Yet the theory is hardly permissive in its implications, for it insists that encouragements and inducements be sufficient to elicit desired action. The practical implication is to use the minimal incentive needed to get behavior to occur, thus encouraging people to attribute their actions to themselves.

This analysis implies that making *decisions* is an important source of dissonance and of subsequent attitude change. When faced with an important decision, sometimes we are torn between two equally attractive but exclusive alternatives—where to attend college, whom to date, which job to accept. Once we commit ourselves to one course of action, we become painfully aware of dissonant cognitions—the desirable features of what we have rejected and the undesirable features of that to which we have bound ourselves.

Experiments indicate that this dissonance is reduced just as you might expect—by upgrading the chosen alternative and denigrating the option passed over. In one clever study, race track bettors indicated significantly more confidence in their chosen horse if they had just bet on it than if they were about to bet on it.[40] In another study, voters indicated more esteem and confidence in their candidate just after voting than just before.[41] Three days after the finishing touches were put on President Carter's energy package and it was committed to print, he confessed to his cabinet that he once had doubts about the program, but that "now I'm feeling better and better about it."[42] Sometimes there may be just a whisker of a difference between the two options, as I can recall in helping make faculty tenure decisions. The one faculty member who barely makes it and the other who barely loses out seem not very different—until after the decision is made and announced. I am a captive of this phenomenon myself. Once this book is committed to print, I will have to fight a natural tendency to be less receptive to the insights of my critics than I have been while writing it.

Self-Perception

A second explanation of the effect of action on attitude is even simpler. Consider how we make inferences about other people's attitudes. We observe a person's behavior and the conditions under which it occurs, and then we either explain the behavior in terms of personal dispositions or in terms of environmental forces.[43] If we were to see a goon squad entering a local restaurant, taking customers one by one and twisting their arms behind their backs until they proclaimed "vote for Barry Bully," we would attribute the customers' behavior to the constraints of the situation, not to their personal dispositions. If we witnessed the same proclamation with less external inducement, we would be much more likely to infer a pro-Bully attitude.

Self-perception theorists reason that much the same information processing occurs when we observe our own behavior.[44] To the extent that our attitudes are weak or ambiguous, we are in the same position as someone else observing us from the outside. Hearing myself talk informs me of my attitudes; observing my actions provides clues to how strong my beliefs are, especially if my behavior is not easily attributable to external constraints. The acts we commit without feeling coerced can be quite self-revealing.

William James proposed a similar explanation for emotion. We infer our emotions, he suggested, by observing our bodies and our behaviors. A stimulus such as a growling bear confronts a woman in the forest. She tenses, her heartbeat increases, adrenalin is secreted, and she runs away. Observing all this, she then experiences fear. On one trip to a place where I was to lecture on this material, I awoke before dawn, unable to sleep. Observing my wakefulness, I concluded that I must be anxious.

Although you may be skeptical of this idea, there are some experiments which support it. In one study, college men saw pictures of *Playboy* centerfolds and were given feedback on the rate of their heartbeats by the experimenter.[45] Actually, the experimenter was contolling the feedback, so that the men heard their heartbeats increase to some pictures and decrease to others. When the men later indicated their preferences for the various pictures, they expressed greatest attraction to those for whom their presumed heartrate had been highest.

An easy personal demonstration of self-perception is suggested by another recent experiment.[46] People induced to make a frowning expression while electrodes were attached to their face—"contract these muscles," "pull your brows together"—reported feeling angry. But it is more fun to try out the other finding: people induced to make a smiling expression felt happier and found cartoons more humorous. I recall being alone in my car one day when I heard the song "Put on a Happy Face" on the radio. How inauthentic I thought. But no one was around, so I tried it, and it works!

We have all experienced this. We are feeling crabby, but then the phone rings or someone comes to the door and warm, polite behavior is elicited. If the crabbiness was not intense, this brief warm behavior can change our whole attitude after the phone is hung up. One of the surest ways to bring a small child out of a foul mood is not to lecture the child out of it, but, more simply, to elicit a smile. In our house a bit of reverse psychology sometimes helps:

"Why, I think Andy's smiles have all gone to Massachusetts today!" Self-perception is surely one reason why Hindus find that physical prostration is conducive to an attitude of humble worship and praise. Our own postures of prayer—kneeling, head bowing—likewise contribute to our sense of humility.[47]

Self-Justification, Self-Perception, and Information Processing

The self-justification and self-perception explanations should not lead us to suppose that the cognitive effects of action are necessarily mindless rationalizations or observations. The context which prompts the person to act also prompts the person to think, to review relevant considerations. In some of the essay writing and role playing experiments, for example, the person retrieves and improvises arguments supporting an opposing point of view. This biased scanning increases the salience of arguments which support the action.[48] A conflict mediator may therefore use role-reversal activities to induce one party to think seriously about the other party's point of view. Another useful strategy is requesting one person to restate the other person's position before giving his or her own.

As self-justification and self-perception theories emphasize, information processing also occurs after an action. As an act is reflected upon, the person becomes "open to and actively searches for new information that lends attitudinal support to his action and thus makes his anticipated role performance more effective, more comfortable, and more rewarding."[49]

Note the emphasis here on the active self-generation of ideas. My own research on group influence is a case in point.[50] We have observed that passive exposure to information about a situation—by reading or listening—has less effect on people's attitudes than when they get the same information through active participation in discussion. Other research further indicates that passive learning about an attitude object will often not change the attitude.[51] The person must actively reformulate or rehearse the information in order to internalize an attitude change. As John Dewey said, "A thought is not a thought unless it is one's own."[52]

Both theories, then, can incorporate thinking processes. But which is right? The assumption that we are motivated to justify our behavior and the assumption that we merely observe our behavior and make inferences from it, have been the subject of experiments which attempt to decide between the two. Ambiguities of both theories have made it difficult to find a critical test which decides between them. They make similar predictions, and each theory can be bent to accommodate the findings we have considered.[53] One major theorist even suggested it boils down to a matter of loyalties or aesthetics. This is a striking illustration of the process of science described in Chapter 2: when data conflict with an accepted theory, they may be regarded as an anomaly or else the assumptions of the theory may be modified to incorporate the data. But this is not to argue that the theories are useless. They provide useful ways of organizing experience, and they have stimulated much new knowledge of practical value.

Self-justification and self-observation both seem partly responsible for the effect of action on attitude. In particular situations, one or the other will seem most relevant.[54] In some instances, as when hypnotized or brain-stimulated people observe themselves carrying out an unexplained action, they may simply infer an appropriate disposition. This was clearly evident in a famous experiment in which people injected with adrenaline and exposed to any angry or euphoric social situation experienced the corresponding emotion— *provided* they had no other explanation for their physical arousal.[55] A similar experiment found that people given an hallucinogenic drug in the context of a Good Friday service labeled their experience in religious terms.[56]

In other instances, discomfort accompanies action, motivating people to reduce the discomfort by coming to believe they were right.[57] And what more powerful rationalization for our acts than religion? By finding a transcendent justification for evil action, people can not only avoid guilt, they can feel positively righteous. A prayer service was held with the Hiroshima bombing crew just before they flew. In establishing Rhodesia's white-ruled government Ian Smith declared that he had "struck a blow for Christianity." Langdon Gilkey's fascinating description of the Shantung Compound makes self-justification processes abundantly clear. The war camp situation elicited numerous self-serving behaviors which often found moral and religious justification:

Rarely does self-interest display itself frankly as selfishness. More often it hides behind the very moral idealism it is denying in action; a legal, moral, or even religious argument is likely to be given for what is at base a selfish action. And what is more, the moral disguise usually deceives even the self who has donned it. For no one is more surprised and outraged than that self when someone else questions the validity of his moral concern.

For this reason, as I saw for the first time, idealistic intentions are not enough; nor is a man's idealistic fervor the final yardstick of the quality of his character. We commit most of our serious sins against our neighbor— and these *are* the serious sins—for what we regard as a "moral principle." Most of us, in spite of whatever harm we may be doing to others, have long since convinced ourselves that the cause for which we do what we do is just and right. Thus teaching high ideals to men will not in itself produce better men and women. It may merely provide the taught with new ways of justifying their devotion to their own security.[58]

How Do We Know?

Less than a century ago psychology and epistemology (the study of the nature and validity of knowledge) were closely related branches of philosophy. After more than fifty years of going its own way, can psychology, the prodigal child, bring something home to its mother discipline?

The theory and research we have reviewed on the cognitive effects of action speaks, does it not, to the nature of human knowing? Many observations of learning by doing could be added which would further sharpen the point. Since we parents fail to recognize that our spoken words are more salient to us (as active speakers) than to our passive hearers, we are often dismayed at our children's capacity to ignore us. If, instead of constant harping, the parent gently asks the child to restate the request (e.g., "Andy, what did I ask you to do?"), the child's act of verbalizing the parental request will often amplify the child's consciousness of it. The child now *knows* the request in a more significant way.

Teachers, even young children functioning as tutors, learn and remember well what they teach.[59] Jerome Bruner and Jean Piaget both stress the contribution of active play, the work of childhood, to intellectual development.[60] Young children come to know reality primarily through their own self-generated activities, not by sitting passively while someone pours knowledge into their heads. This is why it is sad to contemplate that the fifteen thousand hours which the average child spends in front of the television by age eighteen diverts that child from fifteen thousand hours of play and other activities.

These observations, together with the other theory and research described to this point, seem congenial to a epistemology which emphasizes that human knowing is nurtured by action. This viewpoint is not sympathetic to the Platonic view that eternal truths are locked within the soul prior to experience. Daniel Robinson notes that for Plato and Socrates,

knowledge is a reminiscence; that is, the knower *has* the truth. He doesn't learn it; he merely recalls it with the aid of instruction. The centrality of this position to the entire Socratic psychology (and epistemology) cannot be overdrawn, for if we believe that knowledge is memory we will accept the dialectical method of uncovering it. Moreover, we will give to *experience* a place of no special importance; to *reflection,* a place of unparalleled importance.[61]

By contrast, the pervasive cognitive effects we have been considering are more a form of immediate, direct, experiential knowing. The present view seems to share at least a small element in common with Michael Polanyi's ideas about knowledge being obtainable only by personal commitment, as when the scientist acquires "tacit knowledge," not by acquiring rules for doing science, but by actually doing it. John Dewey indicated that this view could not be neatly categorized as either rationalist or empiricist:

Only when a man can already perform an act of standing straight does he know what it is like to have a right posture and only then can he summon the idea required for proper execution. The act must come before the thought, and a habit before an ability to evoke the thought at will. Ordinary psychology reverses the actual state of affairs.

Ideas, thoughts of ends, are not spontaneously generated. There is no immaculate conception of meanings or purposes. Reason pure of all influence from prior habit is a fiction. But pure sensations out of which ideas can be framed apart from habit are equally fictitious.[62]

Given this philosophy of knowledge, it is hardly surprising that Dewey went on to develop a compatible educational philosophy. "There is no such thing as genuine knowledge and fruitful understanding," he wrote, "except as the off-spring of doing."[63] The passive observer of finished, predigested concepts is not so likely to be drawn into the excitement of intellectual development as is the person who engages in creative activity. (In fairness to Plato and Socrates, it should be said that the dialogue method of teaching stimulates more active information processing than does lecture.) This illustrates how our basic assumptions about human knowing have important practical implications, making it important that scholars in philosophy and psychology work to integrate their respective insights.

We are now prepared to connect our social psychological insights to biblical and theological understandings of the nature of faith and discipleship. After achieving this, we will draw from this integration some practical implications for church life and Christian nurture.

NOTES

1. Allan W. Wicker, "Attitudes vs. Actions: The Relationship of Verbal to Overt Behavior Responses to Attitude Objects," *Journal of Social Issues* 25 (1969): 41–78.

2. See Amitai Etzioni, "Human Beings Are Not Very Easy to Change After All," *Saturday Review,* June 3, 1972, 45–47.

3. Robert Brannon et al., "Attitude and Action: A Field Experiment Joined to a General Population Survey," *American Sociological Review* 38 (1973): 625–36. For an excellent analysis of this literature see Brannon's chapter, "Attitudes and the Prediction of Behavior," in *Social Psychology,* ed. B. Seidenberg and A. Snadowsky (New York: Free Press, 1976).

4. The general principle seems to be that attitudes predict behavior only when both are measured at the same level of specificity. If the attitude is very specific to a particular action, as in the voting surveys, then it may predict well. If an attitude measure is global (e.g., general attitudes toward the church), it will only predict global measures of behavior (e.g., behavior that is averaged over many different situations).

5. This observation by José Delgado appears in Maya Pine's fascinating book, *The Brain Changers* (New York: Harcourt Brace Jovanovich, 1973).

6. Roger Brown, *Social Psychology* (New York: Free Press, 1965), pp. 153–54.

7. Irvin L. Janis and Leon Mann, "Effectiveness of Emotional Role-Playing in Modifying Smoking Habits and Attitudes," *Journal of Experimental Research in Personality* 1 (1965): 84–90.

8. Seymour Lieberman, "The Effects of Changes in Roles on the Attitudes of Role Occupants," *Human Relations* 9 (1956): 385–402.

9. Jerald G. Bachman and Patrick M. O'Malley, "Self-Esteem in Young Men: A Longitudinal Analysis of the Impact of Educational and Occupational Attainment," *Journal of Personality and Social Psychology* 35 (1977): 365–80.

10. Jonathan L. Freedman and Scott C. Fraser, "Compliance without Pressure: The Foot-in-the-Door Technique," *Journal of Personality and Social Psychology* 4 (1966): 195–202.

11. Stanley Milgram, "Some Conditions of Obedience and Disobedience to Authority," *Human Relations* 18 (1965): 57–75. Although the victim was not actually shocked, this experiment still has been sufficiently controversial to serve as a stimulus for reforms in professional psychological research ethics.

12. Bertram H. Raven and Jeffrey Z. Rubin, *Social Psychology: People in Groups* (New York: John Wiley & Sons, 1976), p. 241.

13. Ralph K. White, "Selective Inattention," *Psychology Today* 5, no. 6 (November, 1971): 47–50, 78–84.

14. See Keith E. Davis and Edward E. Jones, "Changes in Interpersonal Perception as a Means of Reducing Cognitive Dissonance," *Journal of Abnormal and Social Psychology* 61 (1960): 402–10; David C. Glass, "Changes in Liking as a Means of Reducing Cognitive Discrepancies be-

tween Self-Esteem and Aggression," *Journal of Personality* 32 (1964): 531–49; and Ellen Bersheid, David Boye, and Elaine Walster, "Retaliation as a Means of Restoring Equity," *Journal of Personality and Social Psychology* 10 (1968): 370–76.

15. James Burtchaell uses this line of reasoning to attack situation ethics for identifying evil with evil motives in *Philemon's Problem* (Chicago: Acta Foundation, 1973).

16. Hannah Arendt, "Organized Guilt and Universal Responsibility," in *Guilt: Man and Society*, ed. Roger W. Smith (Garden City, N.Y.: Doubleday Anchor Books, 1971), p. 262 (reprinted from *Jewish Frontier*, 1945, 12).

17. Jonathan Freedman, "Long-Term Behavioral Effects of Cognitive Dissonance," *Journal of Experimental Social Psychology*, 1 (1965): 145–55.

18. Sigmund Freud, *Civilization and its Discontents* (London: Hogarth, 1949), p. 114.

19. John Dewey, *Human Nature and Conduct* (New York: Holt, 1922), p. 32.

20. Burtchaell, *op. cit.*, p. 159.

21. Ross D. Parke, "Rules, Roles, and Resistance to Deviation: Recent Advances in Punishment, Discipline, and Self-Control," in *Minnesota Symposia of Child Psychology*, vol. 8, ed. A. Pick (Minneapolis: University of Minnesota Press, 1974); E. Staub, R. Leavy, and J. Shortsleeves, "Teaching Other Children as a Means of Learning to be Helpful," and E. Staub and W. Jancaterino, "Teaching Others, Participation in Prosocial Action and Prosocial Induction as Means of Children Learning to be Helpful" (unpublished manuscripts, University of Massachusetts, Amherst, 1975). I am grateful to Michael Lougee for acquainting me with this literature.

22. Jean Piaget, *The Moral Development of the Child* (New York: Free Press, 1948).

23. Fletcher A. Blanchard and Stuart W. Cook, "Effects of Helping a Less Competent Member of a Cooperating Interracial Group on the Development of Interpersonal Attraction," *Journal of Personality and Social Psychology*, 34 (1976): 1245–55.

24. Cited by Mark R. Rosenzweig, "Cognitive Dissonance," *American Psychologist* 27 (1972): 769.

25. Richard Grunberger, *The 12-Year Reich: A Social History of Nazi Germany 1933–45* (New York: Holt, Rinehart & Winston, 1971), p. 27.

26. *The Report of the President's Commission on Campus Unrest* (Washington, D.C.: U.S. Government Printing Office, 1970), pp. 78–79.

27. See, for example, James D. Shaughnessy, ed., *The Roots of Ritual* (Grand Rapids: Eerdmans, 1973), p. 158. I use the term *myth* not in its derogatory sense, but in the sense of a story which reflects a people's understanding of some particular mystery.

28. Gerhard von Rad, *Old Testament Theology*, vol 2, trans. D. M. G. Stalker (New York: Harper & Row, 1965), p. 104.

29. Erik H. Erikson, "Ontogeny of Ritualization in Man," *Philo-

sophical Transactions of the Royal Society of London, Series B, no. 772, vol. 251 (1966): 337–50.

30. Edgar H. Schein, "The Chinese Indoctrination Program for Prisoners of War: A Study of Attempted 'Brainwashing'," *Psychiatry* 19 (1956): 149–72.

31. William J. McGuire, "Inducing Resistance to Persuasion: Some Contemporary Approaches," in *Advances in Experimental Social Psychology*, vol. 1, ed. L. Berkowitz (New York: Academic Press, 1964).

32. C. Daniel Batson, "Rational Processing or Rationalization?: The Effect of Disconfirming Information on a Stated Religious Belief," *Journal of Personality and Social Psychology* 32 (1975): 176–84.

33. Susan Darley and Joel Cooper, Cognitive Consequences of Forced Non-Compliance," *Journal of Personality and Social Psychology* 24 (1972): 321–26.

34. Some preachers call this phenomenon "pew-hardening."

35. Regina E. Holloman, "Ritual Opening and Individual Transformation: Rites of Passage at Esalen," *American Anthropologist* 76 (1974): 265–80.

36. Albert Bandura, "Self-Efficacy: Toward a Unifying Theory of Behavioral Change," *Psychological Review* 84 (1977): 191–215.

37. Jacques Barzun, *Simple and Direct* (New York: Harper & Row, 1975), pp. 173–74.

38. An authoritative review of dissonance theory is presented by Robert Wicklund and Jack W. Brehm, *Perspectives on Cognitive Dissonance* (Hillsdale, N.J.: Erlbaum, 1976). An accessible summary of the theory appears in Elliot Aronson's popular textbook, *The Social Animal* (San Francisco: W. H. Freeman, 1976).

39. Matt. 6:24 RSV; Jas. 1:8 KJV.

40. Robert E. Knox and James A. Inkster, "Postdecision Dissonance at Post Time," *Journal of Personality and Social Psychology* 8 (1968): 319–23.

41. Oded J. Frenkel and Anthony N. Doob, "Post-decision Dissonance at the Polling Booth," *Canadian Journal of Behavioral Science* 8 (1976): 347–50.

42. NBC News, April 20, 1977.

43. A systematic analysis of how we make these inferences is provided by *attribution theory*. This is discussed in Chapter 10.

44. Daryl J. Bem, "Self-Perception Theory," in *Advances in Experimental Social Psychology*, vol. 6, ed. L. Berkowitz (New York: Academic Press, 1972).

45. Stuart Valins, "Cognitive Effects of False Heart-Rate Feedback," *Journal of Personality and Social Psychology* 4 (1966): 400–08.

46. James D. Laird, "Self-Attribution of Emotion: The Effects of Expressive Behavior on the Quality of Emotional Experience," *Journal of Personality and Social Psychology* 29 (1974): 475–86.

47. Indeed, Robert Coughenour informs me that the Hebrew word for "bow down" (*shātāch*) literally means to bow one's whole self down—a conscious act of self-humbling worship.

48. Irvin L. Janis and J. Barnard Gilmore, "The Influence of Incentive Conditions on the Success of Role-Playing in Modifying Attitudes," *Journal of Personality and Social Psychology* 1 (1965): 17–27.

49. Herbert Kelman, "Attitudes are Alive and Well and Gainfully Employed in the Sphere of Action," *American Psychologist* 29 (1974): 310–24.

50. See, for example, David G. Myers and Helmut Lamm, "The Polarizing Effect of Group Discussion," *American Scientist* 63 (1975): 297–303; or "The Group Polarization Phenomenon," *Psychological Bulletin* 83 (1976): 602–27.

51. Anthony G. Greenwald, "Cognitive Learning, Cognitive Response to Persuasion, and Attitude Change," in *Psychological Foundations of Attitudes*, ed. A. G. Greenwald, T. C. Brock, and T. M. Ostrum (New York: Academic Press, 1968).

52. John Dewey, *School and Society* (Chicago: University of Chicago Press, 1970), p. 66.

53. Anthony G. Greenwald, "On the Inconclusiveness of 'Crucial' Cognitive Tests of Dissonance versus Self-Perception Theories," *Journal of Experimental Social Psychology* 11 (1975): 490–99.

54. For an attempt to specify these situations see Russell H. Fazio, Mark P. Zanna, and Joel Cooper, "Dissonance versus Self-Perception: An Integrative View of Each Theory's Proper Domain of Application," *Journal of Experimental Social Psychology* 13 (1977): 464–79. Fazio, Zanna, and Cooper argue that dissonance operates when our actions are clearly discrepant from our attitudes and that self-perception processes operate when our actions are compatible with our attitudes, although a step or two beyond them.

55. Stanley Schachter and Jerome E. Singer, "Cognitive, Social and Physiological Determinants of Emotional State," *Psychological Review* 69 (1962): 379–99.

56. This experiment by W. N. Pahnke is discussed by John Bowker, *The Sense of God* (Oxford: Clarendon Press, 1973), p. 151. The experiment provides another example of how an event which is a religious experience for one person can be understood at quite a different level (e.g., a physiological level) by someone on the outside. As was stressed in Chapter 1, these varying understandings—religious and scientific—are *not* logically incompatible. There is a fundamental unity to all things true. This point can also be made with regard to the reports of mystical near-death experiences discussed in Chapter 4.

57. For a review of confirming evidence see Charles A. Kiesler and Michael S. Pallak, "Arousal Properties of Dissonance Manipulations," *Psychological Bulletin* 83 (1976): 1014–25.

58. Langdon Gilkey, *Shantung Compound* (New York: Harper & Row, 1966), p. 112.

59. Vernon L. Allen, ed., *Children as Teachers* (New York: Academic Press, 1976). Robert Zajonc even speculates that the reason first-born children with younger siblings tend to have higher intelligence than only children is because the chance to teach boosts intellectual development

(Robert B. Zajonc and Gregory B. Markus, "Birth Order and Intellectual Development," *Psychological Review* 82 (1975): 74–88.

60. Jerome S. Bruner, "Play is Serious Business," *Psychology Today* 8, no. 8 (January, 1975): pp. 81–83. This is also the general conclusion of a National Institute of Mental Health Report: "The child lives and grows through action" (Philip Lichtenbert and Dolores G. Norton, *Cognitive and Mental Development in the First Five Years of Life: A Review of Recent Research,* National Institute of Mental Health, 1970).

61. Daniel N. Robinson, *An Intellectual History of Psychology* (New York: Macmillan, 1976), p. 53.

62. Dewey, *Human Nature and Conduct, op cit.,* pp. 30, 31.

63. Dewey, *School and Society, op. cit.,* p. 117.

CHAPTER 6

Christian Action and Christian Faith

We have seen that action and attitude, like chicken and egg, "are linked in a continuing reciprocal process, each generating the other in an endless chain."[1] Yet, as other influences intrude, action may depart substantially from stated principles. We will later confront some examples of research which indicate that Christian belief is less predictive of Christian action than most of us presume. A verbal, intellectual assent to certain creeds and propositions does not constitute true piety and complete devotion. Faith is not passive acceptance of dogma or the mere word game which so many have made it. More than 95 percent of Americans say they believe in God, but each week less than half that number find the God in which they believe worthy of their public worship.

The biblical idea is one of a faith which engages the whole person—a person in whom attitude and action, belief and behavior, cognition and commitment, are a unity. Although American Christendom often intimates that religion has only to do with religion (as in the perverse notion that only religious professionals are called to "full-time Christian service"), the truth is that biblical religion has to do with all of life, with the whole of creation. We see in Jesus the Christ, the epitome of wholeness, that words and deeds, both public and private, were consistent. He had one whole life, not a compartmentalized "social life," "occupational life," "spiritual life," and so forth. (Indeed, we do well to avoid labels like "spiritual life," for they facilitate a compartmentalized thinking which is foreign to the Scriptures.)

How can personal wholeness be nurtured? Because my emphasis will be on the importance of the actions of discipleship for a whole faith, I think it appropriate to first recognize that there is a danger in becoming so exclusively preoccupied with external action that we arrive at a new legalism, seeking to justify ourselves by good behavior. The Reformation was a response to religion of good works, it being the conviction of the Reformers that neither reason nor the formal actions of religion effect a right relation with God. Social practices cease to have religious significance—they become superficial parodies of religion—when they lack a transcendent dimension. Jesus and Paul both pointed out that it is the inner reality which counts, not trivial external practices like circumcision and diet. We are to be "transformed by the renewal of our minds." My concern is therefore to help point the way to a deepened sense of the transcendent, to a strengthened inner religious impulse.

The analysis to follow is not a complete description of the origins of Christian commitment. Our beliefs and attitudes have other sources besides our previous actions, and it is certainly not my intent to demystify the inner reality of religious experience. Furthermore, just as attitudes have some effect on action, so also is religious piety a source of behavior as well as a consequence of it. There is an important sense in which faith is the *beginning* rather than the end of religious development. If popular opinion was not already so strongly weighted in this direction I might have felt a need to write on just this point.[2] For example, the experience of being "called" provides convincing demonstration of how faith can precede action in the lives of the faithful. Moses is transformed at the burning bush. Elijah is overwhelmed by the Holy as he huddles in a cave. Paul is touched by the Almighty on the Damascus Road. Ezekiel, Isaiah, Jeremiah, and Amos are likewise invaded by the *Word*, which internally explodes into active response to the call. Yet it is interesting that God's revelation in Jesus was not first of all a revelation of words, but of the Word made flesh. It is more correct to say Jesus *was* the Word, than that he had the word. Our concern then is this: how may Christians *know*—have their whole lives penetrated by—this living Word?

THE CONTRIBUTION OF ACTION TO
RELIGIOUS KNOWLEDGE AND FAITH

Biblical View of Knowledge

Earlier I noted how various educational and persuasive techniques emerge from implicit philosophies of human knowing. The practices of church life and Christian nurture are likewise rooted in some implicit assumptions about the nature of religious knowledge. Many scholars have called attention to the contrasting assumptions of Greek and Hebrew thought. A rudimentary understanding of these views is valuable, not only because they teach us about history, but also because these views permeate our present thinking. As Reinhold Niebuhr has noted, "All modern views of human nature are adaptations, transformations and varying compounds of primarily two distinctive views of man: (a) the view of classical antiquity; that is, of the Graeco-Roman world, and (b) the Biblical view."[3] Thus it is helpful in understanding and evaluating our own ideas to recognize their classical and biblical sources, especially since there has been a "more or less complete triumph of the modernized classical view of man."[4]

In the Platonic view, described earlier, one finds truth by reason and reflection, not by direct experience. Enlightened thinking produces virtuous action—the rational person is the good person. This is evident in Plato's declaration, "There will be no end to the troubles of states, or of humanity itself, till philosophers become kings in this world, or till those we now call kings and rulers really and truly become philosophers. . . ." Michael Novak has suggested, perhaps a bit too strongly, that this idea is still alive today as "the fundamental American myth . . . the myth of the head, of the mind, of the importance of words, rationality and impersonal logic."[5] When translated into Christian terms, this view equates faith with cerebral activity—reason and doctrinal propositions. The church may then become preoccupied with true belief and the defense of dogma. The evangelistic concern is often with what we believe *about* Christ rather than with the devotion of one's total self to God. This cerebral view of religion is evident in the popular observation that Jimmy Carter's religion is a personal matter that has nothing to do with the politics of the presidency. Religion is equated with private thought, rendering it impotent.[6] One of the scandals of present day Christianity, suggests G. C. Berkouwer, is its tendency to elevate *orthodoxy* (right thinking) above *orthopraxis* (right action).[7]

The contrasting biblical view of knowledge follows from its view of the person as a whole entity, not a dichotomy of mind and body. Reality was known by the Hebrew not only by rational contemplation, but also through obedient commitment. It is therefore personal knowledge—immediate, direct, intuitive—and cannot be fully communicated in propositional language. Personal knowledge grows out of active encounter with the object in question, as when the knowledge of good and evil was discovered in conjunction with the act of eating the forbidden fruit. O. A. Piper observes in the *Interpreter's Dictionary of the Bible* that in Old Testament thought,

knowledge of God is experience of the reality of God, not merely knowledge of propositions concerning God. . . . Only the righteous man can therefore be said truly to know God (e.g., Deut. 4:39; Jer. 22:15–16). This feature, more than any other, brings out the wide gulf which separates the Hebraic from the Greek view of knowledge. In the latter, knowledge itself is purely theoretical, and it is left to man's discretion whether or not he will derive rules of conduct from his insight, whereas in the Old Testament the person who does not act in accordance with what God has done or plans to do has but a fragmentary knowledge. . . .[8]

This Hebraic view of knowledge is familiar to us as the sense in which we *know* love. The Hebrew words for *know* and *love* are generally used as verbs—something you do. To know love, we must encounter and experience it—we must act lovingly and be the recipient of loving acts. To know love is more than to know *about* love. Likewise, to *hear* the Word of God means both to listen and to obey.

In the New Testament, greater emphasis is placed upon the inner realities—right attitudes and purity of heart—which produce righteous action. Nevertheless, even here "knowledge of God is not the result of speculative insight, but rather is based upon the experience of being used by God for his saving work."[9] "The New Testament opposition to words without deeds is fierce," writes Berkouwer.

It is possible for a person theoretically to recognize the law as the incarnation of knowledge and truth, and to see himself as its orthodox teacher . . . and yet not do the works of the law. A person can preach the commandments and yet steal or commit adultery or rob the temple (Rom. 2: 21, 22). By such inconsistencies, says Paul, the name of God is blasphemed. Here, one cannot talk about a primary or secondary accent, but only of a deep unity of faith and works.[10]

The bond between right action and true belief is evident in other places in the New Testament besides James's well known admonition to 'do the word.' Paul's lament—"The good which I want to do I fail to do; but what I do is the wrong which is against my will"— suggests how keenly aware he was that an abstract idea in one's head is not the same as a full personal commitment to that idea.[11] So also does his use of the phrase "obedience of faith" and his conclusion that "circumcision makes no difference at all, nor does the want of it; the only thing that counts is faith active in love."[12]

The writer of 1 John declares that his full knowledge of the truth involved more than just his head: "We have heard it; we have seen it with our own eyes; we looked upon it, and felt it with our own hands."[13] By loving action one "knows God," for "it is the man who does right who is righteous," and "in the man who is obedient to his word" that "the divine love has indeed come to its perfection."[14] Right doing and right knowledge are intimately connected.

Jesus declared that he and the Father would come and dwell within those who "heed what I say," and that "whoever has the will to do the will of God shall know . . ."[15] Merely *saying* "Lord, Lord" does not qualify one as a disciple; discipleship means *doing* the will of the Father.[16] Thus Jesus responds to Zacchaeus' act of repentant charity by declaring, "Salvation has come to this house today!"[17] The "Great Commission" to go and call all humanity was addressed to a group which included doubters; it appears that Jesus' therapy for doubt was discipleship.[18] Since we, furthermore, find ourselves not by some mystical inward search, but by losing ourselves as we take up the cross, it becomes evident that Jesus affirms the Old Testament witness that full knowledge of God and of self is possible only with active personal commitment.

Instructions on how to really understand the Bible are given over and again in both the Old and New Testaments. "He who does what is true comes to the light."[19] The wise man—the one who builds his house on rock—differs from the foolish man in that he *acts* upon the word.[20] The power of Jesus' words is known in the doing of them. As Paul Rees has commented, "Jesus was the Word really embodied; we are the Word rhetorically embalmed. Many of us . . . should cease to embalm the gospel in correct creed and begin to embody it in glowing deed."[21]

Practical consequences of the biblical view of knowing will be suggested later. For the present, it is sufficient to note that the ancient biblical and the modern social psychological perspectives stand together in contrast to the classical rationalism which permeates western culture.

Theological View of Faith

The theological understanding of faith is built upon the biblical view of knowledge. Faith is not the product of reason and self-contemplation alone. It is not merely a quiet intellectual certainty on matters of doctrine. One can know *about* matters of faith, in fact one can be an excellent theologian, without *knowing* or having faith in the biblical sense. Even the devils believe, said James.[22]

Faith, rather, is an *attitude* of obedient submission. Some belief content is assumed, yet faith is also "a trust and commitment even when there are no guaranteed beliefs or infallible dogmas. Faith takes us beyond a detached and speculative outlook into the sphere of personal involvement."[23] Reason cannot finally decide what ultimate truth is. Some therefore preach skepticism, advocating that we wait until sufficient evidence for religion is found. But, as when considering marriage, not to decide is to decide. The skeptic's advice, concluded William James, "is tantamount therefore to telling us, when in the presence of the religious hypothesis, that to yield to our fear of its being error is wiser and better than to yield to our hope that it may be true."[24]

But how can our hope that it is true produce authentic faith? This was the question Pascal faced after stating his famous wager: We must wager either that God is or that God isn't; reason cannot finally decide which is true. Considering the potential gains and losses of both wagers should bring any sensible person to stake all on the God hypothesis. But this calculating analysis may not enable our authentic belief. When then? Pascal's advice:

You would like to attain faith, and do not know the way; you would like to cure yourself of unbelief, and ask the remedy for it. Learn of those who have been bound like you, and who now stake all their possessions. These are people who know the way which you would follow, and who are cured of an ill of which you would be cured. Follow the way by which they began; by acting as if they believed, taking the holy water, having masses said, etc. Even this will naturally make you believe. . . .[25]

Immanuel Kant had much the same idea. Williams James summarized it this way: "We can act *as if* there were a God . . . and we find then that these words do make a genuine difference in our moral life."[26]

These philosophical speculations of the effects of behavior on belief are joined by the theologian's understanding of the integral relation between religious piety and religious practice, between faith and obedient discipleship. "But not only faith, perfect and in every way complete, but all right knowledge of God is born of obedience," said Calvin.[27] "Only the doer of the word is its real hearer," wrote Karl Barth.[28]

For Søren Kierkegaard, the leap of faith was an act of obedience, not a rational assent to creeds; we cannot reason our way to genuine faith, he said. In *For Self-Examination* he wrote eloquently of how a preoccupation with studying and interpreting the Scriptures can become a way of keeping the Word from speaking to us directly, an excuse for not *doing* what the Word so plainly instructs. For Kierkegaard, "The question of faith becomes the ethico-religious question of obedience to God. 'The question is quite simple: Will you obey? or will you not obey?' "[29] Preoccupation with creating rational doctrine can sometimes lead away from faith toward doubt, he argued.

Who is it that has doubted? Surely not any one of those whose life bore the marks of a 'follower'? Surely not any one of those who forsook everything to follow Christ? Surely not any one of those who were marked by persecution. . . . For the proof of Christianity really consists in 'following.'[30]

Recall the parallel to Kierkegaard's contention in the research results described earlier. The effortful actions of experimental subjects cultivate a deepened commitment to that for which they have suffered and witnessed. Surely, the same is true for a life of radical discipleship, of crossbearing in the face of opposition and rejection.

Christians are called to walk obediently on the basis of what little they understand, with the hope that as they risk these acts of discipleship their understanding will grow. The outward journey nourishes the inward journey. Faith and faithfulness, like attitude and action, build on each other. Remove either ingredient and religion soon turns sterile. This is why the priesthood of all believers makes perfect psychological sense, for not only does it get the work of the church done, it also stimulates the faith-action spiral. The exercise of faith strengthens faith. Protestant Christianity has maintained well its Reformation emphases on justification by grace and on the authority of Scripture, but has undersold its insight that all believers are priests.

This understanding of faith is given an eloquent defense in Dietrich Bonhoeffer's analysis of "The Call to Discipleship" in his book *The Cost of Discipleship*. Bonhoeffer begins by noting that the call of Jesus is not to a confession of faith but to simple obedience to his authority. The way in which the Spirit of God moves people to respond to the call is beyond the scope of this chapter. The important point for our present discussion is that Jesus called people, not to believe in a creed, but to follow him. Peter drops his nets, leaving all behind, and only much later does he verbalize his certain conviction that "You are the Christ." The meaning of faith is learned through obedient action.

C. S. Lewis captures this dynamic of faith in one of his *Chronicles of Narnia*.[31] The great lion Aslan has returned to Narnia to redeem its captive creatures. Lucy, a young girl with a trusting childlike faith in Aslan, catches a glimpse of him and eventually convinces the others in her party to start walking toward where she sees him. As Lucy follows Aslan, she comes to see him more clearly. The others, skeptical and grumbling at first, follow despite their doubts. Only as they follow do they begin to see what was formerly invisible to them—first a fleeting hint of the lion, then his shadow, until finally, after many steps, they see him face to face.

We must be careful not to confuse human acts of commitment

with justification, lest we recreate a salvation through works. Justification is the gift of God—Peter does not achieve his own conversion. God's acceptance and call to us, frail and insecure as we are, is his grace.[32] But it is a call out of living death and into a new life of obedience, from which faith emerges. Bonhoeffer speaks to the point:

> *Only he who believes is obedient, and only he who is obedient believes.*
> It is quite unbiblical to hold the first proposition without the second.
> . . . If, however, we make a chronological distinction between faith and
> obedience, and make obedience subsequent to faith, we are divorcing the
> one from the other. . . . From the point of view of justification it is neces-
> sary thus to separate them, but we must never lose sight of their essential
> unity. For faith is only real when there is obedience, never without it, and
> faith only becomes faith in the act of obedience. . . .
> The gracious call of Jesus now becomes a stern command: Do this! Give
> up that! Leave the ship and come to me! When a man says he cannot
> obey the call of Jesus . . . because he does not believe, Jesus says: "First
> obey, perform the external work, renounce your attachments, give up the
> obstacles which separate you from the will of God. Do not say you have
> not got faith. You will not have it so long as you persist in disobedience
> and refuse to take the first step. . . . If you believe, take the first step, it
> leads to Jesus Christ. If you don't believe, take the first step all the same,
> for you are bidden to take it. No one wants to know about your faith or
> unbelief, your orders are to perform the act of obedience on the spot. Then
> you will find yourself in the situation where faith becomes possible and
> where faith exists in the true sense of the word. . . .[33]

Practical consequences follow from this position. A person who awaits intellectual certainty before becoming a disciple is likely to persist in unbelief or to find faith losing its vitality.

One can imagine him conversing thus with his pastor: "I have lost the faith I once had." "You must listen to the Word as it is spoken to you in the sermon." "I do; but I cannot get anything out of it, it just falls on deaf ears as far as I'm concerned." "The trouble is, you don't really want to listen." "On the contrary, I do." And here they generally break off, because the pastor is at a loss what to say next. He only remembers the first half of the proposition: "Only those who believe obey." . . . And yet this ought to be the turning-point of the interview. . . . It is now time to take the bull by the horns, and say: "Only those who obey believe." . . . In the name of Christ he must exhort the man to obedience, to action, to take the first step. He must say: "Tear yourself away from all other attachments, and follow him." For at this stage, the first step is what matters most.[34]

This is what Jesus does in urging the rich young ruler to drop his academic question about eternal life and obediently respond to the revealed will of God. Not only does conversion entail repentance,

repentance nurtures true conversion. "You can only know and think about it by actually doing it," Bonhoeffer concluded. "You can only learn what obedience is by obeying. It is no use asking questions; for it is only through obedience that you come to learn the truth."[35]

The truth of Bonhoeffer's analysis can be seen in the nature of biblical commandments. The calls to rejoice and to praise are calls to acts of the will, not to spontaneous emotions. The commandment to love is a call to just and loving action, not to mere sentimentality. As the writer of 1 John reminds us, "Love must not be a matter of words or talk; it must be genuine, and show itself in action."[36] Notice the sequence of events in these words from 1 Peter: "By obedience to the truth you have purified your souls until you feel sincere affection toward your brother Christians."[37] Thus, when Tevye in *Fiddler on the Roof* asks, "Do you love me?" Golde gives a very Hebraic answer: "For twenty-five years I've washed your clothes, cooked your meals, cleaned your house, given you children, milked your cow. . . ." The actions of marital commitment nurtured and sustained their love. We cannot compel from others—or even from ourselves—the *feelings* of love. But if we will act toward that other person in a loving way, we may discover, as did Tevye and Golde, that the authentic feelings of love eventually follow.

IMPLICATIONS FOR CHURCH LIFE AND CHRISTIAN NURTURE

We can now direct our attention to some practical applications of the psychological analysis of attitudes and the corresponding biblical/theological understanding of religious faith and knowledge. How might these insights be usefully applied in public worship? in Christian education? in the cultivation of personal piety? and in the renewal of a powerful and dynamic church? I venture some tentative ideas as illustrations, but I claim no expertise. Anyone who understands these principles is capable of brainstorming their practical application. As we dream visions and examine critically the practices of our church, we need only keep in mind the experimental evidence which indicates that behavior commitments which are substantial, openly public, irrevocable, repeated, and personally chosen are especially likely to stimulate an internal change.

Disciplined Membership

The most obvious implication of the insights we have gained is that a first priority for congregations and Christian groups must be to make their members *active* participants, not mere spectators. Frequently, a congregation does little to implement the idea of the priesthood of every believer. We expect our pastors to do the work, our contribution being to listen to their sermons, drop money in the offering, and occasionally usher. Here we can learn a lesson from effective self-help groups such as Alcoholics Anonymous. These groups make no distinction between recipient member and professional teacher—all are active contributors to the group purpose.

Elton Trueblood has emphasized this point in many of his writings, especially in *Alternative to Futility:*

We must think of all recruits as entering a new estate, beyond clergy and beyond laity. In the new order there are no clergymen and no laymen, but all are engaged in the same divine vocation, which means putting the claims of the Kingdom of God first, no matter what profession one may follow. The *formula is that vocation has priority over profession.*

In nearly all the examples we have mentioned, in which there has been a burst of new Christian life, this criterion has been observed. In the beginning of the Christian cause all were ministers. *Member* equaled *evangelist* equaled *missionary.* There was no place within the society for the observer, the mere supporter or the nominal member.[38]

Those churches which have practiced the discipline of the early church are living testimony to its effectiveness. The Quaker movement in the seventeenth century was strengthened by its recruitment of active workers only. The disciplined commitment of Orthodox Jews has helped enable them to hold their convictions more firmly and enduringly than have Reform Jews. The behavioral expectations which fundamentalist churches have of their members—often including a midweek service in addition to two services on Sunday—have nourished a religious devotion which surpasses that in most nonfundamentalist churches, whose members are often inclined to worship and study only when they feel like it, if they have not already slid into that invisible religious alumni association.

Some ideas for how lukewarm Christians might have their faith rekindled are suggested by examining the way by which people become fanatically committed to the expanding cults which thrive outside the borders of mainline Christianity. No religious group takes the universal priesthood more seriously than the Jehovah's Witnesses. Before military service was made voluntary, for instance, all claimed exemption from the draft because every Witness is a minister. A recent sociological study of the history of the movement revealed that when the early Jehovah's Witnesses ceased merely handing out pamphlets outside churches and undertook daily, house-to-house canvassing, they achieved a heightened identity.[39] This missionary zeal has made the Witnesses one of the fastest growing religious groups in the world—from 50,000 members in 1938 to almost 1.5 million today. There is no provision for passive membership. In addition to regular meetings in Kingdom Hall, the average member logs about ten hours a month in public witness. Regardless of our feelings about their beliefs and behavior, we should be humbled by their courageous dedication. Most of these people must struggle to overcome the same laziness, shyness, and sensitivity which would face any of us asked to tramp door to door.

Another dynamic group is the Mormons, who have tripled their membership since 1950. Here, too, all members are in the priesthood, and their active commitments influence their beliefs. After a young Mormon man commits two years of his life to missionary activity and instructing converts, his loyalty has probably been cemented for life. As with the Jehovah's Witnesses, new converts recognize that membership is no peripheral matter. To be a member in good standing, a Mormon contributes 10 percent of gross income to the church and an additional amount to the upkeep of the local parish.

Seventh Day Adventists are yet another group which is noted for its disciplined giving and for its mission work, including active health and welfare programs. Giving is so substantial that three out of every hundred Adventists are full-time, salaried employees of the church. Evangelistic efforts have multiplied membership several times over during this century. Strict habits of personal discipline are also expected of all members.

An even more extreme example is provided by Sun Myung Moon's Unification Church. This curious mixture of Christianity, fascistic anticommunism, and glorification and enrichment of Mr. Moon has attracted a worldwide following of young people and a growing public concern about the techniques of mind control it employs. Member indoctrination procedures sometimes begin with a voluntary weekend retreat (a foot-in-the-door) which eventually grows to more arduous activities—soliciting contributions, active proselytizing, and public prayer. Since these actions entail considerable personal sacrifice, they understandably engender in some an attitude of commitment and a belief in the teachings of Mr. Moon.

Each of us could add to this list of dynamic Christian communities examples which may be closer to our own tradition. The Catholic orders and the Mennonites, for example, are further examples of deep religious piety linked with sacrificial discipleship. Charismatic groups recognize the dynamic potential of actively engaging members in the priestly functions of sharing and caring. Traditional Protestantism has also contributed many examples of powerful Christian community. Active participation in weekly small group meetings was the chief dynamic of the Methodist movement under John Wesley. Those who heard the powerful preaching but did not experience the mutual edification and commitment which occurred in these "classes" and "bands," as they were called, sooner or later slid back to their former ways.[40]

Some professional observers of religious trends have independently arrived at similar conclusions regarding the effect of behavior commitments on religious beliefs and attitudes. In his controversial book, *Why Conservative Churches are Growing,* Dean Kelley argues that "the quality which enables religious meanings to take hole is . . . the *demand* they make upon their adherents and the degree to which that demand is met *by commitment.*"[41] Martin Marty speculates similarly that mainline Protestant denominations are declining partly because they elicit fewer of the distinctive behavior patterns which formerly enabled their members to establish a church-related identity.[42] Surely, though, there are limits to the number of people willing to respond to any particular set of high demands. If high demands stimulate church growth it is probably growth in commitment more than in numbers. If high expectations guaranteed numerical growth the demanding churches would long ago have displaced the undemanding churches. When Jesus told potential disciples his expectations of full commitment, most turned away. Some scholars have, in fact, suggested that the numerical growth in conservative denominations may be partly a statistical illusion, although they do grant that "conservative groups are simply far more efficient in keeping their children within the tradition."[43]

These observations are only suggestive: spiritual vitality is surely causing these external actions, and we can only suppose that, as the psychological and biblical evidence predicts, the reverse is true as well. Furthermore, my descriptions of the discipline of the early church and of the growing sects are a bit idealized; all these groups have suffered variability in the depth of member commitment. But at least it seems clear that dynamic religious communities are distinguished by the active and disciplined behavior of their members. "All the evidence shows that any society, anywhere, which will adopt this practice will be dynamic in any culture," wrote Trueblood. "If we want to make a difference, here is the clear way. *Make all, within your society, members of the crew and permit no passengers.*"[44]

But how can this be accomplished given the practical reality of American congregations? First, churches could raise their standards for admitting new members. It is always tempting to make numerical success rather than faithfulness the ultimate criterion of church growth. Hitler avoided this in his organization of the Nazi party. The masses were exhorted by propaganda, but the party organization found its strength in restricting membership to those totally devoted. American Christendom, which is largely populated by nominal members who associate faith with verbalized belief, not discipleship, would do well to attend to this practical wisdom. "The great tragedy of modern evangelism," writes Jim Wallis, "is in calling many to belief but few to obedience."[45] When a famous evangelist declares that getting a ticket to heaven is as easy as getting an airplane reservation, he runs the risk of being understood to say that conversion is static, in contrast to Christ's instruction to make *disciples* of all peoples, "teaching them to observe" all that was commanded and taught. Salvation is to be worked out "with fear and trembling." (A smaller, more committed membership would also enable the church to fulfill its mandate as a prophetic saving remnant within the culture. This is now very difficult since the people who compose American society and the people who compose the membership of American churches are substantially the same.)

The call for more rigorous membership standards is not without its dangers. Foremost is the creation of a new Pharisaism in which some people set themselves up to judge whether others are good enough to gain admission. Although such snobbism always appeals to the ego, which may be one reason for the numerical success of religious groups with strict behavior standards, it violates the biblical idea of the church as a group of admitted sinners who bear one another's burdens. But a disciplined membership is not restricted to those who are deserving, for all are undeserving. It is rather a call to commitment. The discipline which Rotary Club members undergo in attending all meetings is a useful model, for it represents not an elitist standard, but simply an insistence that all those who join make membership a priority.

If instituting more rigorous standards of membership is a practical impossibility in all but newly established religious communities, it may still be possible for churches to make the ritual of inducting new members a more significant event. Other social induction rites serve an important function, and there is no reason that induction into church membership could not do the same. In some cultures, for example, male puberty rites help break the child's dependence on the mother by eliciting new masculine behavior.[46] Experiments confirm that substantial initiation demands can enhance the attractiveness of the group; we value more something we have worked to obtain. Fraternities and sororities make conscious use of this principle in placing enormous action demands upon their new pledges. With a few exceptions, churches can be joined with far less effort and commitment than many such social organizations. The seriousness with which most Lutherans, for instance, regard confirmation (as contrasted with merely "joining the church") is at least a step in the right direction, especially for those churches which do not practice adult baptism.

The issue of raising standards extends beyond membership initiation. The experimental finding that people are more committed to those things for which they have suffered adds credence to the idea that faith is nurtured by commitment. If our faith costs little, we may not only wonder how faithfully we have followed but also how deep our faith has grown. How many American Christians, nurtured on a religion of success and positive thinking, would stand by their faith if it implied suffering and despisement rather than social and economic success?

Existing members might therefore be engaged in periodic recommitment. Stewardship drives could elicit behavior pledges as well as money pledges. These programs for action should be as specific as possible, not just vague resolutions. Elton Trueblood recalls in his autobiography:

The strongest single religious influence was that of the Christian Endeavor Society in the local Friends Church. I signed the pledge to take some part, other than singing, in every meeting of the society, and also to engage daily in both Bible reading and prayer. Honoring my signature, I kept the promise, thus early learning something of the power released by the voluntary acceptance of discipline. Years later, when I began to dream of a new redemptive society, to be called Yokefellows, my experience when I was fifteen and sixteen was influential.[47]

One pastor I know found his church rejuvenated by the establishment of a network of "prayer covenants." Members would contract with another member or with the pastor to pray daily for each other. The covenant terminated after a specified number of days unless renewed by the two people involved. Besides being a concrete action which helped to strengthen fellowship, this brought pastor and members more closely in touch with one another's needs and enabled them to sense the concern of others in their community.

If all aspects of our lives are to be subject to the lordship of Christ, we must be careful not to confine action commitments only to overtly "spiritual" matters. The truth is, as we shall later see, that mere church-going behavior in the United States is largely unrelated to the practice of Christian ethics.

In recent times the church has suffered from an unbiblical schism between evangelism and social concern. On the one hand, calling people merely to believe intellectually and to join the church cheapens the call to repentant discipleship. Grace without discipline is cheap grace. Faith without works is a sham. Honking to a bumper sticker is *not* the way to love Jesus. But on the other hand, social concern that is not nurtured by continuing experience of transcendent power and meaning may, like a cut flower, wither if social approval evaporates. Christian commitment must therefore be understood as *both* a personal event, by which the liberating power of divine acceptance and love is experienced, and a public event, as it empowers a person to challenge the "principalities and powers" which oppress humanity. This sense that we are all members of the priesthood, not just believers, might be enhanced among insurance salespeople, nurses, teachers, and parents, as well as the clergy, by a personal statement of commitment or some ritual or ordination which would help people identify and proclaim the religious meaning of their profession.

So much is being written on the use of small groups in the church that little more need be said here. The power of small groups, although newly rediscovered, is not new to the church. Adherents of the early Christian church, the Quakers, and the early Methodist movement were all strengthened by the active participation and commitment elicited by the small group context. There is, however, always the danger that small group discussion may become diverted from significant witness and action, transforming religion into something merely to be talked about.

Much less is written about congregational size. While there is much to say for the educational and worship experiences afforded by large churches, as I know well from having grown up in a Presbyterian church of four thousand members, there is also a case to be made for "small is beautiful." Retention of membership increases when a high proportion of members have an active role. This was evident, for example, in research on adult discussion groups participating in the Great Books program, a once successful program of adult liberal education.[48] It is therefore significant that as congregational size increases, member participation decreases.[49] Members of small schools and small churches report greater feelings of responsibility and involvement and they commit more of themselves to their institutions.[50] This is easy to understand when you consider the leadership opportunities and sense of fellowship likely to exist in the Jehovah's Witnesses Kingdom Halls, which average less than 100 people and which divide when numbers exceed about 250, compared to the average United States Roman Catholic parish, which numbers about 2,000. Large churches might therefore consider combining the advantages of large and small, as some universities have attempted to do in establishing small colleges within the large institution. The establishment of satellite house churches or fellowship groups within large parishes is one example of what could be done.

No one of the preceeding suggestions is foolproof or, taken by itself, of crucial importance. The important point is the overarching objective upon which the examples converge: to create conditions which enable individuals to enact publicly their convictions, thereby confirming and strengthening their self-awareness as Christians.

After deriving these suggestions from the principles formulated earlier, I was intrigued to note how similar were the principles which Dean Kelley believes enabled the Anabaptist and Wesleyan movements to preserve the integrity of their organizations without violating the integrity of individual persons:

a. *They were in no haste to take anyone into membership.* A long period of training and preparation preceded admission. . . . Various tests of readiness were passed and solemn vows taken in the presence of the congregation to show that he knew what he was getting into and made his choice with full awareness and determination.

b. *The tests of membership were attitudinal and behavioral* rather than solely or chiefly doctrinal. . . . Theirs was not just an acceptance of the present content of the faith but an ardent willingness to pursue it in its future unfolding, to search the Word of God together in utter seriousness and to obey its implications in their lives with total dedication. . . .

c. *Membership was conditional upon continuing faithfulness.* . . .

d. *Members made their life pilgrimage together in small groups.* . . .

e. *No one who had not undertaken the rigorous training and accepted the obedience and discipline of the group had any voice in making the decisions of the group.*[51]

One church that has put many of these ideas into practice is the Church of the Savior in Washington, D.C. Elizabeth O'Connor has described this congregation in several books, including *Call to*

Commitment and *The New Community*.[52] To provide "integrity of church membership," all potential members undergo a serious program of Christian studies leading to a personal statement describing their Christian experience, current practice of spiritual disciplines, areas of personal need, and current and intended commitments to the mission of the church. New members pledge themselves and old members annually recommit themselves to some concrete behavior objectives, including the minimum disciplines expected of all members:

> We covenant with Christ and one another to:
>   Meet God daily in a set time of prayer
> Let God confront us daily through the Scriptures
> Grow in love for the brotherhood and all people,
>   remembering the command, "Love one another as I
>   have loved you"
> Worship weekly—normally with our church
> Be a vital contributing member of one of the groups
> Give proportionately, beginning at a tithe of our incomes
> Confess and ask the help of our fellowship should we fail
>   in these expressions of devotion.[53]

Perhaps most important, every person is involved in ministry—in mission groups dedicated to Christian outreach and in sponsoring and guiding prospective members through the initiation phase. Leadership and responsibility is decentralized. The community outreach of this church demonstrates that the meaning which is embodied by action commitments is not necessarily conservative; it may, according to current social convention, be liberal, or even radical.

Once again, we must recognize the danger in becoming too exclusively behavioral; we risk constructing a new legalism with which to achieve self-righteousness. The purpose of discipline is not to make us perfect through good works but to assist us in enacting the two great commandments. The rituals of worship and personal piety express and cultivate our love of God, while acts of obedient discipleship express and enhance our love for people. Søren Kierkegaard's synopsis is apt: "Christianity's requirement is: Thy life shall as strenuously as possible give expression to works— and then one thing more is required: that thou humble thyself and admit, 'But nonetheless I am saved by grace.' "[54]

I hope that I have not overstated the need for a more disciplined membership to the point of narrow exclusivism, or advocated purism to the point of making the church remote from the masses, or given the impression that Christian action has mostly to do with directly serving the institutional church rather than with the whole of our existence. But even if I have, I am confident that the inertia of the status quo and the present extent to which the church is captive of the culture will more than balance any over-emphasis. Few established congregations, encumbered as they are with traditions and nominal members, can hope to implement these principles wholesale. Kelley is especially pessimistic on this point:

The persons who now occupy positions of leadership and followership in the church . . . prefer a church which is not too strenuous or demanding—a church, in fact, which is dying. . . . Like all energy systems, social organizations are entropic—they gradually run down—they are subsiding toward a state of rest. . . . Another way to put it is that *traits of strictness are harder to maintain in an organization than traits of leniency.*[55]

I am a bit more hopeful. The psychological and theological understandings of the effect of behavior on belief not only confirm one another but are further confirmed by the examples of their practical validity within dynamic religious communities. While this principle provides no magical formula for church renewal, it does suggest some goals for local congregations to work toward which might gradually transform them from mild Christian lip service organizations into more committed communities. Just remember: *all believers are priests*—this is the great forgotten Reformation doctrine.

Participative Worship

My emphasis on active participation in all realms of Christian experience—from the daily rituals of personal piety to prophetic social action—should not be understood to undermine the importance of the "word rightly preached." While our analysis has much to tell us about the *dynamics* of religious vitality, it offers no substantive content. Although separate from this discussion of the dynamics of commitment, the truth or falsity of various doctrines is an important matter, and one with which the the pastor is appropriately concerned, lest we be ships with engines but no rudders. Sermons serve an important function in instructing the congregation on matters of belief and action.

Yet even in the planning of worship, there may be some useful applications of research on the cognitive consequences of action. If the rehearsal and reformulation of information is one way by which actions become internalized, then sermons might attempt to directly stimulate this information processing in listeners. As a teacher I constantly have to remind myself not to lay out finished results. It is better to provoke students to first derive in their own minds what the result should be if theory X is correct. Rather than barging ahead with predigested answers to questions which no one may have asked, the minister might raise issues, pause for a moment to give the congregation a chance to actively assemble their own thoughts, and then offer his pastoral insights. The goal is to make the members active rather than passive listeners. Too often, lay people are mere spectators of religious theatre rather than active participants in worship. Even taking notes on the sermon, as any serious student does in class, deepens the impression through active expression. William James made the same point more than seventy-five years ago: "No reception without *reaction*, no impression without correlative expression—this is the great maxim which the teacher ought never to forget."[56]

Those of us who are teachers or preachers become so easily enamoured with our spoken words that we are tempted to overestimate their power. Ask college students what aspect of their college experience has been most valuable and surprisingly few will say it is the classes in which they have sat. Many more students, at least among those at residential colleges, will attribute their personal growth primarily to their interactions with friends and fellow students. It can therefore be somewhat disconcerting for teachers to ask college seniors what they remember or found most significant from their freshman year. Rarely will it be the content of a brilliant lecture which they passively heard or a book they read. (Indeed, it saddens me to think that within the next year you will have forgotten most of what you read in this book.) Much more often it is something they did—an encounter with a person, an essay they wrote, or something else which actively engaged them. Would you agree that the same is probably true of church members? You can test this out by asking some parishioners to recall the previous week's sermon. Do not ask what they learned that was new or what impact it had on their lives; ask merely if they remember what it was about. Or ask yourself, how much do you remember of the last sermon you heard?

A recent award-winning experiment suggests, in fact, that passively received sermons have little effect on the hearers, at least when the topic is one about which the members already have strong feelings.[57] In a large midwestern city undergoing considerable racial tension, the Roman Catholic bishop decreed a program to combat racism. This included, on two successive Sundays, preaching prescribed sermons opposing racial hatred and injustice. To study the effect of the sermons, a sample of parishoners from each of twelve parishes were interviewed at home before and after the sermons. Investigators also attended masses in each parish and observed the sermon content. When asked within ten days after the two sermons whether they had heard or read anything about racial prejudice or discrimination since the previous interview, only 10 percent of those who had attended at least one of the masses spontaneously recalled the sermon. When the remaining 90 percent were asked directly whether their priest "talked about prejudice or discrimination in the last couple of weeks" more than 30 percent denied hearing such a sermon! It is therefore hardly surprising that the sermons had no measurable impact on racial attitudes. But it seems that although the preaching did not influence the audiences, the audiences influenced the preaching. Priests in more prejudiced parishes preached sermons which were considerably more bland or abstract than those preached in the less prejudiced parishes. This apparent tendency of the priest to adjust his preaching so as not to offend his audience partly explained why so many people could not even recall hearing a sermon about prejudice.

Other research also suggests that the power of preaching is limited. Laboratory studies indicate that even if an attitude *is* shaped by persuasive communication, it is less likely to endure and to have an impact on later behavior than when the same expressed attitude emerges from behavioral experience.[58]

Findings such as these should motivate pastors not only to consider how they might activate their listeners, but also how they might more actively involve the congregation in other aspects of worship. Those of us in the Reformed tradition, for example, would do well to more fully appreciate the value of ritual in the more liturgical churches—Lutheran, Episcopalian, and Roman Catholic. Religious ideas have always been expressed and transmitted in ritual. The early Christian ritual of washing one another's feet must have generated as deep a sense of humility as did any doctrinal proposition about human equality before God. Even if Jimmy Carter's carrying his own bags is something of a calculated gesture, such acts may still help remind him that he is only a mere mortal like the rest of us.

Two observations are appropriate here. First, if religious symbols and rituals serve to interpret historical experience, then we must not fear the ongoing renewal of ritual which interprets the experience of people today. Just as nineteenth-century hymns expressed the pietistic mood of people yesterday and some still today, so also we in the twentieth century need to develop images and practices which are authentic to people growing up in our time. Of course, not all of us have had the same experience. The old and the young, for example, have grown up in vastly different cultures. One group, therefore, should be careful not to impose its symbols and rituals on the other. Margaret Mead has observed that "people fight changes in ritual more fiercely than they fight changes in anything else. . . . Only if a ritual is conducted in the same way, only if the same words are spoken in the same order and accompanied by the same gestures, will the same feeling of security be present."[59] If our liturgy is radically altered rather than slowly modified, we become too conscious of our actions and the ritual feels artificial. With time, however, new rituals are absorbed into our consciousness, just as we internalize new roles which at first feel inauthentic.

The second observation is to again stress the value of active, public participation in the rituals of worship. The public act of choosing to get out of one's seat and kneel publicly before the congregation in taking communion has much to commend it. Richard Avery and Donald Marsh offer a number of practical ideas for increasing mindful participation.[60] The Psalms, for example, can be done as they originally were, in improvised chant with congregational echo. Children and adults can be helped to internalize the meaning of their baptism by placing a hand on their head and saying:

> I am baptized;
>   I belong to God.
> I am a child of God;
>   Thanks be to God.

Elton Trueblood, who as a Quaker is understandably sensitive to the benefits of group-centered worship, has suggested that

One of the simplest ways in which an ordinary church could begin to become an Order of the Concerned would be for the clergy to encourage the participation of the laity in the conduct of public worship. Most of the churches have permissive rubrics, but they do nothing about this, partly because it is easier to stay in the same old rut. The great advantage which accrues when a lay member reads the Scripture or offers vocal prayer is that this becomes his means of public witness. It may not do the others good, but it does him good. The most fortunate single feature of preaching is the beneficient effect on the one who does the preaching. Witness strengthens his Christian commitment because he has taken a public stand before his fellows. That the laymen know very well that this is what it means is shown by the manner in which some refuse to participate when invited. They are afraid to make a public witness because more will be expected of them by their neighbors, once they make such a witness.[61]

The Hebrew word for "teach" is also the word for "learn," showing the intimate connection between the activity of teaching and one's own learning. Just within the past month I have observed three instances of someone's attitudes and commitments being significantly strengthened by the act of preparing, presenting, and defending a talk on a position to which they were previously only moderately committed.

Christian Nurture

The light from psychological and biblical/theological insights can also be directed upon Christian education and Christian nurture. If active participation is important for worship, it is even more natural and practical in Christian education. Fortunately, there is an increasing supply of helpful curriculum materials for those who want to activate their students. One technique, which first elicits learning biblical facts and then *knowing* the event in the richer Hebraic sense, is meant to engage people in simulations of biblical events.[62] If experiments on the effects of role playing generalize to Christian education, then we may expect that reenacting biblical events would enable people to identify more closely with the persons and groups involved.

Unfortunately, many parents, especially in our conservative churches, assume that teaching the literal, surface content of Bible stories, sometimes with fictionalized embellishments, constitutes an adequate Christian education. By now I hope it is evident why this assumption is *dead wrong*—scientifically wrong and biblically wrong. It is wrong because it is based on the false assumption that mere head knowledge inevitably penetrates the whole person. Wisdom, commitment, discipleship—these goals for Christian education presume biblical substance, to be sure. But they are not likely to be realized by *merely* pouring factual biblical content into a child's head. Even at the purely intellectual level, it is unlikely that a child will be able to transfer biblical principles of love and justice to the real situations of daily existence unless there has been explicit practice in doing so. This is also the biblical witness: "A man who listens to the message but never acts upon it is like one who looks in a mirror at the face nature gave him. He glances at himself and goes away, and at once forgets what he looked like."[63]

Evidence bears this out. As Jesus recognized long ago in his observations about hypocrites and Pharisees, little relationship exists between church background and moral behavior. One review of research concludes bluntly: "As far as moral behavior is concerned, religion appears to have little effect."[64] Another recent report compared the tendency of religious and nonreligious college students to do good (volunteer to help retarded children) and avoid evil (not cheat when given an easy chance to do so).[65] Conservative Christian students who were orthodox in their belief about God and Jesus Christ and active in groups such as Campus Crusade for Christ and Navigators were just as likely to cheat and to not volunteer as were nonreligious and atheist students. Furthermore, these two types of moral behavior were totally unrelated—students who were honest were not more likely to volunteer than those who cheated—even among those active in religion.

I live in a community blessed with ten churches for every tavern. Recently our state announced plans for a medium-security prison at an abandoned seminary six miles from town. The state promises that only prisoners accused of nonviolent crimes will be housed there, that the prison will be secured with a sophisticated security system which has been virtually escape proof elsewhere, and that community volunteers would be welcome in the prison. Do we see this as a unique opportunity for ministry "to the least of these" so that it might be said of us, "I was a prisoner and you visited me?" No, our response has been to fill gymnasiums by the hundreds to protest bringing these sinners into our nice Christian community and to write letters by the thousands lamenting what this addition might do to our property values and our feelings of personal security. Although sympathy and understanding are due those genuinely afraid, whether their fear is unfounded or not, we can also wonder why the response of our Christian community has been so similar to that of other communities.

The bulk of available research indicates that the relationship of religious belief to social behavior is simply insignificant compared to the effect of cultural variables, such as social class. The vast majority of self-described Christians appear to be far more captive of their culture than responsive to their verbalized beliefs. This conclusion is a strong indictment of American Christendom. If I were a pastor, it would cause me to ponder whether my parishioners were really more selfless and more committed to justice and reconciliation than their nonchurched neighbors.

Although the evidence of religion's negligible relation to significant moral action and other personal traits may discourage us, these findings may also be God's way of pulling us away from a view of the church to which we never should have succumbed.

The church is not a company of morally pure, successful, and beautifully adjusted people, as some well-known preachers and religious groups imply, but rather a community of admitted sinners who have come to acknowledge their frailty, to worship God, to hear and celebrate the good news of his grace, and to respond in grateful discipleship. The proper worship of God should not be primarily because worship does something for us, but simply because God is God.

There is, fortunately, some cause for optimism based on research which subdivides people on the basis of their religious motivation rather than lumping all self-described Christians together. That small subset of church members who are intrinsically and deeply committed to their religion *are* more likely to practice Christian ethics than those only nominally committed to the same expressed beliefs.[66] Perhaps these deeply committed members are the "remnant" of whom the Scriptures speak. And should it really shock us that intellectual assent to a creed does not much relate to moral action, except for a few areas of personal life-style? Merely saying yes to a creed is not what the Scriptures mean by hearing and following, in any case. "Not everyone who says . . . 'Lord, Lord,'" is a disciple of the kingdom.[67] Christians can also take heart that when the relation of faith and moral action *is* explicitly taught and practiced—as it often is with sexual behavior, drug and alcohol abuse, and other more trivial behaviors—moral action *can* be influenced.[68]

That President Nixon and many of the young men who assisted in the Watergate coverup were graduates of church-related colleges should cause us to wonder whether Christian colleges really promote a heightened moral literacy. The problem with the typical Christian perspective on liberal education, suggested Will Herberg, is that we live "in two spiritual worlds—biblical-Hebraic in religion, Greek-idealist in thought, education, and culture."[69] In the biblical view, the ultimate end of education is not passive contemplation of truth but obedience to God through responsible concern for our neighbor. Herberg's point is that we too often combine this biblical goal, if we are serious about it at all, with a nonbiblical educational philosophy which is based on the assumption that the rational person is the good person. As Reinhold Niebuhr wrote:

If modern culture conceives man primarily in terms of the uniqueness of his rational faculties, it finds the root of his evil in his involvement in natural impulses and natural necessities from which it hopes to free him by the increase of his rational faculties. This essentially Platonic idea manages to creep into many social and educational theories. . . . The anti-aristocratic tendencies of Biblical religion stand in sharpest contrast to all forms of rationalism which assume that the intelligent man is also the good man, and which do not recognize to what degree reason may be the servant of passion; and that the genuine achievements of mind and conscience may also be new occasions for expressing the pride of sinful man.[70]

Taking these observations seriously implies that a Christian college should cultivate along with the intellect a sense of stewardship regarding the use of intellectual power. A Christian college should also stimulate some conscious reflection on the inevitable two-way interaction between faith and life-style.[71] It should encourage intellectually rigorous decisions and commitments on real issues, and it should create an institutional atmosphere which is conducive to moral action. As Robert Hutchins concluded: "The virtues are habits. . . . They are formed by acts. The virtue of punctuality, if it is one, is formed by being on time.[72] A college can declare itself a community of scholars who work cooperatively to advance knowledge and wisdom. If, however, its academic and social practices elicit mostly competitive behavior, then, despite the nice communal ideal, its people will be socialized into individualism. The *real* values of a college are defined by what it does, not by what it says in its catalogue.

But we all know that it is the home—not the school or church—which has first responsibility for Christian nurture. Here the research evidence is again helpful for it suggests that children learn more moral behavior from observing what others *do* than from what they preach. Children exposed to a hypocrtitical model who does one thing and says another tend to do what the model does and say what the model says.[73] It appears that young lives are formed not as much by the parental intellectual beliefs as by habitual family practices. Although we may nod our heads in agreement, few Christian families begin to appreciate and reap the benefits of family ritual. Old Testament family rituals helped participants actively remember the mighty acts of God. When today's Jewish family celebrates the Passover by eating special foods, reading prayers, and singing psalms, all of which symbolize their historical experience, it helps the family members know and remember who they are. Such behaviors, done without question, renew the roots of deep convictions and feelings. To quote Tevye again, "Because of our traditions everyone of us knows who he is and what God expects him to do. . . . Without our traditions our lives would be as shaky as a fiddler on the roof."

Many churches outside the liturgical tradition are beginning to recognize the value of family ritual during one brief season: Advent. With energy, imagination, and the help of excellent resource materials the family celebration of Advent can be extended through all the other seasons of the church year.[74] Here lies a great undeveloped challenge for pastors and Christian educators—to motivate and equip families for year-round home celebration and ritual.

Those of us who have associated ritual with hocus pocus are unaware of the simple and creative forms which ritual can assume and of the extent to which the natural ritual of our own personal histories has shaped who we are. Many of the things we did without question in childhood have long since become an enduring part of our self-identities. As Aidan Kavanagh has written, we are inevitably so immersed in ritual "that it takes an extraordinary degree of perception even to note its presence, much less to analyze its influences on us. This presence and its effects are nonetheless real, and they are not confined to stadiums on Saturday afternoons, to military parades, to inaugurations, or to Sunday services in church."[75] Indeed, our internalization of our own rituals is what makes their recognition so much more difficult than the rituals of societies we call "primitive." This is why a sociologist like Erving Goffman can make a living by pointing out the rituals going on right under our noses.[76]

Far from being superficial, meaningless, and empty, as many Americans seem to suppose, everyday ritual patterns can convey profound meaning. This is implicit in the Christian view of sex, which presumes that the rituals of sexual intimacy, if not diminished by acting as if sexual behavior has no depth of meaning, can celebrate and strengthen a sense of lifelong, unconditional self-exposure between two persons. The surrender of privacy which is literally embodied in sexual acts nourishes this merger of purposes and decisions.

In the end, after considering how to facilitate the Christian nurture of *other* people, Christians must not ignore their own continuing need for growth. The biblical heroes of the faith serve as models. Although it is true, as I have noted, that their call did not originate in action, for something had to first motivate that action, it did nearly always *begin* with action. Abraham, Moses, and the rest did not wait for their feelings to mature. They were called to acts of obedience beyond what they really felt like doing. To be continually risking, pushing the frontiers of our faith with new acts of commitment, is to stimulate the inner life. "Truth must be lived into meaning before it can be fully known," wrote Horace Bushnell. If, however, Christians settle into some niche in life where they enjoy security and the comfort of warm friendships, there they may also find that the contemplative aftereffects of bold action—prayer, searching study, deep discussion—are diminished. Keith Miller's experience bears on this issue:

In our small group of becomers I was forced to this amazingly simple discovery about "Christian education." For years I had been urging men and women to study the Bible, pray, and attend church so they could become "stronger in the faith." And all they did was resist my efforts. But as members of our group actually began to risk themselves and their securities, they started asking how they could learn more about the Scriptures, theology, and prayer. And I realized that for many lay people motivation to get "educated about the faith" is a natural by-product of a vulnerable life-style. If a Christian is consciously in need of God, because he is risking his safety, he is highly motivated to learn what the tools and content of his faith are.[77]

One of the marks of contemporary Christianity, in contrast to the dynamic periods of Christian history, is its tendency to leave public witness to the religious professionals. Christians have failed to appreciate that public expression is not only central to both evangelism and the prophetic tradition, it is also precisely the type of action—overt, irrevocable, chosen, effortful—that will nurture faith. The new cults appreciate this in making public witness a clear expectation, just as it is in effective political groups. When Billy Graham declares, "Now I am going to ask you to get up out of your seat," he recognizes well the importance of public commitment for internalization. The church should train people in the relative safety of the fellowship to profess their faith, genuinely, sensitively, and prophetically, just as those engaged in assertion training and some of the other action therapies do with their participants.

I hope you agree that the fruits of recent social psychological research reinforce some ancient but underappreciated biblical truths. Biblical and psychological perspectives both remind us that faith is like love: if we hoard it, it will shrivel; if we use it and give it away, we will have it more abundantly. And that's the way it is with all God's gifts.[78]

NOTES

1. Herbert Kelman, "Attitudes are Alive and Well and Gainfully Employed in the Sphere of Action," *American Psychologist* 29 (1974); 310–24.

2. Two authors have already done this: Merton Strommen, "Religous Beliefs: Powerful Predictors of Actions and Behavior" (Paper presented to the American Psychological Association Convention, September 1976); and Richard Gorsuch, "Religion as a Significant Predictor of Important Human Behavior" (unpublished paper, University of Texas at Arlington). They report that strong religious beliefs predict active religious participation and low indulgence in drugs, alcohol, and non-marital sex. Other research exploring the relationship between Christian belief and the practice of Christian ethics will be discussed later in this chapter and in Chapter 10. As we will see, verbal adherence to Christian creeds is surprisingly unrelated to altruism and racial brotherhood.

3. Reinhold Niebuhr, *The Nature and Destiny of Man*, vol. 1, *Human Nature*, (New York: Scribner's, 1964), p. 5. Not all scholars accept Niebuhr's sharp distinction between Greek and biblical thought. John Ferguson, for example, notes that Greek thinking is very diverse and that Greek influences on New Testament thinking are more extensive than Niebuhr grants, although Ferguson agrees that *rationalism* and *dualism* provide "a reasonable, though limited, account of some aspects of Plato's thought" ("Athens and Jerusalem," *Religious Studies* 8 [1972]; 1–13).

4. *Ibid.*, p. 5.

5. Michael Novak, "The Experience of Nothingness," Introduction to Helmut Thielicke, *Nihilism* (New York: Schocken 1969).

6. Compare this view with Senator Mark Hatfield's experience: "Radical allegiance to Jesus Christ transforms one's entire perspective on political reality. Priorities become totally changed; a whole new understanding of what is truly important bursts forth" (*Between a Rock and a Hard Place* [Waco, Texas: Word, 1976], p. 27).

7. G. C. Berkouwer, "Orthodoxy and Orthopraxis," in *God and the Good*, ed. Clifton Orlebeke and Lewis Smedes (Grand Rapids: Eerdmans, 1975), pp. 13–21.

8. *Interpreter's Dictionary of the Bible*, vol. 3 (Nashville: Abingdon Press, 1962), p. 44. My thanks to Arthur Jentz for pointing this out to me.

9. *Ibid.*, p. 47.

10. Berkouwer *op. cit.*, p. 16.

11. Rom. 7:19, NEB.

12. Rom. 1:5, 16:26, RSV; Gal. 5:6, NEB.

13. 1 John 1:1, NEB.

14. 1 John 4:8, NEB; 1 John 3:7, NEB; 1 John 2:5, NEB.

15. John 14:23, NEB; John 7:17a, NEB.

16. Matt. 7:21.

17. Luke 19:9, NEB.

18. Matt. 28:16–20. Merold Westphal called this to my attention.

19. John 3:21 RSV.

20. Matt. 7:24–29.

21. Paul S. Rees, "Lift Up Your Eyes," *World Vision*, September, 1976, p. 23.

22. James 2:19.

23. Ian Barbour, *Myths, Models, and Paradigms* (New York: Harper & Row, 1974), p. 180.

24. William James, *The Will to Believe* (New York: Longmans, Green & Company, 1937), p. 27.

25. Blaise Pascal, *Thoughts,* 233 (W. F. Trotter, trans.), in *World Masterpieces,* vol. 2, ed. M. Mack (New York: W. W. Norton, 1965), p. 38.

26. William James, *Varieties of Religious Experience* (1902), Mentor Books, 1958), p. 59.

27. John Calvin, *Institutes of the Christian Religion,* I, VI, 2, (John T. McNeil, ed., Ford L. Battles, trans.), (Philadelphia: Westminster Press, 1975), p. 72.

28. Quoted by John H. Westerhoff III, *Values for Tomorrow's Children,* (Philadelphia: Pilgrim Press, 1971), p. 44.

29. Merold Westphal, "Kierkegaard and The Logic of Insanity," *Religious Studies* 7 (1971); 204.

30. Søren Kierkegaard, *For Self-Examination and Judge for Yourselves,* trans. Walter Lowrie (Princeton: Princeton University Press, 1944), p. 87, 88.

31. C. S. Lewis, *Prince Caspian* (New York: Collier Books, 1970).

32. An important tangent here would consider how the experience of God's affirming grace reduces our need for self-justification.

33. Dietrich Bonhoeffer, *The Cost of Discipleship* (New York: Macmillan, 1963), pp. 69, 73–74.

34. *Ibid.,* p. 76.

35. *Ibid.,* p. 86.

36. 1 John 3:19, NEB.

37. 1 Peter 1:22, NEB.

38. Elton Trueblood, *Alternative to Futility* (New York: Harper, 1948), pp. 73–74.

39. J. A. Beckford, *The Trumpet of Prophesy: A Sociological Study of Jehovah's Witnesses* (New York: John Wiley & Sons, 1975), p. 9.

40. Martin Schmidt, *John Wesley: A Theological Autobiography,* vol. 2, trans. Norman P. Goldhawk (Nashville: Abingdon, 1972).

41. Dean M. Kelley, *Why Conservative Churches are Growing* (New York: Harper & Row, 1972), p. 53.

42. Martin M. Marty, *A Nation of Behavers* (Chicago: University of Chicago Press, 1976), pp. 75–76.

43. N. J. Demerath III and W. C. Roof, "Religion—Recent Strands in Research," *Annual Review of Sociology* 2 (1976): 19–33.

44. Trueblood *op. cit.,* p. 74.

45. Jim Wallis, *Agenda for Biblical People* (New York: Harper & Row, 1976).

46. J. W. M. Whiting, R. Kluckhohn, and A. Anthony, "The Functions of Male Initiation Ceremonies at Puberty," in *Readings in Social Psychology,* 3rd ed., ed. E. E. Maccoby, T. M. Newcomb and E. L. Hartley (New York: Holt, 1958), pp. 359–70.

47. Elton Trueblood, *While it is Day* (New York: Harper & Row, 1974), p. 15.

48. James Davis, "Compositional Effects, Role Systems, and the Survival of Small Discussion Groups," *Public Opinion Quarterly* 25 (1961): 574–84.

49. David Moberg, "Religious Practices," in *Research on Religious Development*, ed. M. P. Strommen (New York: Hawthorn Books, 1971), pp. 551–98.

50. For a recent study which includes a brief review of other relevant research, see Allan W. Wicker and Claudia E. Kauma, "Effects of a Merger of a Small and a Large Organization on Members' Behaviors and Experiences," *Journal of Applied Psychology* 59 (1974): 24–30.

51. Kelley, *op. cit.*, pp. 125–27.

52. Elizabeth O'Connor, *Call to Commitment* (New York: Harper & Row, 1963) and *The New Community* (Harper & Row, 1976).

53. *Ibid.*, 1963, p. 34.

54. Kierkegaard, *op. cit.*, p. 44.

55. Kelley, *op. cit.*, pp. x, 96.

56. William James, *Talks to Teachers on Psychology: And to Students on Some of Life's Ideals* (New York: Holt, 1922), p. 33 (originally published, 1899). Cited by W. J. McKeachie,"Psychology in America's Bicentennial Year," *American Psychologist* 31 (1976): 819–33.

57. Thomas J. Crawford, "Sermons on Racial Tolerance and the Parish Neighborhood Context," *Journal of Applied Social Psychology* 4 (1974): 1–23.

58. See W. A. Watts, "Relative Persistance of Opinion Change Induced by Active Compared to Passive Participation," *Journal of Personality and Social Psychology* 5 (1967): 4–15; and D. T. Ryan and R. Fazio, "On the Consistency Between Attitudes and Behavior: Look to the Method of Attitude Formation," *Journal of Experimental Social Psychology* 13 (1977): 28–45.

59. Margaret Mead, "Ritual and Social Crisis," in *The Roots of Ritual,* ed. James Shaughnessy (Grand Rapids: Eerdmans, 1973), p. 92.

60. Avery and Marsh's publications are available through Proclamation Productions, Orange Square, Port Jervis, New York, 12771.

61. Trueblood, *Alternative to Futility, op. cit.*, pp. 66–67.

62. See, for example, Donald E. Miller, Graydon F. Snyder, and Robert W. Neff, *Using Biblical Simulations*, vol. 2 (Valley Forge, Pa.: Judson Press, 1975).

63. James 1:23–24 NEB.

64. Michael Argyle and Benjamin Beit-Hallahmi, *The Social Psychology of Religion* (Boston: Routledge & Kegan Paul, 1975), p. 122.

65. Ronald E. Smith, Gregory Wheeler, and Edward Diener, "Faith Without Works: Jesus People, Resistance to Temptation, and Altruism," *Journal of Applied Social Psychology* 4 (1975); 320–30. This readable study also provides a short overview of other research which further demonstrates the lack of connection between religious belief and moral behavior. For a similar conclusion from a review of the sociology research literature see Gary D. Bouma, "On Preaching and Practicing: Religious Beliefs and Behavior," *Intellect* 104 (January, 1976): pp. 333–34.

66. This research is briefly described in Chapter 10 as part of a discussion of Christian belief and racial prejudice.

67. Matt. 7:21 RSV.

68. Merton Strommen, *Four Cries of Youth* (New York: Harper & Row, 1974).

Recall from Chapter 5 that behavior is usually predictable from an attitude only if the behavior is very directly implied by the attitude. This suggests that Christian belief may influence action if the belief-action connection is unambiguous in the minds of the believers. Some of the research which reports that Christian belief is unrelated to the practice of Christian ethics seems, more precisely, to show that practice of the *researcher*'s ethics is unrelated to the believers' beliefs. Perhaps the believers' ethical practices are more consistent with their own belief systems, even if neither their behaviors nor beliefs are intrinsically very Christian. Researchers who wish to study the impact of religious beliefs should therefore ascertain what the *believers* see as the significant ethical implications of their faith and see if *they* practice what *they* believe. If they do, then there is hope that educating a more truly Christian belief structure with clear ethical imperatives might, in fact, result in more Christ-like ethical practice.

See also note 2.

69. Will Herberg, "Toward a Biblical Theology of Education," *The Christian Scholar* 26 (1953): 259–72.

70. Niebuhr, *op. cit.*, pp. 23, 227.

71. Thanks to Sang Lee for this observation.

72. Robert M. Hutchins, "The Intellectual Community," *The Center Magazine* 10, no. 1 (January/February, 1977): 2–9.

73. James H. Bryan and Nancy H. Walbek, "Preaching and Practicing Generosity: Children's Actions and Reactions," *Child Development* 41 (1970): 329–53; and "The Impact of Words and Deeds Concerning Altruism Upon Children," *Child Development* 41 (1970): 747–57.

74. Two of the best "idea" books on Christian family ritual our family has discovered are Harold J. Belgum, *Great Days for the Family* (St. Louis: Concordia, 1969); and David and Elizabeth Gray, *Children of Joy: Raising Your Own Home-Grown Christians* (Branford, Conn.: Reader's Press, 1975).

75. Aidan Kavanagh, "Introduction," in James Shaughnessy, *op. cit.*, p. 8.

76. See, for example, Erving Goffman, *Interaction Ritual: Essays on Face-to-Face Behavior* (Garden City, N.Y.: Doubleday, 1967).

77. Keith Miller, *The Becomers* (Waco, Texas: Word, 1973), pp. 166–67.

78. My thanks to John Stewart for this closing illustration and for his encouragement of these ideas.

PART IV

Superstition and Prayer

If we are to be genuine in celebrating the emerging unity of scientific and biblical perspectives on human nature, then we must also probe areas of apparent tension. One tension zone is suggested by new research on the nature and extent of superstitious thinking. Because of the highly technical nature of many of the available reports, some of them have been a well-kept scientific secret. I suspect, however, that as people become more aware of these findings they may wonder whether superstitious thinking can penetrate prayer behavior. Does superstitious thinking sometimes give people an inflated perception of the manipulative power of their prayers of petition and intercession? Theologians have sometimes warned against "false prayer." Perhaps psychological research on human thinking can help us understand its origins.

Those who may be discomfited by the challenge to identify and excise superstitious infections of Christian thinking should remember that Christians have often been moved to a more correct understanding of biblical truth by the revelations of scientific research. The insights of modern ecology, for example, have revolutionized our understanding of what it means to have dominion over the earth. God's revelation to humanity is ever-continuing, and both the scientific and the biblical data are a part of this revelation. This does not mean biblical teachings should be forsaken in the face of seemingly threatening evidence. But it does mean that there need be no fear of exposing Christian faith to the most cogent evidence of science. Whatever the truth may be, it is God's truth.

CHAPTER 7

Superstition

The Bible gives humanity a mixed review of itself. We are esteemed as the pinnacle of the creation, the image-bearers of the omniscient God, yet we are also demeaned as fallen, full of pride, and frail and imperfect in wisdom. Both halves of this human picture need to be appreciated lest we succumb to the extreme of either naive optimism or cold cynicism in our view of human nature.

If we were in great danger of taking too low a view of our own beliefs and motives then we would need to read more tributes to human wisdom, such as Hamlet's hymn of praise:

> What a piece of work is man!
> How noble in reason!
> How infinite in faculties!

Human pride, however, already inclines us so naturally in this direction that we need more to be reminded of the magnitude of human folly. It is increasingly evident to those who study human thinking that Hamlet's noble portrayal of human reason symptomizes our capacity for self-delusion. We are far more ignoble in reason and finite in faculty than Hamlet appreciated. Furthermore, our naivete about the illusions and fallacies of our thought sometimes leads to pernicious consequences. Some of these consequences might be avoided if we were more realistic and humble in our self-appraisal.

THE FRAILTY OF HUMAN THINKING

What the Scriptures describe as the finiteness of human thinking is abundantly evident in research on how thought is subject to biases, errors, and distortions. Visual perceptions are easily victimized by subtle illusions and by manipulation of expectations. Consider the phrase in Figure 10.

Figure 10.

Did you notice something unusual about it? Now count the *F*'s in this sentence:

FINISHED FILES ARE THE RESULTS
OF YEARS OF SCIENTIFIC STUDY
COMBINED WITH THE EXPERIENCE
OF YEARS.

You had better count again.* There is obviously more to vision than meets the eye.

Creative problem-solving ability is likewise impeded by the mental habits and frames of mind which people carry to the task. Consider the following questions:

1. How much dirt is in a hole two feet deep and two feet square?

2. In what state is it not legal for a man to marry his widow's sister?

3. A farmer had seventeen sheep. All but nine died. How many were left?

4. I have two U.S. coins which total fifty-five cents. One is *not* a nickel. What are the two coins?

Perhaps my forewarning enabled you to correctly overcome the frames of mind usually induced by the questions.†

As was emphasized in Chapter 2, our beliefs and values influence our understanding and description of phenomena. Sometimes this even leads us to impute meaning and order where none

---

*The word *the* appears twice in Figure 10. There are six *F*'s in the paragraph.

†Answers: (1) no dirt, (2) no man has a widow, (3) nine, (4) one nickel and one half dollar.

is present. James Dittes prepared a parable in biblical idiom and invited students to interpret it.[1] Although sprinkled with familiar religious symbols, the parable was actually prepared to be incoherent. Nonetheless, many students, especially those whose self-esteem had been temporarily lowered, unhesitatingly assigned a meaning to the parable. They did this even though it meant ignoring some parts and distorting others to fit the supposed meaning. Not surprisingly, no two of these literalists ever found the same meaning.

The bounds of human reason are evident in many settings. When the destructive consequences of otherwise rewarding activities are delayed and accumulated imperceptibly, people can become willful agents of their own degradation. For example, we often act in ways which benefit us in the short run—smoking, wasting time watching television, overusing credit cards, depleting our resources—even when these actions will reduce our net long term satisfaction. We misperceive other people. We tend to see them as more in agreement with us than they really are.[2] Having been taught from childhood that good is rewarded and evil is punished we come, as did Job's friends, to believe that those who are rewarded must be good and that those who suffer must be wicked. This causes us to be unresponsive to injustice, not only out of callous indifference but also because we often do not see the injustice.[3]

We also create myths from small shreds of evidence. The human tendency to perceive a sequence of events in causal terms is so irresistible that it occurs despite a person's being intellectually aware that the sequence is coincidental.[4] Even given a random sequence of numbers, most of us can "discover" a pattern to them. When people assume that the sequence of events is *not* coincidental then they are likely to be positively certain of their cause-effect perceptions, even if the events are still, statistically speaking, coincidental. Do you think this phenomenon occurs among believers in ESP, astrology, faith healing, or even, sometimes, believers in the causal effects of intercessory prayer?

The inventive capacity of the human mind sometimes enables us to create myths from nothing. In one experiment the right half of a girl's face was projected to split brain patients' right hemispheres and the left half of a *woman's* face was projected to their left hemispheres. When they were then asked to indicate which of several faces was seen, they confidently *pointed* to a completed picture of the girl, but *said* they saw a woman. Both answers were given confidently; each hemisphere simply invented the missing half face. Asked to explain the contradiction, patients typically denied or rationalized their pointing. It seems that, psychologically, there is little or no difference between an artificially constructed reality and an objectively correct belief.

If people are told something often enough, they may come to believe it, even if the assertion is known to be of dubious credibility. Lynn Hasher and colleagues had students rate, on three different occasions, the truth or falsity of dozens of plausible statements.[5] They were told that these statements might or might not be true. In fact, half were true (e.g., Cairo, Egypt has a larger population than Chicago, Illinois) and half were false (e.g., The People's Republic of China was founded in 1947). Some of the statements were repeatedly presented in all three test sessions. These repeated statements became more believable to the students, regardless of whether they were in reality true or false.

We are also too easily persuaded by personal homilies which, though heart-warming, are more subject to multiple interpretations than is experimental evidence. A friend of mine (who happens to be a brilliant philosopher) commented after reading several of these chapters that he found the everyday illustrations more persuasive than the experiments. This tendency to place greater confidence in concrete examples than in more valid, general information has been demonstrated in several experimental situations.[6] Such quirks in human reasoning have practical effects in real life. Students (and surely administrators, also) are more influenced by a few other students' vivid testimonies to their good or bad experience with a given teacher than they are by a less concrete but more representative statistical sample of student evaluations.[7] If the available survey data are trustworthy, then, rationally, a single testimonial should only be used to increase the survey sample by an iota of one more person. But the effects of a good testimonial are in reality far more dramatic. Airplane accidents, because of the large numbers of fatalities involved, are much more vividly dramatic events than auto accidents. Thus most of us have come to *feel* less vulnerable while traveling in a car, even if we are aware of statistical evidence that we are actually much safer traveling in airplanes.

This tendency to overuse salient information and to underutilize less distinctive statistical information also biases our predictions. Pretend a stranger told you about a person who is short, slim, and likes to read poetry and then asked you to guess whether this person was a professor of classics at an Ivy League university or a truck driver. Which would be your best guess? If even for a moment you considered guessing the professor, you committed the common error of giving too much weight to the distinctive information and of underusing your general knowledge of the number of truck drivers—there are obviously at least several thousand times as many truck drivers as Ivy League classics professors. Thus there are sure to be many more truck drivers who fit the description, even if the description is hundreds of times more typical of classics professors.

In one study, clinicians grew more confident in their judgments about a case as they got more information about it, but they did not grow more accurate.[8] By the end of the study, most of them had therefore become markedly overconfident. This demonstrates that the confidence we place in our beliefs is not a sure sign of their truth. Newer experimental research confirms that we humans tend to be consistently overconfident in judging the certainty of our beliefs.[9] My colleague, John Shaughnessy, has also demonstrated the overconfidence phenomenon with college students. Students who performed poorly on exams were quite likely to not know when they didn't know something.

Clinicians, students, and stock experts all share this overconfidence phenomenon. Stock experts, reading the latest information on specific companies and industries, market their services on the presumption that they can beat the market average. But incredible as it may seem, reports Burton Malkiel, many studies indicate that "over long periods of time mutual fund portfolios [which are selected by the best investment analysts in the business] have not outperformed randomly selected groups of stocks."[10] Current stock prices reflect the distributed judgments of all stock buyers and this baseline provides the best predictions of future stock values. It is difficult to avoid this foible of human thought: vivid testimonies and specific, dramatic information overwhelm our knowledge of the actual base rates of events, leading us to erroneous judgments and beliefs which are held with gross overconfidence.

Another common thinking error contributes to distortions in our self-images. This was evident when Lee Ross and his colleagues randomly assigned some students to play the role of questioner and some to play the role of contestant in a simulated quiz game.[11] Questioners were invited to make up difficult and esoteric questions which would demonstrate their general wealth of knowledge. Despite the fact that everyone was fully aware that the roles assigned to questioner and contestant guaranteed that the questioner would have the advantage, both participants and observers of the experiment succumbed to the erroneous impression that the questioners *really were* more knowledgeable individuals than the contestants. In real life, people in positions of social power tend to initiate and control conversation, leading their underlings to often overestimate their knowledge and intelligence. It has been my experience that students often over-estimate the brilliance of their teachers and underestimate their own abilities by comparison. (Teachers, of course, enjoy the prerogatives of questioners on subjects of their own choosing.) When some of these students later become teachers, they are usually amazed to discover that teachers are not so brilliant after all.

More examples could be compiled from the experimental literature.[12] What makes most of these mental imperfections so striking is the extent to which people are oblivious to them. Several experiments by Baruch Fischhoff and colleagues have found that when people are told the outcome of an experiment, the outcome seems more inevitable and less surprising than when people are simply told about the experiment and its possible outcomes. (This finding may itself, therefore, seem inevitable and unsurprising now that you know it!) This highlights a difficulty faced by psychological researchers in presenting their results or in writing a book such as this. Almost any result an experiment might obtain seems understandable and obvious—after you know the result. Moreover, people who are made aware of this "hindsight bias," as you have just been, still exhibit it.[13]

This phenomenon makes problems for many psychology students. When they read the results of experiments in their textbooks the material often seems easy, even common-sensical. When they subsequently take a multiple choice test on which they must choose among several plausible outcomes to an experiment the task becomes surprisingly difficult. "I don't know what happened," the befuddled student later exclaims, "I thought I knew the material."

One reason for the intellectual conceit of hindsight judgments is that our recall of what we expected—or would have expected had we been the decision-maker—is instantly distorted by our learning what did happen. For example, Fischhoff found that subjects told the correct answers to almanac-type questions overestimate how much they would have known about the answer had they not been told. Since outcomes therefore seem as if they should have been foreseen, we are more likely to blame decision-makers for their "obvious" bad choices than to praise them for their "obvious" good choices. In retrospect everyone agrees that the Attica Prison riot or the Japanese attack on Pearl Harbor should have come as no surprise to anyone who could read the signs. But although hindsight enables us to easily interpret events so as to predict what we know happened, the inevitability of these tragedies was not nearly so apparent beforehand.

As this book goes to press Egypt's President Sadat has just made his momentous decision to visit Israel. Is this visit "premature" or is it a "breakthrough" in Arab-Israeli relations? Experts are agreed that Sadat is taking a big risk. The visit may bring the Middle East closer to a negotiated peace, but it could also backfire, undercutting Sadat's position in the Arab world and frustrating hopes for peace. No one seems sure how this risky decision will turn out.

From my present vantage point you who read this book are living in the future, able to look back on events which transpired during and after the Sadat visit. Has your knowledge of its outcomes made the outcomes seem more foreseeable and inevitable than they were beforehand? And has this outcome knowledge made Sadat into either a fool or a courageous visionary, possibly even a future candidate for the Nobel Peace Prize?

Other evidence confirms that we frequently fail to realize Socrates' maxim to "Know thyself." In everyday life we are frequently asked questions about why we act as we do—why we like particular political candidates, have chosen a particular job, or behaved as we did in a social situation. Research psychologists have also asked people why they behaved, chose, or evaluated as they did. They have then compared these introspections with factual evidence concerning what *actually* influenced the subjects' behavior.[14] It turns out that our self-knowledge often strays far from the truth. People seem to be accurate in reporting the causes of their behavior only if their hunches about what causes behavior are correct in that situation. If the influences upon their actions are subtle, then their self-reports may be quite inaccurate. For example, although experiments have clearly shown that bystanders become less willing to help others in distress as the number of other bystanders increases, the people who participated in these experiments persistently denied any such influence.

Moreover, we are sometimes woefully incapable of accurately reporting our own prior behavior and attitudes. People who undergo attitude change during an experiment are often unaware of it; they tend to recall their pre-experiment attitudes as being similar to their post-experiment attitudes. (This is another example of hindsight bias.) Long term observations of parents and children reveal that parents' recollections of how they handled their children better fit their current views of child rearing than their actual past behavior. Freudians and other believers in unconscious mental processes can rejoice; these and other findings indicate that people often cannot directly observe the workings of their own minds. As Pascal put it, "The heart has its reasons, which reason does not know."[15] (Incidentally, to the extent that Pascal's dictum is true, limits are placed upon subjective personal reports as a method of psychological inquiry.)

Our finiteness is also evident in other everyday situations. Magicians play skillfully upon the limits of our ability to identify causation. Millions believe in astrological predictions, despite near complete consensus among scientists that the claims of astrology have no basis in fact. Just the other day I received an advertisement for a book of "Avatar Power Chants." There are chants for every purpose—to make others obey, to dispel evil, to attract "love slaves," to win contests. One woman used the power chant for winning contests and then won $750,000 in a lottery. A man used the power chants and picked six consecutive winners at the track. Of course, if power chants really worked or if even a few people had the prophetic abilities which some ESP proponents claim, there would be no lotteries, no horse racing industry, and no Las Vegas. But this evident fact does not erode the convictions of the millions who believe, nor does it undermine our own little superstitious behaviors. How, then, do these false ideas emerge, and why are they so resistant to change?

CORRELATION AND CAUSATION

One of the most pervasive mistakes of human thinking is our inclination to assume that two events which occur coincidentally are necessarily causally connected. Because educational attainments correlate with income, we assume that it pays to go to school. Because marriage is associated with health (young bachelors have twice the mortality rate of their married counterparts), we conclude that marriage is good for health. Because children whose television diet is heavily saturated with violence tend to act more aggressively than children who see less violence, we criticize the networks for the brutalizing effects of their violent programs. Because the probability of lung cancer increases with the number of cigarettes smoked, we point the guilty finger at the tobacco industry. Because good breakfast nutrition predicts good school achievement, advertisers of breakfast food would have us believe that we can improve our children's grades by changing their morning bowl of cereal.

The point is not that these conclusions are false—in some of these instances, experimental manipulations (e.g., of exposure to television violence) indicate that the conclusion is correct. The point is that the evidence I provided does not convincingly indicate that the first variable of each pair has caused the second. In each case there are other plausible interpretations of the data, and a little ingenuity can provide them. For example, although it seems highly unlikely, one scholar has seriously proposed that the temperament and constitution of people who take up heavy smoking predisposes them to cancer for reasons having nothing to do with smoking.

This is a stale lesson which any student of psychology or logic has heard many times. Yet the tendency to infer causation from mere correlation is so deeply imbedded that even we who teach this lesson often succumb to it. If we find that a particular child-rearing style is associated with certain personality characteristics of children, we are tempted to conclude that the former causes the latter. But might it not also be that the attributes of the child force the parent to react in predictable ways or that both parent and child attributes are symptomatic of some third factor, like their shared heredity? If we could confirm Freud's suspicion that harsh toilet training is associated with compulsive, up-tight personalities, would this prove that toilet training makes a difference? Not necessarily.

It is hard to remember this point and to apply it to our experiences. I pound it into my students' heads. I warn them to watch for it on examinations. And still many of them forget—except when a causal interpretation would violate what they already believe. At one time, the number of storks in various Dutch towns correlated with the number of babies born in each, but this never convinced anyone to repudiate their sex education. (Storks like to nest on roofs, so there were more storks in larger towns.)

Sometimes the mere co-occurrence of two events produces humorous results. During the East Coast blackout a few years back, one lad was walking gaily down the street with a stick in hand. Just as he whacked a nearby telephone pole the power went off, sending the boy home in tears. At the same moment, a woman living in a high-rise apartment was cautiously plugging in her rusty old toaster. As she did so, the lights in the apartment dimmed, and through her window she could see the whole city blackening. Overwhelmed with guilt, she called her husband to confess her horrible deed.

These examples suggest the ease with which we falsely connect something we do with an improbable coincidence. It is, of course, improbable coincidences which are most likely to be remembered. Do dreams have any predictive value? Some years ago, when the Lindbergh baby was kidnapped, but before its body was discovered, two Harvard psychologists invited the public to send them dream reports concerning the whereabouts of the child.[16] Of the 1,300 dream reports received, only 5 percent correctly perceived the child as dead and only 4 of the 1,300, a seemingly chance number, correctly predicted death, burial in the ground, and location among trees. I have always wondered about the writers of those 4 reports. Surely, they remembered the success of their dream better than the other 1,296 remembered their failure. Did some of the 4 also sell copies of their letters to newspapers and magazines, enabling others to read their glowing testimony to the clairvoyant power of dreams? Is there a parallel tendency to recall and report only dramatic instances of prayer preceding an unusual happening?

The power of coincidence is demonstrated by experimental studies of superstitious behavior. Imagine a rat that is trained to press a lever in order to obtain food pellets. Then suppose we change the rules, and give food pellets every so often, *regardless* of the rat's behavior. What do you think the rat will now do? It will probably continue pressing the lever for awhile. Occasionally, because pellets are still delivered, the presses will be followed by pellets. These accidental sequences of behavior and reinforcement are conducive to superstitious behavior, so the rat will keep on pressing as if its presses produce the pellets.

The erratic, intermittent schedule by which superstitious behavior is reinforced makes it especially persistent. During recent droughts in England and in the United States the news media reported several instances of rain dances, a few of which were followed by rain. In some prescientific cultures rain dances have occurred frequently enough to receive occasional reinforcement. This is all that is needed to maintain them, especially since the believer has ways of accounting for failures. There is considerable evidence documenting the resilience of people's beliefs and impressions to contradictory facts. It is much easier to somehow assimilate a new fact within one's existing beliefs than to revise one's beliefs in light of the fact.[17]

It is not necessary that the superstitious behavior ever have caused its apparent reward for superstition to persist. In the best-known experimental study of superstitious behavior, B. F. Skinner presented food to hungry pigeons every fifteen seconds for a few minutes each day. Can you guess what happened? Remember that the food appeared at regular intervals, regardless of the bird's behavior. In Skinner's words:

In six out of eight cases the resulting responses were so clearly defined that two observers could agree perfectly in counting instances. One bird was conditioned to turn counter-clockwise about the cage, making two or three turns between reinforcements. Another repeatedly thrust its head into one of the upper corners of the cage. A third developed a 'tossing' response, as if placing its head beneath an invisible bar and lifting it repeatedly. Two birds developed a pendulum motion of the head and body, in which the head was extended forward and swung from right to left with a sharp movement followed by a somewhat slower return. . . . Another bird was conditioned to make incomplete pecking or brushing movements directed toward but not touching the floor.[18]

Perhaps if we had walked into the laboratory at this point, we would have diagnosed the pigeons as severely neurotic. What produced these strange behaviors? Whatever the bird was doing as the food tray appeared was, of course, strengthened, and therefore more likely than other behaviors to reoccur and be further reinforced fifteen seconds later.

Over time, the superstitious behavior sometimes gradually shifted to a different act. One bird added a hopping step to its sequence. When the food tray was presented once every minute, the bird would hop vigorously for the forty seconds preceding the appearance of the food. It was no small effort to convince the bird that this ritual was ineffectual. After the food mechanism was turned off, the bird hopped more than ten thousand times before quitting! Said Skinner:

The bird behaves as if there were a causal relation between its behavior and the presentation of food, although such a relation is lacking. There are many analogies in human behavior. Rituals for changing one's luck at cards are good examples. A few accidental connections between a ritual and favorable consequences suffice to set up and maintain the behavior in spite of many unreinforced instances. The bowler who has released a ball down the alley but continues to behave as if he were controlling it by twisting and turning his arm and shoulder is another case in point. These behaviors have, of course, no real effect upon one's luck or upon a ball half way down the alley, just as in the present case the food would appear as often if the pigeon did nothing—or, more strictly speaking, did something else.[19]

Subsequent laboratory experiments confirm that children and adults will develop superstitious behaviors in much the same way. In one study, preschool children were given a piece of candy after pressing a red button or a blue button, or both, for a combined total of thirty responses.[20] Next, the rules were changed, and for a brief period of time the children were rewarded for *not pressing* the *blue* key. Most of the children then came to press the red key at a high rate, even though these responses were irrelevant. There were a few exceptions. One child dropped a piece of candy on the floor and left the apparatus to crawl around and search for it. While he was doing so, the next piece of candy was delivered on schedule. He then spent the rest of the experimental session crawling around the floor, reaching up to get the candy after each delivery.

Animal superstitions are idiosyncratic, that is, unique to each animal. So are some adult superstitious acts. We call these "compulsions," or aspects of personal style. But many human superstitions are shaped by culture and are therefore shared. Some of these superstitious conventions may be traced to a time when they had survival value, just as the child's button pressing can be traced to when it was an effective act. Other superstitions probably originated in accidental associations that, for example, shaped the perception that Friday the thirteenth is ominous but Tuesday the tenth is not.[21]

All of us engage in harmless superstitious behaviors from time to time.[22] The coach wins a couple of big games while wearing red socks and thereafter continues the practice. I catch a nice salmon while fishing in a particular spot or wearing a particular hat, so I persist in these actions and eventually catch another.

I know of a woman who, rightly believing that God cares for the little things in her life as well as the big, will pray for a parking space when she goes shopping. If she is persistent in her prayer (and if she continues driving), no doubt her prayers are eventually answered. This encourages her to continue. The phenomenon is equally evident when animals or humans seek to avoid an unpleasant event. Behaviors which enable a rat to avoid a shock or a person to avoid confronting some fearful event endure because the avoidance behavior is reinforced by fear reduction—even if the threat no longer exists. If a person does some act or carries some good luck charm to ward off an unlikely trauma, like an accident while traveling, the act is quite likely to meet with apparent success and thus be continued.

ILLUSORY CORRELATION

A second source of superstitious thinking is our tendency to perceive correlation where none exists. People have great difficulty objectively recognizing chance events for what they are.

Experiments on "illusory correlation" have demonstrated its relevance to clinical psychology. Many clinicians believe that projective tests like the Rorschach inkblots are useful in diagnosing patient problems; patients' symptoms are presumed to be reflected in their performance on these subjective tests. Yet research has consistently failed to substantiate these claims. There is actually very little correlation between symptoms and test performance when the two are assessed independently. Why does belief in the validity of projective tests persist? Studies indicate that when naive students view a series of projective test performances *randomly paired* with various symptoms, the students "rediscover" much of the clinical lore.[23] For example, patients with worries about their intelligence were believed to have emphasized the head on the "Draw-a-Person" test; suspicious patients were thought to have drawn peculiar eyes. Actually, no such relationships existed in what had been viewed—the perceived correlation between symptoms and drawings was illusory. The effect persisted even when subjects were told a twenty-dollar prize would be given to the most accurate subject.

Twenty years ago, one influential research psychologist was already lamenting, "Personally, I find the cultural lag between what the published research shows and what clinicians persist in claiming to do with their favorite devices even more disheartening than the adverse evidence itself."[24] Experiments on test interpretation continue to confirm that people perceive relationships they expect to find, even if they do not exist. Even random data are easily construed as supporting one's existing beliefs.[25] That many clinicians persist in using projective tests despite additional disconfirming evidence testifies to the potency of superstitious thinking even within the psychology profession. It seems highly likely, then, that *if people believe a relationship exists between two things, confirming instances are noticed more than disconfirming instances, thus reinforcing their belief in it*. Might this effect ever extend to people's perceptions of the correlation between their prayer and its outcomes?

Illusory correlation also occurs because people are more attentive to unusual than to ordinary events. This makes the simultaneous occurrence of unusual events particularly noticeable—more noticeable than each of the times the unusual events do *not* occur together. This was evident in one clever experiment in which various hypothetical people, members of "Group A" or "Group B," were paired with desirable or undesirable behaviors.[26] For example, on one slide the subjects read, "John, a member of Group A, visited a sick friend in the hospital." Members of Group A outnumbered Group B by two to one, but both groups received nine desirable descriptions for every four undesirable descriptions. Since both Group B and the undesirable acts were less frequent events their co-occurrence caught people's attention. Subjects overestimated the frequency with which the "minority" group (B) exhibited undesirable behaviors, and consequently they judged this group more harshly. Remember now, Group B members actually exhibited undesirable traits in the same proportion as Group A members. This result suggests that illusory correlation may be one basis for racial stereotypes. It also confirms that *the joint occurrence of two distinctive events draws our attention.*

The mass media reflect and feed this phenomenon. For example, when an avowed homosexual murders someone, the homosexuality is likely to get mentioned. When a heterosexual person murders someone, this is a less distinctive event and thus the person's sexual orientation is unlikely to be mentioned, which, in turn, contributes to an inflated perception of the likelihood of homosexual persons committing violent crimes.

Illusion of Control

Our tendency to interpret chance events as though they were meaningfully correlated provides the foundation for yet another thought distortion—the illusion that chance events are subject to our personal control.

In a brilliant series of experiments performed mostly in real life situations, Ellen Langer demonstrated the illusion of control in gambling situations.[27] When some features of situations involving skill (like choice, active involvement, and familiarity with the task) were introduced into gambling situations, people became more optimistic about their possibilities, despite the fact that these changes still could not possibly affect the outcomes. For example, people had more confidence in a lottery number which they chose than in one which someone else chose for them. This illusion of control was so powerful that many people who had chosen their own ticket number later declined an opportunity to switch to a lottery where their objective chances of winning were actually better. Using several different methods and types of people, Langer consistently observed that people will behave as though chance events are subject to their control.

Observations of real-life gamblers have confirmed these experimental findings. Dice players often behave as if they could control the outcome by throwing softly for low numbers and hard for high numbers.[28] Putting the experimental results to practial use, Langer suggests that state lotteries can maximize betting by giving participants maximum choice on their tickets. The extent to which the gambling industry thrives because gamblers are victimized by their illusion of control is strong testimony to how resistant to reason the phenomenon is. Gamblers' hopes that they can beat the laws of chance sustain their gambling. Even the gambling industry itself can suffer the illusion: Las Vegas table dealers who experience a string of losses for the house can lose their jobs.[29]

Another of Langer's studies indicates that if people experience some unusual early successes in a chance situation, later failures may be discounted.[30] People predicted the outcomes of thirty coin tosses. The experimenter rigged the feedback so that some people experienced mostly wins during the first ten flips while others experienced either mostly losses or a random sequence of wins and losses. Across all thirty trials, however, each person accumulated the same total outcome: fifteen wins and fifteen losses. Nonetheless, those who started with a fairly consistent sequence of wins made inflated estimates of how many flips they had actually predicted and how many they could predict given another hundred trials. Having experienced early success, people evidently came to perceive themselves as skilled, and therefore did not give as much weight to later failures. It appears that the motivation to see events as controllable is so strong that just one cue like early positive results can induce an illusion of control over what is obviously a mere chance task.

In my home we have occasionally flipped a coin to settle disputes. At one point my older son began arguing that he always lost coin tosses. I reminded him that each flip was a fifty-fifty proposition. To my dismay, he suffered several more consecutive losses. Now no amount of rational persuasion will convince him that he really has a fifty-fifty chance on the next toss. What makes Langer's results so striking is that her subjects were not ten-year-old boys, but bright, sophisticated, Yale University students.

Amos Tversky and Daniel Kahneman have identified many more fascinating ways by which human judgment becomes predictably distorted.[31] For example, we fail to recognize and properly interpret the statistical phenomenon of "regression toward the average," even though it often occurs in real life. The phenomenon is simply illustrated: students who obtain extremely high scores on an exam are likely to obtain a lower average score on the next exam. Their first scores are at the ceiling and the only way to move is down. This is why a student who does consistently good work, even if never the best, will sometimes end a course at the top of the class. Conversely, those who do worst on the first exam are likely to improve. Thus if those who scored lowest are tutored after the first exam, the tutors are likely to be rewarded for their efforts, even if the tutoring had no effect. Likewise, a counselor who is visited by people at their most depressed is more likely to be gratified by their subsequent improvement than to observe further deterioration. Similarly, a compensatory education program which admits disadvantaged students who are judged on the basis of test scores to have the best chance of success is less likely to "produce" improvements in these scores than a program which admits those with the lowest initial scores.

Tversky and Kahneman show how the failure to recognize this regression phenomenon can have pernicious consequences. Experienced flight instructors have noted that praise for an exceptionally smooth landing is typically followed by a poorer landing on the next try, while harsh criticism after a very rough landing is typically followed by improvement. This led the instructors to conclude that verbal rewards are detrimental to learning, while punishments are beneficial. Parents and teachers may reach the same conclusion after reacting to extremely good or bad behaviors. It seems, therefore, that "the human condition is such that, by chance alone, one is most often rewarded for punishing others and most often punished for rewarding them."[32] Indeed, *any desperate behavior* in response to an exceptionally bad situation is more likely to be followed by improvements in the situation than by further decrements. This phenomenon is surely the source of many of the "cures" of unorthodox medicine. When we are physically sick or emotionally down, whatever we do—altering our diet, going to a faith healer or psychotherapist, practicing transcendental meditation—may seem to work.

Our final experiment is perhaps the most thought-provoking because of its striking parallel to some types of prayer. Fred Ayeroff and Robert Abelson engaged Yale University students in an ESP experiment.[33] On each of one hundred trials one student tried to send mentally one of five possible symbols to another student in a different room. After each trial, the receiver guessed what was transmitted. Both the sender and the receiver indicated whether they were "confident" or "not confident" that a hit had been scored. Half of these pairs were given a *choice* as to which of several sets of symbols they wished to use. For the other half, the experimenter did the choosing. Some of the pairs were also given a warmup period, during which they practiced telepathy and discussed verbally their techniques in order that they could "hook up" their transmissions. In all pairs, the sender was actively involved by shuffling and dealing the cards.

Can you predict the results? Under all conditions, the percentage of actual telepathic hits was at chance levels. The telepathic success rate of 19.25 percent was insignificantly different from the chance baseline of 20 percent. Nevertheless, if subjects actively chose their telepathic symbols and if they were given the warm-up communication experience, they became wildly optimistic in their belief that something was really happening. Both the sender and receiver indicated they were "confident" of a hit on more than 50 percent of the trials! When neither choice nor the warm-up was allowed, confidence judgments matched much more closely the chance rate of hits. The senders also tended to be more confident than the receivers. This is not surprising because senders were more actively engaged in the experiment.

This experiment is important not as one more laboratory failure to find ESP but for what it indicates about how people come to believe things that are not true. Although it would have been difficult to rationally explain or defend, the subjects nonetheless had an intuitive conviction that something was truly transpiring. But despite the subjects' good feeling, the objective data showed this euphoria to be groundless, a mere illusion. The choice, involvement, and warm-up factors which produced the strong subjective feelings of success were actually irrelevant. Here is yet another demonstration of our great propensity to internalize our actions, to believe in what we have done.

Note, finally, that the participants in the above experiment received no feedback as to how well they were doing. If a few seemingly confirming experiences, as in the coin-tossing experiment, were to be added to these other factors, we would probably complete the recipe for an enduring, although utterly false, belief in an occult phenomenon. A critical feature in the autobiography of many true believers in ESP is, in fact, an unusual experience which seems to confirm the ESP belief.

So it is with my own faith in the power of petitionary prayer. As a boy growing up in Seattle I longed for snow, which we rarely had. One night I clearly heard God say to me, "David, it is going to snow tonight." When I awoke the next morning I discovered, to my delight, that the ground was white. I would be hard pressed to defend my interpretation of that experience, and hence have seldom spoken of it, much less publicly confessed it as I have just done. Nonetheless, experiences like this helped shape a subjective conviction of the mysterious efficacy of prayer from which no amount of rational evidence will ever fully dissuade me. As Martin Luther declared, "No one believes how strong and mighty prayer is and how much it can do except he whom experience has taught, and who has tried it."[34]

SUMMING UP

The evidence is clear and consistent. Human beings are remarkably inclined to:

perceive causal connections among events which are merely correlated,

perceive correlations where none exist, and

think they can control events which are really beyond their control.

Furthermore, we are largely ignorant of the extent to which these illusions permeate our thinking. Indeed, we *must* be oblivious to these illusions, or we wouldn't maintain them. While most of us are adept at recognizing *others'* superstitions, our own superstitions are more often regarded as beliefs or facts of life. As Jeremiah knew, "The heart is deceitful above all things."[35]

Although it is wise that we be sensitized to these truths, it is also true that superstitious thinking serves some important functions which have enabled it to flourish and which will sustain it in the future. What are these functions? Why does superstitious thinking occur?

First, simple rules of thought by which we infer conclusions that are generally true will sometimes lead us astray. For example, the clarity of an object helps determine its perceived distance. This is usually a valid rule because in any scene, distant objects *are* seen less sharply than near objects. But our reliance on this rule sometimes distorts our perception. If visibility is poor and objects become blurred, distances are overestimated.

Superstitions also originate in correct causal inferences. It is useful to presume that positive outcomes are produced by the acts which precede them because this is often true. But very often, *both* chance and skill contribute to an outcome. This makes it advantageous to believe that the event is controllable because in that way we maximize our own influence. Sometimes, however, events are uncontrollable, in which case what is usually a useful rule can lead us astray.

Second, people are motivated to control their environment. Superstitious thinking is actually a sort of amateur science because, like science, it seeks "to reduce natural phenomena to a comprehensible system in order that it can be mastered."[36] Much research in social and animal psychology and several personality theories converge in pointing to our need to master our environment.[37] When a painful or anxiety-arousing event is thought to be controllable or predictable, its destructive effects on the psyche are not so bad, whereas a sense of helplessness engenders resignation.[38] Since many superstitious acts provide the person with a sense of control over uncontrollable events, it is not surprising that people with less perceived social power (e.g., women and less educated working-class persons) typically evidence more superstitious beliefs.[39] Jean Piaget has likewise demonstrated the extent to which children's thinking includes magical concepts of causality which empower the child. The child "regards his gestures, his thoughts, or the objects he handles as charged with efficacy."[40]

Because superstitious acts provide a sense of control, they are especially prevalent in times of stress and tension. Primitive magic reduces tension by subjecting the mysteries of nature to human will. It therefore helps maintain hope where despair might otherwise reign.[41] The effect is not limited to primitive cultures. In dire circumstances, any of us may become desperate to control the external environment. Surveys reveal that many more people pray than attend church. In a crisis, even avowed atheists may act as if they think there really is a supernatural power.

If the perceived control is sometimes illusory, it still may engender the confidence needed to continue one's struggle. We therefore pay a price for undercutting superstitious thinking, and if we want to do away with it, we had best be prepared to put something better in its place. The widespread belief in occult phenomena and the romantic urge for mystical or charismatic experience indicate a yearning for something beyond the cold rationality of naturalism.

To close the chapter on a playful note, I must admit that students of illusory thinking are not immune to their own phenomena. My ideas about illusory thinking may be partly illusory thinking. Imagine the irony were I to insist that all human thinking is corrupted by biases, errors, and distortions—and that is an absolute truth. It would be logically equivalent to my arguing that all generalizations are false, including this one.

NOTES

1. James E. Dittes, "Justification by Faith and the Experimental Psychologist," *Religion in Life* 28 (1959): 567–76.

2. For a review of laboratory demonstrations of this phenomenon see Lee Ross, David Greene, and Pamela House, "The 'False Consensus Effect': An Egocentric Bias on Social Perception and Attribution Processes," *Journal of Experimental Social Psychology* 13 (1977): 279–01; for evidence from national opinion surveys see Hubert J. O'Gorman & Stephen

L. Garry, "Pluralistic Ignorance—A Replication and Extension," *Public Opinion Quarterly* 40 (1976): 449–58.

3. This is shown by research on the "just world phenomenon." Martin Bolt explores the implications of this research for Christians in his excellent forthcoming book, *The Christian in a Social World: Applications of Social Psychology to the Christian Community* (tentative title).

4. A. Michotte, *The Perception of Causality*, Basic Books, 1963.

5. Lynn Hasher, David Goldstein, & Thomas Topping, "Frequency and the Conference of Referential Validity," *Journal of Verbal Learning and Verbal Behavior* 16 (1977): 107–12.

6. Richard Nisbett, Eugene Borgida, Rick Crandall, and H Reed, "Popular Induction: Information is Not Always Informative," in *Cognition and Social Behavior*, ed. J. S. Carroll and John W. Payne (Hillsdale, N.J.: Erlbaum, 1976), pp. 113–133.

7. Eugene Borgida and Richard E. Nisbett, "The Differential Impact of Abstract vs. Concrete Information on Decisions," *Journal of Applied Social Psychology*, in press.

8. Stuart Oskamp, "Overconfidence in Case-Study Judgments," *Journal of Consulting Psychology* 29 (1965): 261–65.

9. Baruch Fischhoff, Paul Slovic, and Sarah Lichtenstein, "Knowing with Certainty: The Appropriateness of Extreme Confidence," *Journal of Experimental Psychology: Human Perception and Performance*, in press.

10. Burton G. Malkiel, *A Random Walk Down Wall Street* (New York: W. W. Norton, 1975). My thanks to Douglas Heerema for bringing this book to my attention.

11. Lee Ross, "The Intuitive Psychologist and His Shortcomings: Distortions in the Attribution Process," *Advances in Experimental Social Psychology*, vol. 10, ed. L. Berkowitz (New York: Academic Press, 1977), pp. 174–220.

12. See Richard Gorsuch's discussion, "Man and Finitude," in Richard L. Gorsuch and H. Newton Maloney, *The Nature of Man: A Social Psychological Perspective* (Springfield, Ill.: Charles C. Thomas, 1975).

13. These experiments are summarized in Paul Slovic and Baruch Fischhoff, "On the Psychology of Experimental Surprises," *Journal of Experimental Psychology: Human Perception and Performance*, in press. See also Fischhoff, "Perceived Informativeness of Facts," *Journal of Experimental Psychology: Human Perception and Performance* 3 (1977): 349–58 and Fischhoff and Ruth Beyth, " 'I Knew It Would Happen': Remembered Probabilities of Once-Future Things," *Organizational Behavior and Human Performance* 13 (1975): 1–16.

14. Richard E. Nisbett and Timothy D. Wilson, "Telling More Than We Can Know: Verbal Reports on Mental Processes," *Psychological Review* 84 (1977): 231–59.

15. Pascal, *Thoughts*, 227.

16. H. A. Murray and D. R. Wheeler, "A Note on the Possible Clairvoyance of Dreams," *Journal of Psychology* 3 (1936): 309–13.

17. Amos Tversky & Daniel Kahneman, "Causal Schemata in Judgments Under Uncertainty," in *Progress in Social Psychology*, ed. M. Fishbein (Hillsdale, N.J.: Erlbaum, 1977).

18. B. F. Skinner, " 'Superstition' in the Piegeon," *Journal of Experimental Psychology* 38 (1948): 168–72.

19. *Ibid.*

20. Michael D. Zeiler, "Superstitious Behavior in Children: An Experimental Analysis," in *Advances in Child Development and Behavior*, Vol. 7, ed. H. W. Reese (New York: Academic Press, 1972), pp. 1–29.

21. Richard J. Herrnstein, "Superstition: A Corollary of the Principles of Operant Conditioning," in *Operant Behavior: Areas of Research and Application*, ed. W. K. Honig (New York: Appleton, Century, Crofts, 1966), pp. 33–51.

22. Human superstitions have been catalogued by the thousands. See, for example, Eric Maple, *Superstition and the Superstitious* (New York: A. S. Barnes & Co., 1972, and Gustav Jahoda, *The Psychology of Superstition* (New York: Penguin, 1969).

23. See, for example, Loren J. Chapman and Jean P. Chapman, "Genesis of Popular but Erroneous Psychodiagnostic Observations," *Journal of Abnormal Psychology* 72 (1967): 193–204.

24. Paul E. Meehl, "The Cognitive Activity of the Clinician," *American Psychologist* 15 (1960): 19–27.

25. See Ross, *op. cit.,* p. 196.

26. David L. Hamilton and Robert K. Gifford, "Illusory Correlation in Interpersonal Perception: A Cognitive Basis of Stereotypic Judgments," *Journal of Experimental Social Psychology* 12 (1976): 392–407.

27. Ellen J. Langer, "The Illusion of Control," *Journal of Personality and Social Psychology* 32 (1975): 311–28.

28. M. Henslin, "Craps and Magic," *American Journal of Sociology* 73 (1967): 316–30.

29. Erving Goffman, *Interaction Ritual* (Garden City, N.Y.: Doubleday Anchor, 1967).

30. Ellen J. Langer and Jane Roth, "Heads I Win, Tails It's Chance: The Illusion of Control as a Function of the Sequence of Outcomes in a Purely Chance Task," *Journal of Personality and Social Psychology* 32 (1975): 951–55.

31. Amos Tversky and Daniel Kahneman, "Judgment under Uncertainty: Heuristics and Biases," *Science* 185 (1974): 1124–31.

32. *Ibid.*

33. Fred Ayeroff and Robert P. Ableson, "ESP and ESB: Belief in Personal Success at Mental Telepathy," *Journal of Personality and Social Psychology* 34 (1976): 240–47.

34. Quoted in George A. Buttrick, *Prayer* (Nashville: Abingdon-Cokesbury, 1942), p. 82.

35. Jer. 17:9 RSV.

36. Maple, *op. cit.,* p. 184.

37. See Chapter 10 for further discussion of this.

38. For a review of relevant experiments, see Herbert M. Lefcourt, "The Function of the Illusions of Control and Freedom," *American Psychologist* 28 (1973): 417–25.

39. Eleanor Maccoby and Carol N. Jacklin, *The Psychology of Sex Differences* (Stanford: Stanford University Press, 1974). Studies con-

ducted fifty years ago (see C. J. Gregory, "Changes in Superstitious Beliefs Among College Women," *Psychological Reports* 37 [1975]: 939–44) and recently (see S. H. Blum, "Some Aspects of Belief in Prevailing Superstitions," *Psychological Reports* 38 [1976]: 579–82) find that the average woman engages in more superstitious behaviors than the average man.

40. Jean Piaget, *The Child's Conception of Physical Causality* (Boston: Routledge & Kegan Paul, 1931), p. 261.

41. Bronislaw Malinowski, *Magic, Science, and Religion* (Garden City, N.Y.: Doubleday, 1948).

CHAPTER 8

Prayer

The many demonstrations of how easily human thinking is distorted by falsehood do not prove that illusions corrupt prayer behavior with equal ease. Although superstition easily invades our thinking, not all of our ideas are tainted by its influence. Perhaps superstitious acts are a substitute for genuine prayer in situations where prayer and a simple faith in God's providence are needed. Superstitious beliefs are often rooted in causal inferences which are generally true but sometimes erroneous. The same conclusion may hold for belief in the power of prayer. Perhaps this belief, also, is rooted in truth, but occasionally subject to distortion.

The evidence that people are easily victimized by causal illusions does, however, make plain how some prayer *could* be infected by superstition. This infection is especially possible since the circumstances of prayer, such as earnest involvement, closely correspond to the conditions under which illusions of control are evident. When we consider further that both superstition and prayer can give a sense of personal power or confidence to individuals otherwise feeling powerless, that stressful situations which are conducive to superstition are also conducive to petitionary prayer, and that the types of people most inclined to be superstitious (women and people in the lowest socioeconomic classes) are also most inclined to a simple faith in the controlling power of petitionary prayer, then a deeper look at our conception of prayer seems called for.[1]

Every age has been steeped in beliefs which, judged in retrospect or from the outside, seem superstitious. Christians, for example, most easily identify the silly superstitions of other people, especially non-Christians. But are Christians likely to be found different in this respect? Voltaire wrote:

It is hard to mark out the boundaries of superstition. A Frenchman travelling in Italy finds almost everything superstitious, and is hardly wrong.

The archbishop of Canterbury claims that the archbishop of Paris is superstitious; the Presbyterians levy the same reproach against His Grace of Canterbury, and are in their turn called superstitious by the Quakers, who are the most superstitious of men in the eyes of other Christians.[2]

The Scriptures, however, remind Christians that they should first examine themselves: "Judgment must begin at the house of God."[3] We all live under the Fall. The illusions of thought should therefore come as no surprise, whether evident outside the church or inside of it.

Since one of my purposes in writing this book is to give a fresh and credible expression to Christian truth, I certainly do not wish these chapters to undercut faith in prayer. My anxiety is that I might reach wrong conclusions or, even if right, move some people to despair. Surely, though, the God who is light and truth would rather we struggle honestly to approach truth, even if it is temporarily discomforting. Perpetuating untruth does faith no service. We do not need to defend every popular use of prayer in order to maintain our commitment to its general value and validity.

I have dared to write these chapters on superstition and prayer because conversation with students and friends convinces me that many thinking Christians and skeptics are already troubled by the problem. Moreover, the type of person who would read this book is likely to be already entertaining questions about the power of prayer and in search of a positive, sensible understanding of it. The net result of being sensitized to superstition should not be to give up petitionary prayer—such prayer is too basic to our creaturely needs for that—but to move Christians to consider prayer as more than merely a fire escape in times of stress. Tearing away mental illusions can help get us to the reality beneath. Trying to rid prayer of superstition is done at some risk, but it can help create a balance among prayers of adoration, praise, confession, thanksgiving, dedication, meditation, and petition. Furthermore, our concept of prayer is so closely tied to our concept of God that thinking about prayer can be a part of our seeking God.

How, then, are Christians to know if they suffer the illusions and superstitious thinking which penetrate human thought? One way to find out, it has been suggested, is to put prayer to the test.

TESTING PRAYER

Do prayers of petition for oneself and intercession for others effectively manipulate events, as many Christians presume? Some have suggested that people who genuinely believe that prayer can influence God to alter future events should welcome an opportunity to demonstrate the power of their faith to unbelievers.[4]

At first blush this is a repulsive idea, partly because the very idea of researching prayer implies doubts about it. The scientific mentality is one of skepticism. It examines claims, questions authority, and tests theoretical doctrines in every way possible before accepting them. It prompts us to step back from our commitment and make a spectacle of it. Subjection of prayer to critical scrutiny could make it hard for the intellectual person to pray with spontaneity and passion.

Furthermore, the idea of testing prayer seems to disregard the reality of phenomena and spheres of knowledge that are beyond science. Religious knowledge is different from scientific knowledge. That "God exists" is not a scientifically testable hypothesis for it entails no verifiable conclusion. It is confirmed by personal and historical experience, not by scientific method. Our faith contains mysteries that are not penetrable by science. Gerardus van der Leeuw has reminded us that for religion, "God is the active Agent in relation to man, while the sciences in question can concern themselves only with the activity of man in his relation to God; of the acts of God himself they can give no account whatever."[5]

Nevertheless, some popular claims for prayer *are* of a straightforward, empirical character. Numerous testimonies proclaim the observable results of prayers. Prayer is said to be effective for specific bodily healings, receipt of money, good weather, landing a job, or finding a parking place. Not long ago I had a student who never studied very hard, but who would before each exam, pray fervently that God would direct her answers. (She got a C− in the course.) Some Christians petition different saints, depending on their need. Prayers to St. Francis, for example, are said to be effective for finding lost items.

These empirical claims for the predictable effects of prayer are reminiscent of claims for the material blessings which follow tithing. If all the testimonies uttered during annual stewardship drives were to be believed, tithing could be commended for its profit and taught as an investment principle in Business Administration courses. One widowed mother sent five dollars to Bishop Sheen, only to learn a few days later that she had won a one hundred dollars savings bond. After joyously declaring to her son that God rewards those who give, the son exclaimed, "This is wonderful— let's put the hundred dollars back on Bishop Sheen!" This self-serving concept of stewardship is, of course, not the biblical concept of stewardship, so we need not be disheartened if the material payoffs cannot be demonstrated.

The idea of putting prayer to the test was a source of serious controversy one hundred years ago.[6] To those who believed in the effectiveness of prayer, some British scientists proposed a crucial experiment. Since prayer is recommended for the sick, why not test the efficacy of prayer, just as we test any other proposed remedy: identify a group of patients who are suffering from a disease, administer the remedy, and observe its effects in comparison to a comparable group which did not receive the remedy. This proposal touched off the "prayer-test" debate which raged for several months in 1872–73.

The proposal and the response which followed were similar to George Price's challenge issued to proponents of ESP in *Science* during 1955. Given what we know about nature, said Price, ESP is impossible. Errors, nonverbal communication, selective reporting of results, or plain dishonesty account for the positive results reported by some. What we need, he argued, was just one bias-free experiment conducted before a panel of honest skeptics. Price would propose the experiment, and parapsychologists could send their ESP all-star team. Parapsychologists refused to accept a showdown. Sensitive ESP subjects cannot perform under such pressure, they said; ESP is too elusive, uncertain, and unpredictable to be judged by such an experiment.

Some of the reasons why the proposed prayer test of the last century was declined have already been noted. Religious beliefs are not to be tested experimentally. Besides, Christians believe that God often denies prayer requests for our own good. Most importantly, the proposal was not just to test prayer, but to test *God* in a way that is explicitly prohibited by the narrative of Jesus' temptations—"You are not to put the Lord your God to the test."[7]

Why not, then, suggested Francis Galton, examine the efficacy of prayers that have been uttered under natural circumstances.[8] Galton revealed that for several years he had been collecting data which showed that certain groups of people who were the objects of much prayer—kings, clergy, missionaries—had mortality rates at least as high as other groups. Furthermore, Galton observed, the proportion of still-births suffered by praying and by nonpraying parents appeared to be identical.

The challenge to set up a crucial experimental test of prayer can easily be faulted. It ignores the fact that "crucial experiments" are virtually as rare in science as in religion. It also ignores that scientists, like religionists, always interpret data from some assumed theoretical framework and hesitate to abandon that framework because of a few disconfirming observations. The prayer-test challenge should, nevertheless, stimulate us to clarify our concept of prayer. Should Christians assume that prayer has observable physical effects? Are God's actions affected by our prayers? Or is belief in the physical effects of prayer a self-aggrandizing illusion of control?

USES AND ABUSES OF PRAYER

It should not take experimental evidence to make us realize that some uses of prayer not only may be superstitious, they also may make little theological sense. Consider first those prayers which treat God as a cosmic Santa Claus to whom we appeal for our personal benefit—to gain a better job, prosperity, health, success, self-fulfillment.

Rather than "praying without ceasing," we pray mostly when we want to gain something immediately. When army equipment was immobilized by rains during the winter of 1944, General George S. Patton impatiently ordered all chaplains to pray for dry weather.

General Patton: "Chaplain, I want you to publish a prayer for good weather. I'm tired of these soldiers having to fight mud and floods as well as Germans. See if we can't get God to work on our side."

Chaplain O'Neill: "Sir, it's going to take a pretty thick rug for that kind of praying."

General Patton: "I don't care if it takes the flying carpet. I want the praying done."

Chaplain O'Neill: "Yes, sir. May I say, General, that it isn't a customary thing among men of my profession to pray for clear weather to kill fellow men."

General Patton: "Chaplain, are you teaching me theology or are you the Chaplain of the Third Army? I want a prayer."

Chaplain O'Neill: "Yes, sir."

The prayer, which was printed by the Army and distributed with Patton's Christmas greetings, called upon God

to restrain these immoderate rains with which we have had to contend. Grant us fair weather for Battle. Graciously harken to us as soldiers who call upon Thee that, armed with Thy power, we may advance from victory to victory, and crush the oppression and wickedness of our enemies, and establish Thy justice among men and nations. Amen.[9]

More recently, we have witnessed the spectacle of American Christians lobbying God for *and* against the American war effort in Vietnam, often simultaneously. One side or the other would occasionally declare a national day of prayer, possibly under the assumption that there is strength in numbers before God.[10]

Such self-serving uses of prayer parallel Bronislaw Malinowski's description of the superstitious magic of primitive cultures (as contrasted with true religion). Magic consists "of acts which are only a means to a definite end expected later on; religion [is] a body of self-contained acts being themselves the fulfillment of their purpose."[11] The implication is that religious acts become superstitious when they are no longer seen as being intrinsically worthwhile but function instead as a self-serving technique for manipulating some practical result.

Indeed, laments Jacques Ellul, prayer has for a long time been understood as a technique for "having power over everything over which God has power, over demons, over sickness, over other people, over nature. It is a way of acting upon God, and over everything through him."[12] The ultimate effect of this conception of prayer, surmises Ellul, has been a massive setback for the faith. Modern techniques, such as medicine, which seem merely human, have tended to make calling on God seem superfluous. Though prayer still flourishes when it comes to the uncontrollable realms beyond the borders of human technology, it fades as these borders expand.

The problem with self-serving petitionary prayers is not only our vanity, but also the miserly conception of God which these prayers involve. Does God really need to be told what we need? And does he need be persuaded to give it? Is he so grudging that we must extort favors from him? Or is he already more anxious to give than we are to understand? James Burtchaell questions sharply:

Is it not absurd in the first place to suppose that creatures could ever persuade or cajole or entice God to change his mind? . . . Indeed, does not the entire spectacle of prayer of petition somehow assume that God is not quite so discreet, nor yet so generous as we? It is as though God's more modest and reticent plans for the furtherance of the world's welfare might stagnate without our words to the wise. Who are we to counsel the Most High, or to presume our hearts are more extravagant than his own?[13]

Some petitionary prayers seem not only to lack faith in the inherent goodness of God but also to elevate humankind to a position of control over God. God, the Scriptures remind us, is omniscient and omnipotent, the sovereign ruler of the universe. For Christians to pray as if God were a puppet whose strings they yank with their prayers seems not only potentially superstitious but blasphemous as well.

We have all heard amazing testimonies of the power of prayer to change things. Television evangelists, especially those with charismatic leanings, offer us remarkable accounts of how God was persuaded by their prayers to perform miraculous healings and life changes. I do not wish to dispute all these claims, but one can wonder whether those who recount these stories are not inclined to overstate their experience to make it newsworthy. The glamorizing of Christian experience in dramatic testimonies sometimes may give a falsely romantized impression of what being a Christian is like. It is better to base evangelism on truth than on exaggerated claims. Exaggeration not only provokes a sense of inferiority in listeners who feel ordinary by comparison, it also sets the stage for disillusionment among converts when their experience fails to confirm the purported manipulative power of prayer and religious belief. When prayer is sold as a device for eliciting health, success, and other favors from a celestial vending machine, we may wonder what is really being merchandised. Is this faith or is it faith's counterfeit, a glib caricature of true Christianity?

Personal needs are, however, what prompt many people toward the Christian faith. Ask people why they go to church, and few will say it is to worship God. The promised satisfaction of social and emotional needs is what sells religion to millions. Almost all the new religious movements of our culture focus on the problems of personal life.[14] They are examples of what Richard Bube calls "therapy theology," offering smiles and success in exchange for life's physical and psychological afflictions. But there is a danger here, as Elton Trueblood has noted:

In some congregations the Gospel has been diminished to the mere art of self-fulfillment. Some current religious authors, far from emphasizing what it means to believe that God was in Christ, reconciling the world unto Himself, write chiefly of themselves. Egocentricity is all that is left when the objective truth about the revelation of Christ is lost or even obscured. In one recent religious book the pronoun "I" appears 1600 times! . . . We are simply experiencing a recurrence of a malady which has been suffered before and will be suffered again. The departure from Basic Christianity is easy, having occurred many times in our history.[15]

Surely, though, the God who loves us more than we can know *does* care for our personal needs. The biblical faith is in a God who is not only the sovereign creator but also a personal, immanent being. Although God does not promise that Christians will be spared sorrow, humiliation, misfortune, and death, he does provide a perspective from which to view these events and "patience and longsuffering" with which to endure them. The Christian faith endows life with meaning and purpose, it calls forth commitment to that which is of ultimate value, and it enables one in all circumstances to trust in the providence of the loving Creator. Christians know that triumphs frequently come in paradoxical ways— through defeat and suffering. Out of the "failure" of the cross came life. Furthermore, research suggests that there are some practical effects of having Christian hope: religious involvement correlates with life satisfaction in old age and it facilitates coping with the prospects of death.[16]

CHRISTIAN PRAYER

If prayer is vulnerable to vain abuses, what is the Christian's proper prayer? First of all, it is a declaration of praise and thanksgiving to God for his infinite goodness and an acknowledgment of sin and the need for forgiveness.

> Our Father which art in heaven,
> Hallowed be thy name.
> Thy kingdom come.
> Thy will be done on earth,
>   as it is in heaven.
> Give us this day our daily bread,
> And forgive us our debts,
>   as we forgive our debtors.
> And lead us not into temptation,
>   but deliver us from evil:
> For thine is the kingdom,
>   and the power,
>   and the glory,
>   forever.
>   Amen.[17]

Christ's prayer, the model prayer for Christians, contains no attempt to manipulate God. It does not attempt to cajole a miserly god into doing what he would not have the good will and good sense to do anyway. It has the quality of a confessional statement, affirming God's nature and human dependence upon God's grace. In fact, just before instructing his followers with this prayer, Jesus explicitly counseled against pagan prayers which seek to manipulate God by their many words. He indicated that God "knows what your needs are before you ask him."[18]

The Lord's prayer therefore prepares one to receive that which God by his nature is already providing. The petitions that God's will be done and that forgiveness be given for debts seek what is intrinsic to God's nature. The petition for daily bread serves to reinforce the sense of God as gracious Father, of humanity as his dependent and anticipating children, and of our lives as daily saturated by God's providence.[19] "The prayer of a Christian," J. I. Packer has written, "is not an attempt to force God's hand, but a humble acknowledgement of helplessness and dependence."[20]

But what then of the many clear Scriptural imperatives to petition God with the promise of answers?

If you ask the Father for anything in my name, he will give it to you. . . . Ask and you will receive.[21]

A good man's prayer is powerful and effective. . . . Elijah was a man with human frailties like our own; and when he prayed earnestly that there should be no rain, not a drop fell on the land for three years and a half; then he prayed again, and down came the rain and the land bore crops once more.[22]

Jesus exemplified the fulfillment of these promises when he healed those who earnestly sought after him—the man with the epileptic child, the blind beggar, the band of ten lepers, and the paralytic who was finally forced on him through the roof.

Karl Barth sums up the conviction of the Reformers in urging us to approach prayer

from the given fact that God answers. He is not deaf, he listens; more than that, he acts. He does not act in the same way whether we pray or not. Prayer exerts an influence upon God's action, even upon his existence. This is what the word "answer" means.[23]

But what is the nature of this answer? George Buttrick, no doubter of the efficacy of prayer, was honest enough to recognize that:

People have prayed for fine weather, and it has rained in torrents. People have prayed for health, and their sickness has become chronic. People have prayed for deliverance, and danger has turned only to imprisonment and wounds. People have prayed to live, and they have died. People have prayed that loved ones might be spared, and loved ones have perished even while the prayer was being offered. . . . Why deny these facts?[24]

Job's experience, which we are prone to forget, reminds us that God does not play favorites. The rain falls both on those who pray and those who do not. The writer of Ecclesiastes was willing to face this truth:

Oh yes, I know what they say: "If you have reverence for God everything will be all right, but it will not go well for the wicked. . . ." But this is nonsense. Look at what happens in the world: sometimes righteous men get the punishment of the wicked and wicked men get the reward of the righteous. . . . The same fate comes to . . . those who are religious and those who are not, to those who offer sacrifices and those who do not.[25]

How shall we square the emphatic teachings of the effectiveness of prayer with these empirical facts and with the equally emphatic teachings of God's sovereignty and unconditional grace? We can trust that God is always present; he hears our prayers before we utter them. "Before they call to me, I will answer."[26] Indeed, it has sometimes been our experience that the answer to a prayer is in process before the need even arose, as when help from a passerby is on the way before an accident occurs.

Without presuming to penetrate the mystery of what it means to talk with our creator, Donald MacKay suggests that we may be helped by remembering that conclusions which are legitimate for a detached observer are inappropriate for people who are contemplating their own action.

The logical standpoint valid for us in petitionary prayer is that of an agent, pleading (in time) with the all-powerful Giver of all good for an outcome which from that standpoint is *not yet determined*. . . . Yet . . . none of this contradicts . . . what can be said *in retrospect*, as from the standpoint of God-in-eternity, to affirm his total sovereignty in the whole transaction.[27]

From the Creator's perspective, says MacKay, not only the answer to our prayer, but also our asking is ordained. From our viewpoint, prayer is, as Augustine said, "effective in obtaining those things which he foreknew he would grant to those who pray."[28]

C. S. Lewis reasons similarly:

When we are praying about the result, say, of a battle or a medical consultation the thought will often cross our minds that (if only we knew it) the event is already decided one way or the other. I believe this to be no good reason for ceasing our prayers. The event certainly has been decided—in a sense it was decided 'before all worlds'. But one of the things taken into account in deciding it, and therefore one of the things that really cause it to happen, may be this very prayer that we are now offering. Thus, shocking as it may sound, I conclude that we can at noon become part causes of an event occurring at ten o'clock. (Some scientists would find this easier than popular thought does.) The imagination will, no doubt, try to play all sorts of tricks on us at this point. It will ask, 'Then if I stop praying can God go back and alter what has already happened?' No. The event has already happened and one of its causes has been the fact that you are asking such questions instead of praying. It will ask, 'Then if I begin to pray can God go back and alter what has already happened?' No. The event has already happened and one of its causes is your present prayer. . . .[29]

This explains how prayers might be viewed as effective without denying God's total sovereignty. It allows for God to act differently when we are praying than when we are not, without our having to view our prayers as manipulative of God. It does, however, prompt MacKay to deduce a startling empirical prediction: "We may confidently expect to see correlation in retrospect between people's praying and the occurrence of events . . . that provide appropriate answers."[30]

This seems to suggest that we *should*, for example, be able to observe that expectant parents who pray have a higher proportion of healthy babies than those who do not, other things being equal. Here we do well to remember William Pollard's observation that God's providence is not merely an added force in nature "whose operation produces discernable and verifiable empirical consequences by means of which it can be objectively established."[31] The concept of God is diminished when he is considered a small factor which disturbs nature's distributions in statistically verifiable ways, for he is present and sovereign in *all* the seemingly chance events of his creation.

Some people's desperate need to believe that prayer changes the outside world seems rooted in a sense that God would be dead if it did not: if we believe that praying parents have 5 percent more normal births than otherwise equivalent nonpraying parents, then we may reassure ourselves that God is active in this world. This is another version of the natural/supernatural dichotomy introduced in Chapter 1. In the biblical view, the "God factor" is not merely this 5 percent but 100 percent, regardless of whether it is empirically evident in the results of prayer. One does not need a manipulative conception of prayer to *induce* God's involvement in the world; God is everywhere and at all times already involved. Moreover, God's ever-presence in the world is vastly more important to us than the immediate granting of our wishes. The Psalmist seems to sense this when exulting, "The Lord is my shepherd; I have everything I need."[32] When the Pharisees pressed Jesus for some criteria by which they could validate the kingdom of God, Jesus answered: "You cannot tell by observation when the kingdom of God comes. There will be no one saying, 'Look, here it is!' or 'There it is!'; for in fact the kingdom of God is among you."[33]

This is one reason why many theologians do not insist on empirically observable effects of prayer. C. S. Lewis, for instance, thought that the

impossibility of empirical proof is a spiritual necessity. A man who knew empirically that an event has been caused by his prayer would feel like a magician. His head would turn and his heart would be corrupted. The

Christian is not to ask whether this or that event happened because of a prayer. He is rather to believe that all events without exception are *answers* to prayer in the sense that whether they are grantings or refusals the prayers of all concerned and their needs have all been taken into account.[34]

Others say that "no prayer is unanswered because the answer is already contained in the question. We wouldn't *be* praying if *God* were not praying with us."[35] When we pray, wrote Paul, the spirit bears witness with our spirit.[36]

Still others contend that while our prayers do not change God's purpose, the act of praying can change our own minds. Sinking to our knees reminds us of our humble dependence. The Christian mystic who prays without ceasing, "Lord Jesus Christ, have mercy on me a sinner," eventually finds that the prayer of the mouth becomes the prayer of the heart. Prayers for others make us more acutely aware of their needs. This idea is not peculiar to modern writers. William Law advised in his devotional classic, *A Serious Call:*

Be daily on your knees praying for others in such forms, with such length, importunity, an earnestness as you use for yourself. You will then find that all little, ill-natured passions die away and your heart will grow great and generous. When our intercession is made an exercise of love and care for those among whom our lot is fallen, or who belong to us in a nearer relation, it becomes the greatest benefit of ourselves and produces its best effects in our own hearts. For there is nothing that makes us love a man so much as praying for him. When you can once do this sincerely for any man, you have fitted your soul for the performance of everything that is kind and civil toward him. By considering yourself as an advocate with God for your neighbors and acquaintances you would never find it hard to be at peace with them yourself.[37]

The notion that prayer changes the pray-er appears to have some validity, as research on action and attitude makes plain. Still, a psychological explanation of prayer's effectiveness is not fully satisfactory, for on this view it makes no difference if God does not exist. Prayer becomes listening to one's own echo, a "therapeutic monologue."

Prayer, then, is not only the occasion for people to talk to God, but also to listen quietly. The unreflective person, said Kierkegaard,

thinks and imagines that when he prays, the important thing, the thing he must concentrate upon, is that *God should hear what HE is praying for.* And yet in the true, eternal sense it is just the reverse; the true relation in prayer is not when God hears what is prayed for, but when the person continues to pray until he is the one who hears, who hears what God wills.[38]

The modern movement toward meditational practices, as in Transcendental Meditation, should remind Christians of meditational practices in their own heritage, such as the passive openness to God experienced by the Christian mystics. Jesus lived a continual rhythm of engagement and retreat; he made ample room for quiet meditation and prayer. Prayer is not magic, but it *is* mystical. In quiet prayer, the living God speaks to us; we sense his presence.

Thinking clearly and rigorously about prayer can help root out the pagan corruptions of our prayers. "In this day and age when the conviction seems widespread that a heart of gold will more than compensate for a head of feathers," writes Howard Hageman, "I still remain convinced that if there is anything our so-called religious revival needs, it is a healthy dose of intellectual discipline."[39] By abandoning some of the false gods of popular religion we can clear the decks for the God of the Bible and move toward prayer which is motivated by love of the Lord God, rather than solely by love of self. As Henri Nouwen concludes, "Only by the final unmasking of the illusion of all our works, thoughts, and feelings can we reach the Spirit of Truth."[40]

The danger in being put on guard against false prayer is that we may in the process sterilize our faith by destroying from within the desire to pray at all. "The defect of the proof-demanding mind," wrote George Buttrick, "is that it can never reach any conclusion. . . . It just sits, and waits for certainties. It is . . . a cash register for ringing up pros and cons."[41] A certain amount of suspicion about ourselves is conducive to true piety. But the danger in carrying our analytic method too far is that it commits us "to an approach so alien to the subject matter as to preclude the possibility of any deep understanding. To study love with a microscope or electrons with the tools of a literary critic is to be methodologically prejudiced against one's subject matter."[42]

In the last analysis, our prayer is not prompted by any rationally defensible theory. Prayer is a spiritual act, an obedient response to the summons to "watch and pray." It is prompted, not by the force of reason, but by a mysterious faith that craves dialogue and personal relationship with its source. Given the distortions and limited nature of our rational capacities, we ought not be surprised that human minds cannot resolve the mysteries of existence and faith.

When concerned about the effect of our prayers, James Burtchaell reminds us to consider Jesus' prayers as our model.

He prays for those he serves. . . . It is not simply that his prayer spurs him to serve; the same Spirit that gives him force for his task gives breath to his utterances. . . .

A distinctively Christian sense of prayer reveals that, rather than it being an appeal to God, it is itself a reply to his call. It is not we who solicit his generosity; it is he who summons ours forth, in word and work harmonized. We are only distracted if always trying to validate prayer by its effects. . . . Prayer is itself an effect more than a cause. Rather than releasing grace, it flows from grace. Though cast into the syntax of request, prayer to the Father of Jesus is addressed to one who is supremely giving—giving even the faith wherewith we pray. Our concern for prayer should not be in what it will produce, so much as in how resonant it is with God's work in the world, and our own.[43]

Jacques Ellul reinforces the same point: "Prayer, however fervent, spontaneous and new, is never other than a sequel, a consequence, a response, to the word of invitation first made known in Scripture."[44]

The remedy for superstitious corruptions of prayer, then, is not to self-critically analyze every prayer, but to direct one's thoughts first to the worship and service of God. Augustine's dictum, "Love God and do as you please," says it well. Jesus' own counsel powerfully expresses this same principle:

No, do not ask anxiously, "What are we to eat? What are we to drink? What shall we wear?" All these are things for the heathen to run after, not for you, because your heavenly Father knows that you need them all. Set your mind on God's kingdom and his justice before everything else, and all the rest will come to you as well.[45]

This sense of trust in the providence of our creator liberates us from the need to make prayer into a pagan superstitious act intended to manipulate God into gratifying our cravings. Listen to Paul:

The Lord is near; have no anxiety, but in everything make your requests known to God in prayer and petition with Thanksgiving. Then the peace of God, which is beyond our utmost understanding, will keep guard over your hearts and your thoughts, in Christ Jesus.[46]

Paul urges us to petition God, and we are promised an answer: not that of scientifically provable effects, but that peace of God which satisfies the deeper cravings of our being. As Elton Trueblood has noted, "If anything is worth worrying about, it is worth praying about. . . ."[47]

Jesus himself prayed that, if it was God's will, the "cup" might pass. It did not, but his strength was made equal to the burden. Jesus confessed honestly the private longings of his soul. In that communion with the Father he found the grace to endure. If our Creator loves us as an all-loving parent would love a child, then we, like children, can commune with him without ceasing. We can share even the little concerns of daily existence, as a child does with its parents or as two intimate friends do with one another.[48] We can surrender every corner of our lives in prayer, not with a superstitious intent of manipulating magical results, but in the confidence that *petitionary prayer is a means of grace* whereby we will grow and be sensitized to the presence of God. Surely this is part of what is meant when the Westminster Shorter Catechism teaches that our purpose is "to glorify God, and to enjoy him forever."

CONCLUSION

The circumstances which prompt superstitious behavior and which prompt petitionary prayer have so much in common that it is easy to see how superstitious ideas could contaminate prayer. Given the limtations of our rationality, this infection is probably inevitable. Can we nevertheless conclude that prayer yields observable, statistically significant results beyond those mediated by its effects on the person who prays? Christians are divided on this question. For my own part, I continue petitionary prayer partly because this is so natural a way of sharing concerns with my creator. The petitionary mode of prayer, writes Harold Ellens, "places us in a stance of a *child* expecting his father's love and, therefore, when receiving it, recognizing it redemptively for *what it is:* The Father's care."[49]

Being sensitive to possible superstitious infections of Christian prayer can serve two purposes. First, it may alleviate some of the arrogance which so easily accompanies a confident belief in prayer's manipulative effects; the Scriptures nowhere suggest that nature is out of control except when we induce God to intervene. The Christian hope lies not in magical solutions to life's problems, but in the conviction that nothing can ultimately separate us from God's love. Second, it can also move Christians to discover other deep meanings in prayer, meanings they have hardly begun to fathom. Christian prayer thanks and praises God for the wisdom and goodness of his purposes, humbly admits sin, confesses one's deepest desires and one's dependence upon God's continuous providence and grace, and asks help in being an instrument in the answering of prayer.

NOTES

1. Michael Argyle and Benjamin Beit-Hallahmi, *The Social Psychology of Religion* (Boston: Routledge & Kegan Paul, 1975).
2. From Voltaire's *Philosophical Dictionary*, as cited by Gustav Jahoda, *The Psychology of Superstition* (Penguin, 1969).
3. 1 Peter 4:17, KJV.
4. Daniel L. Hodges, "Breaking a Scientific Taboo: Putting Assumptions About the Supernatural into Scientific Theories of Religion," *Journal for the Scientific Study of Religion* 13 (1974): 393–408.
5. Gerardus van der Leeuw, *Religion in Essence and Manifestation*, vol. 1 (New York: Harper & Row, 1963), p. 23.
6. Stephen G. Brush, "The Prayer Test," *American Scientist* 62 (1974): 561–63.
7. Matt. 4:7, NEB.
8. See Brush, *op. cit.*
9. George S. Patton, Jr., *War As I Knew It* (Boston: Houghton Mifflin, 1949), pp. 184–85, as cited by J. T. Burtchaell, *Philemon's Problem* (Chicago: Acta Foundation, 1973).
10. Or possibly out of a genuine sense of corporate relationship and corporate responsibility for the nation.
11. Bronislaw Malinowski, *Magic, Science, and Religion* (Garden City, N.Y.: Doubleday, 1948), p. 68.
12. Jacques Ellul, *Prayer and Modern Man* (New York: Seabury Press, 1970), pp. 76–77.
13. Burtchaell, *op. cit.*, pp. 164–65.
14. Benton Johnson, "Alternate Religions in Social Context: Past and Present" (Paper presented to the American Association for the Advancement of Science Convention, 1977).
15. From the *Quarterly Yoke Letter* 18, no. 1 (1977).
16. Argyle and Beit-Hallahmi, *op. cit.*
17. Matt. 6:9–13, KJV.
18. Matt. 6:8, NEB.
19. J. Harold Ellens, "Communication Theory and Petitionary Prayer," *Journal of Psychology and Theology* 5 (1977): 48–54.
20. J. I. Packer, *Evangelism and the Sovereignty of God* (Downer's Grove, Ill.: Intervarsity, 1961), p. 11.
21. John 16:23–24, NEB.
22. James 5:15, 17–18, NEB.
23. Karl Barth, *Prayer*, trans. Sara F. Terrien (Philadelphia: Westminster Press, 1952), p. 21.
24. George A. Buttrick, *Prayer* (Nashville: Abingdon-Cokesbury, 1942), p. 80.
25. Eccles. 8:12–14, 9:2, Good News.
26. Isa. 65:24, NEB.
27. Donald M. MacKay, "The Sovereignty of God in the Natural World," *Scottish Journal of Theology* 21 (1968): 13–26.
28. Augustine, *City of God*, bk. 5, chap. 10.

29. C. S. Lewis, *Miracles* (New York: Macmillan, 1947), p. 214.

30. MacKay, *op. cit.*

31. William Pollard, *Chance and Providence* (New York: Harper, 1958), p. 78.

32. Ps. 23:1, Good News.

33. Luke 17:20–21, NEB.

34. Lewis, *op. cit.*, p. 215.

35. Robert K. Hudnut, *Church Growth Is Not the Point* (New York: Harper & Row, 1975), p. 83.

36. See Rom. 8:15–16.

37. William Law, *A Serious Call to a Devout and Holy Life,* ed. John W. Meister (Phildelphia: Westminster, 1955), pp. 135, 136.

38. Søren Kierkegaard, *The Journals of Søren Kierkegaard,* trans. Alexander Dru (New York: Oxford University Press, 1938), pp. 153–54.

39. *Church Herald,* December 24, 1976, p. 30.

40. Henri J. M. Nouwen, "The Prayer of the Heart" (unpublished manuscript, Yale Divinity School).

41. Buttrick, *op. cit.*, p. 69.

42. Merold Westphal, "The Art of Understanding as an Alternate Approach in Philosophy of Religion" (unpublished manuscript, Hope College, 1977).

43. Burtchaell, *op. cit.*

44. Ellul, *op. cit.*, p. 123.

45. Matt. 6:31–33, NEB.

46. Phil. 4:6–7, NEB.

47. Elton Trueblood, *A Place to Stand* (New York: Harper & Row, 1969), p. 85.

48. Indeed, Jesus begins the Lord's Prayer by saying "Abba," which was the homely address of a small child to its father.

49. Ellens, *op. cit.*

PART V

The Mystery of Freedom

The contentions of the preceding chapters—that natural and religious explanation complement one another, that mind and body are a unity, and that attitudes and beliefs are amenable to scientific scrutiny—lead us to a deep and troubling question: what room is left for our convictions and our intuitive sense of personal freedom?

Chapter 9 first defines the issue of human freedom from a philosophical perspective. It then identifies a related theological issue—an apparent tension between divine sovereignty and grace on the one hand, and ultimate moral responsibility on the other. This has been called "the most important question of theology."[1] J. I. Packer provides an insightful overview of this tension:

Man is indubitably responsible to God, for God is the Lawgiver who fixes his duty, and the Judge who takes account of him as to whether or not he has done it. And God is indubitably sovereign over man, for He controls and orders all human deeds, as He controls and orders all else in His universe. Man's responsibility for his actions, and God's sovereignty in relation to those same actions, are thus . . . equally real and ultimate facts.[2]

Christians start with a mysterious pair of assumptions concerning (1) divine control and the natural regularity which this is generally taken to imply, and (2) human freedom and accountability. Most Christians who are psychologists resolve the mystery as most other Christians do; they emphasize human autonomy at the expense of divine sovereignty. This naturally moves them toward a humanistic psychology which emphasizes self-determination. A few other Christians, more impressed with the faithful, orderly movement of nature and history from creation to the end of time, have gravitated toward a mechanistic psychology at the expense of a rich conception of human freedom. I am struggling to find a third approach which rejects, from both Christian and scientific perspectives, the popular image of human autonomy and yet still finds a meaningful place for human initiative and freedom within the order of nature.

Many of us have waffled between thinking on Mondays, Wednesdays, and Fridays that the freedom issue is abstract speculation of no real consequence, and being sure, the rest of the week, that it is *the* crucial question of human existence. My own reading of the literature inclines me increasingly to the latter point of view. We all make implicit assumptions about our own and others' freedom, even if we do not think much about this consciously. The assumptions we make have enormous practical consequences, as we will see in Chapter 10. By documenting the effects of people's naive philosophies I hope to encourage more serious thinking about philosophical and theological issues. Our implicit philosophical and religious ideas are sometimes an important social force.

NOTES

1. G. C. Berkouwer, *The Providence of God* (Grand Rapids: Eerdmans, 1952), p. 159.

2. J. I. Packer, *Evangelism and the Sovereignty of God* (Downer's Grove, Ill: InterVarsity, 1961), p. 93.

CHAPTER 9

Determinism, Divine Sovereignty, and Human Responsibility*

FREEDOM AND DETERMINISM

Research psychologists operate from a working assumption of determinism, even if they do not live their lives from this assumption. I begin by exploring this concept and its implications for human freedom and responsibility.

Determinism and Indeterminism

The issue of determinism is sharply defined by a simple mental experiment. Consider a situation involving two completely identical persons. Physically, they are exact replicas of one another. Their heredity, their past experiences, the states of their nervous systems, are the same. All prior and current circumstances are identical, meaning that different predictions about their choices would not be possible. Assume further that we now present them with identical choices in an identical manner (coffee or tea, madam?) and that each ponders the decision a moment and then announces her choice. Will their choices necessarily be the same? A yes answer—there is nothing to differentiate them—defines a deterministic position. That is, behavior is lawfully related to prior

---

* Every serious student of human nature wrestles with the issue of freedom and determinism. For the Christian, some additional complicating considerations enter in. My uncertainty about some of the issues raised in this chapter mirrors the lack of consensus among philosophers and theologians on these issues. I nevertheless raise them because they so often arise when Christians discuss psychology, because these issues merit deeper scrutiny than psychologists usually give them, and because they provide a background for the concluding chapter on psychology and human freedom. The reader can skip directly to the concluding chapter or, if interested, can struggle with me as I contemplate determinism, divine sovereignty, and human responsibility from my vantage point as a Christian psychologist.

and current events, making future behavior, in principle, 100 percent predictable. An answer of no, not necessarily—the person is to some extent inherently unpredictable—defines a position of indeterminism.

The same question can tease us in a different form. This time our subject is you: you have just been faced with a significant moral choice and have decided to act either righteously or reprehensibly. Now imagine we can wind the universe back to your moment of decision. Everything is identical to however it was before. Will your decision therefore necessarily be the same? Would television broadcasts of your two moments of choice make the second appear as an instant replay of the first? Note that in both of these hypothetical cases the answer to our question is simply either yes or no. As William James wrote, "The issue . . . is a perfectly sharp one, which no eulogistic terminology can smear over or wipe out. The truth *must* lie with one side or the other, and its lying with one side makes the other false."[1]

My own answer to these hypothetical questions is: I don't know. An answer of either yes or no presents some problems which will be detailed below. Believing that the created order always reflects the activity of its creator inclines me to be open to mysteries and miracles which defy causal analysis. At the same time, I feel no need of such miracles, since all events, whether seen as natural or supernatural, are equally rooted in God's power. The natural system is not merely open to God's initiative, it is entirely sustained and ordered by his providence.

As a research psychologist I need only assume that there is considerable order and regularity to human behavior. Indeed, statistically significant results found by psychologists affirm that there is. Whether this order is rooted in an absolute determinism, or whether inherent indeterminacies mean that we can only hope to describe behavior in terms of probabilities is of no great concern. As a practical matter, the enormous complexity of human behavior will in either case always limit us to statistical generalizations.

But does not viewing ourselves as part of the natural order of the universe lead to some intolerable implications? Let us consider objections to the extreme position of absolute determinism. If we can defend determinism against some of these objections, we can even more easily defend a position which simply asserts a considerable regularity and order to human behavior.

Objections to Determinism

Our "thought experiments" help us to see why several popular objections to determinism are equivocal. The problems with these objections are worth identifying, not as a logical strategy for establishing determinism, but so that those who dispute the concept of determinism will not do so for dubious reasons. Please bear in mind, I am *not* arguing for determinism. I am simply asking *what if* we are determined; are the implications as terrible as most people suppose?

Unpredictability. One objection is that we are, in fact, far from being completely successful at predicting and controlling behavior. So much so that John Watson's presumptuous claim seems laughable:

Give me a dozen healthy infants, well-formed, and my own specified world to bring them up in and I'll guarantee to take any one at random and train him to become any type of specialist I might select—doctor, lawyer, artist, merchant-chief, and yes, even beggar-man and thief, regardless of his talents, penchants, tendencies, abilities, vocations, and race of his ancestors.[2]

When we consider evidence ranging from the percent of variation in human behavior which our experimental manipulations fail to predict (we call this the "error" factor) to the ineffectiveness of most attempts to change people, as in prison rehabilitation efforts, it is evident that individuals are very difficult to predict and control. Few among us can escape a sense of the mystery of human personality.

But the determinist only contends that behavior is, *in principle,* predictable. Granted, we are very poor at predicting behavior. We also have great difficulty predicting the weather, but surely this does not mean that storms possess free will. In both cases the assumption is that what is being predicted is complexly determined, that the defect is in our knowledge and intelligence, and that with infinite amounts of each (omniscience), fluctuations in both the weather and behavior would be predictable.

Dehumanization. Another concern is that belief in determinism might destroy our essential freedom. If science is permitted to have its way, it is said, "we may never be able to really think again."[3] Our assumptions about our own and others' freedom *do* have practical consequences. But our belief or disbelief in determinism does not change human nature. Scientific laws are descriptive, not prescriptive. People are not obliged to act in accord with scientific laws. The laws merely describe how people happen to act. To presume that behavior becomes determined merely by believing it to be so implies that somehow scientists can formulate laws just as do political legislators, and that God and nature then act as administrators, seeing to it that these laws are followed.[4]

Relativism. Another common source of discomfort with the idea of determinism is that it seems to suggest that beliefs and values are only relative. Presuming that there is always a hidden explanation for why we believe and act as we do seems to undermine religious convictions. If I understand my belief in God to be merely a product of my socialization, then what confidence can I have in it? This view fails to recognize that the truth or falsity of a belief is independent of its causes (unless the belief is about the causes of belief). An exhaustive psychological explanation of a schoolchild's belief that Columbus discovered America does not tell us whether Columbus did, in fact, discover America. That is another story. A complete explanation of why a mathematician believes in Pythagoras' theorem does not validate or invalidate the theorem. God either exists or he doesn't. That is not affected by the causes of our belief or disbelief. If the atheist's disbelief and the Christian's belief were both completely explained psychologically, this would tell us nothing about the truth of their beliefs.

Fatalism. Many people also are troubled by the fatalism that seems implicit in determinism. We demur on both scientific and religious grounds from the idea that God's activity ceased with an initial creation and that the universe has since been like a clock unwinding through its predictable course. Surely it is not like the poet wrote:

> With Earth's first Clay They did the Last Man knead,
> And there of the Last Harvest sow'd the Seed:
> And the first Morning of Creation wrote
> What the Last Dawn of Reckoning shall read.[5]

A fatalistic, whatever-will-be-will-be attitude—whether expressed in terms of naturalistic determinism or of passive acceptance of whatever happens as "the Lord's will"—is poison to the sense of hope and commitment essential to social reform.[6]

But determinism provides a foundation for vision, not resignation. Our actions have effects; they help determine the world of tomorrow. "A man reaps what he sows."[7] "The stream of causation runs through my deliberations and decision, and, if it did not run as it does run, the [future] would be different. The past cannot determine the [future] except through the present."[8] This lays a heavy responsibility upon us, for we know that we must "train up a child in the way he should go" so that he will not depart from it.[9] Conversely, the sins of the fathers are predictably laid upon their children unto the third and fourth generation.[10] Determinism implies the possibility of moral and Christian education.

If the opposite were the case, then we *would* have cause for

hopeless resignation. If people's actions tomorrow were *not* determined by the circumstances created today, nothing we could do
would make a predictable difference. We can act responsibly only
to the extent that we can predict the effects of our actions. The
prophet must be able to assume that judgments of praise and
blame have the power to influence behavior. Otherwise his voice is
empty wind.

Denies choice. We may also be repelled by the idea of determinism because it seems to deny our self-confirming experience of
choice. It is self-evident that we have a measure of personal control over our destiny in life, that we can rationally choose among
alternatives, and that we have some responsibility for our own outcomes. We can be more sure of these facts of experience than of
any philosophical analysis. It is, moreover, certainly true that our
capacity for self-determination (as opposed to programed instinct)
distinguishes us from other creatures. The great range of vices and
virtues among which we can choose enables us to commit acts
ranging from cruel destruction to selfless sacrifice. But it should
be apparent that determinism denies nothing of this everyday,
practical definition of freedom as summarized by the humanistic
psychologist Rollo May:

Let me speak of my impressionistic picture of the free man. The free man
is conscious of his right to have some part in the decisions of his social
group or nations which affect him; he actualizes this consciousness by affirming the decisions or if he disagrees, by registering his protest for the
sake of a better decision next time. The free man has respect for rational
authority, both that of history and that of his fellow-men who may have
beliefs different from his own. The free man is responsible, in that he can
think and act for the long-term welfare of the group. He has esteem for
himself as an individual of worth and dignity—not the least of the sources
of this dignity being his knowing himself to be a free man (pp. 178–80 in
Psychology and the Human Dilemma, Princeton: Van Nostrand, 1967).

The repugnance of determinism sometimes derives from the
confused notion that behavioral laws compel people to behave
against their will. As already noted, this is a misunderstanding of
scientific explanation. Laws of behavior are not ultimate truths
which lie hidden in nature, waiting for us to trip over them.[11] "It
would be just as correct, and perhaps less misleading, to say that
the Law of Nature depends on our choice, instead of the reverse."[12] Descriptive laws start from the choices people make. To
assert that knowing some biographical information about you enables a prediction of your presidential preference is not to maintain
that you were forced to choose as you did. You may know your

next door neighbors well enough to predict their voting behavior. This does not mean that your neighbors are coerced by inexorable forces. Rather it simply means that their choices are understandable, given what you know about them.

Negates praise and blame. But how can we consider an action blameworthy or praiseworthy if it is, in principle, determined? The implication here is that an action must be unpredictable in order to merit our admiration. This is obviously not so. If you find a wallet full of money and I predict that you will surely return it to the owner, it is no insult that I say I know enough of your background to predict your good act. But if I say that I really have no idea how you would act, because you are a free and unpredictable being, you might be insulted. As R. E. Hobart wrote: "It is the stuff certain people are made of that commands our admiration and affection. Where it came from is another question; it is precious in its own nature; let us be thankful when it is there. Its origin cannot take away its value, and it is its value we are recognizing when we praise."[13]

The same has been said for holding a person accountable for evil. The concept of fault, "so far from being inapplicable, is the specific name for the kind of defect or infirmity which he has displayed—insufficient love of good and aversion to evil."[14] We are justifiably indignant at any act which is intrinsically evil. Understanding its origin does not mean we must condone it. I have an apple tree in my back yard which, despite my efforts, consistently produces inedible fruit. Now, I could say that the earth bears the apples, or just as truly, that the tree bears the apples, for the earth bears the apples by bearing the tree. The accountability of the tree for the apples it yields is not nullified by prior conditions which caused it to be as it is. Indeed, I will probably chop down that tree and cast it into our winter fires.

If there is a troublesome youth in the neighborhood, we see nothing inconsistent in blaming him and venting our anger and, in the next moment, shaking our head over the circumstances that produced his rowdiness. All we require is that he not have been coerced in the matter. If my older son arrived home late from school, I would not hold him responsible if he was late because the bus broke down. If, however, he was late because he chose to go to the candy store instead of coming home, I would hold him accountable because he chose to do it. Were he to say, "You can't hold me responsible because my motives drove me to the candy store," I would say, "Obviously your motives drove you, but I am still holding you responsible for your choice."[15]

Many popular objections to determinism, then, are grounded in misunderstandings of its implications. Those who would refute a complete determinism of human behavior had best do so on some other basis than the obvious mystery and practical unpredictability of behavior; or the dread that believed determinism will make it so or will undermine our beliefs and values; or because determinism seems to imply fatalism, denial of choice, and condoning of evil and inability to praise what is good. There is nothing about causation and natural regularity which prohibits our understanding the person as a rational, creative, volitional, purposive, and even mysterious being.

Choice and Free Will

But surely this is not the whole story, or there would be no point of issue between determinism and freedom. To understand the difference we must distinguish two different meanings of *freedom*. Failure to understand this distinction has contributed to much unnecessary argument and confused thinking.

The commonsense meaning of *freedom* is roughly what we understand as constitutionally guaranteed freedom. This is not ultimate free will, but rather freedom in a practical sense, social freedom, or *choice—the capacity and opportunity to select consciously from among alternatives and do what we choose*. This everyday, practical sense of freedom is what people usually refer to when defending the concept, and it is what I shall mean by *freedom* when using the term hereafter. This freedom is, as we have seen, entirely compatible with determinism. Although our actions may be caused (determinism), we are nevertheless active in consciously selecting from among alternatives, and what we decide to do can make a great difference. Freedom and a nonfatalistic attitude can, when understood in this way, remain as valid concepts within a deterministic framework. Even the biblical sense of freedom as liberation from bondage to sin and law seems incorporated within this understanding of freedom as the absence of compulsion.[16] Remember, when I hereafter use the term *freedom* it will always be in this limited sense, freedom as *noncoerced choice*.

What is not compatible with determinism is the philosophical meaning of *freedom*. This is the idea that people are ultimately autonomous, a first cause of their own behavior, and therefore inherently somewhat unpredictable. We may call this *free will* as contrasted with our more obvious capacity for deliberate choice. Since this is not the ordinary meaning of *freedom* and not what I mean by *freedom*, I shall always denote my references to "free will" as such. The freedom for which people will fight and die is not this metaphysical concept of free will (which, if we possess, no one could take away), but simply the opportunity to decide and control their own futures.

The most significant reason for affirming free will is our conviction that people do bear some ultimate moral responsibility for their choices. While it may be true that determinism leaves us free to judge a person's *behavior* as worthy of praise or condemnation, it does not seem to leave us free to praise or condemn the *person*. Suppose, for example, that a hypnotist was able to plant in a subject an irresistible suggestion to commit a crime and the subject then did so with a sense of having chosen to do it. Surely, we would not hold the person morally responsible, because we know there is an understandable cause for the act. To the extent we are aware of hidden causes for an evil behavior, we are not inclined to blame the person for it.

This cuts the other way, too. We tend to credit and honor people for their good and benevolent acts only when we do not fully understand why they did them. If we know the conditions which brought them to act as they did, we credit the conditions rather than the person.

If behavior is totally explained by a mosaic of hidden causes, how can anyone be ultimately responsible? Demolishing free will seems to leave a vacuum at the very heart of our sense of moral responsibility. In the final analysis, we become morally equal; ultimate distinctions are erased. The District of Columbia Court of Appeals declared in a 1972 decision that our judicial system would be undermined if it were assumed "that the behavior of every individual is dictated by forces—ultimately, his genes and lifelong environment—that are unconscious and beyond his control. . . . Our jurisprudence . . . while not oblivious to deterministic components, ultimately rests on a premise of freedom of will."[17]

Although it is beyond my competence to identify what sense of freedom is really required for moral responsibility, it should be noted that absence of causation does not establish moral responsibility. Some philosophers maintain that scientific predictability has no bearing on our obligation to live morally. Psychology's predictive principles may successfully foretell an act, but doing so does not relieve the actor's responsibility. Moreover, the scientist's description of the *causes* of an action is a different sort of discourse than the ethicist's discussion of the *reasons* why one *should* act this way or that. *Description* of why people have acted as they have done gives no *prescription* for how they should behave. One could conceivably describe the causes of the looting which occurred during the New York City blackout in the summer of 1977, but it would be quite another task to establish reasons which would morally justify those acts.

Most people don't see it this way. Faced with the apparent dilemma of having to believe either that some actions have no causal explanation or that people are not ultimately responsible for what they do, most people do one of two things. First they may hold to both causation and free will, but keep them separate to avoid facing the contradiction. Self-contradiction dominates ordinary human thinking on this issue. For example, a recent survey of some high school students revealed that 84 percent agreed that "everything that happens, including what people think, feel, and do has causes"—despite the fact that much earlier in the survey 72 percent of these students had already agreed that "some of the things people think, feel, and do are acts of a free uncaused will."[18]

The second escape people may take is to favor a compromise which might enable them to avoid both horns of the dilemma. Moral choices are understood to require sufficient predictability to enable us to count on certain effects of our actions, but also sufficient looseness to enable genuine free will. Thus, science is possible because of the extent of lawfulness in the universe, and ultimate moral freedom is possible because of the play in the system. This, we presume, is what enables some people to rise above miserable circumstances, although we can predict that most will not. It is rather like the decay of radioactive atoms. The half-life indicates the typical length of radioactivity, but individual atoms are "free" to vary within certain limits.

This view of the place of free will within nature is reminiscent of the dichotomy of the natural and the supernatural discussed in Chapter 1. If religious and naturalistic explanations sit on opposite ends of a teeter-totter, the potential validity of religious explanation is defined by the gap in the naturalistic account of things, and vice versa. A God-of-the-gaps religion is consequently very defensive about scientific advances. So it is with this freedom-of-the-gap. One has the uneasy feeling, wrote Malcolm Jeeves, that this view "has the character of a convenient, temporary escape-hatch being slowly closed by every new advance in behavioral science."[19]

It is, moreover, difficult to conceive the locus of free will. If the two identical people in our first thought experiment chose differently, we would likely presume the existence of an autonomous self inside the person which made a spontaneous choice. But then we are tempted to wonder: if a little person inside pulled the strings that made the choice, then who pulled the little person's strings? What is the microdecision system inside the little decision system? This opens a series of Chinese boxes that leads us in an infinite regress. As Jonathan Edwards argued, if the will chooses its choice then it must choose to choose this choice and so on.[20] Our imagination cannot conceive the identity of any ultimate free power within us.

Or consider how we might construct the best decision makers using the freedom model. We would probably not decide to free the decision makers from causation, but to endow them with the capacity to appropriately process all information relevant to their goals. Rationality, not unpredictability, would be our concern.

Indeterminacy in Nature

Some free-will advocates take comfort, however, in knowing that there is an indeterminacy in nature for which we have been unable to discover any hidden explanation. The old clockwork image of the physical universe is foreign to modern science. The behavior of elementary particles is now understood to be predictable only in terms of probabilities. This introduction of chance into our conception of the evolution of history undercuts the deistic notion of a god who set the universe on an inexorable course and then stepped back from it. William Pollard argues that the scientific concepts of chance and natural spontaneity therefore strengthen our understanding of the immanence of God's providence in the unfolding of history.[21] As we read in Proverbs, "The lot is cast into the lap, but the decision is wholly from the Lord."[22]

In the biological realm, mutations are also described in terms of chance and probability, leading some to conclude that "organic life partakes then of the same freedom and spontaneity that physicists have found at the root of material being. . . . We may say then that the attempt to prove man a machine, to deny him free will, has been refuted by the sheer facts of science."[23]

An enormous leap is required to deduce human free will from the probabilistic (rather than deterministic) predictions of physics and molecular biology. Several considerations caution us from doing so. First, there is disagreement as to whether quantum mechanics is a complete theory. It is possible that its indeterminacies reflect our ignorance of hidden variables, of some underlying causal infrastructure. Since physical knowledge is acquired at the cost of disturbing what we observe, elementary particles might be unpredictable even though inherently determined. For some scientists, such as Einstein and Planck, randomness has been unacceptable as a final description of nature—a "culprit" must be found. We can admit that we have reached the limits of human understanding without asserting that nature is inherently disorderly. "Does God throw dice?" Einstein asked, or is the order simply unknowable? It must be acknowledged, however, that many more physicists find no need for this assumption of hidden variables. The uncertainty principle provides a satisfactory description of all that is observed.

If it is therefore assumed that indeterminacies are part of the ultimate fabric of nature, we still face two more problems in leaping from indeterminacy to free will. First, indeterminism is claimed only at very elementary levels, not at the macroscopic levels with which we are concerned here. Classical physics succeeded in formulating deterministic laws by depending upon the behavior of enormous numbers of atoms. This makes the next eclipse of the sun perfectly predictable, even though the movements of its atomic particles are unpredictable. Bees construct their honeycomb in a precisely determined manner despite being composed of particles whose action is described in terms of chance and probability. These examples indicate that macroscopic determinism can arise from the averaging of chance fluctuations at elementary levels. For indeterminacy to operate at a human level, one must therefore assume that there exist conditions under which a minute chance factor serves as a fork in the road, producing in the end very large differences. Extending this type of assumption to the human brain, Sir John Eccles has argued that minute indeterminacies applied to neural events could initiate and direct a series of events which, avalanche-like, progressively magnify the effect of the initial event to the level of macroscopic observability. To many physicists, however, it is "far-fetched" to presume that the narrow range of indeterminacies in inorganic matter could produce so large a consequence as a muscle movement.[24]

But even making this favorable assumption brings us up against a final brick wall, for chance is no basis for free will. Physicists do not impute a mystical self-determining power to the indeterminate particle. If random uncertainty describes the indeterminacy of a person's moral choice, then, to that extent, there would be no character. Repeating the same moral choice would yield an unpredictable outcome. This *reduces* personal responsibility, since "by personal responsibility we mean deliberate choice of the will, not an uncontrolled fluctuation in thinking."[25] "So if we admit volition at all, we must not forget first to remove the hypothesis of chance if we have been applying it."[26] Erwin Schrodinger summarized this point well: "This haphazard side of goings-on in the material world is . . . *the very last to be invoked as the physical correlate of man's ethical behavior.*" For moral behavior is anything but haphazard, being determined by motives ranging from the lowest to the most sublime. Furthermore, he argued, the range of indeterminacy at the molar level is so slight as to destroy ethical freedom, if such freedom is irreconcilable with predictability. "To my mind this is the most valuable outcome of the whole controversy: the scale is turned in favour of a possible reconciliation of free will [i.e. moral responsibility] with physical determinism, when we realize how inadequate a basis physical haphazard provides for ethics."[27]

The upshot of all this seems to be that while physical indeterminacy may provide a chink in the deterministic armor, it does not provide a gap into which free will easily steps. If modern physics has sensitized us to the openness and spontaneity of nature, its introduction of random unpredictability gets us no closer to free will than did the clockwork determinism it replaced. Although free will may require at least a dash of indeterminacy, indeterminacy does not establish free will or moral responsibility.

THEOLOGICAL ASSERTIONS OF HUMAN RESPONSIBILITY AND DIVINE SOVEREIGNTY

The dilemma apparent in this elementary philosophical analysis of freedom is intensified when it is translated into theological language. On the one hand, the assumptions of human freedom and moral responsibility permeate the Scriptures. We are not to consider ourselves mere dummies on the lap of a supernatural ventriloquist. Since "whosoever will may come" we are held accountable for our choices. Sin elicits God's judgment. Tampering with the biblical view of true, moral guilt diminishes our understanding of what Jesus accomplished by his death and resurrection.

Freedom is not only biblically assumed, but also a self-evident reality of raw human experience that overrides any denials of it, making further defense of freedom unnecessary. The vividness of our sense of freedom and its centrality in the Bible can be counted on to balance any exclusive emphasis on God's controlling power. That is why theology has not often had to call God's people to remember their freedom. We are already prone to do this.

The reverse is *not* equally true. When the centrality of human will and responsibility is emphasized, our sense of God's omnipotence and transcendence may soon diminish, with the result that religion degenerates into self-righteous individualism. The most tempting heresy since the early days of Christianity has been to flatter ourselves, to glorify the human will, to presume we have power to act meritoriously independent of God's initiative. The refutation of such heresy was a principal task of several theological masterminds—St. Augustine, Martin Luther, John Calvin, and Jonathan Edwards—whose teachings are now being reinforced by revelations from the behavioral sciences. Perhaps it is time to again sound the warning against this irrepressible heresy. Writes Ralph Wendell Burhoe:

I think that the sciences will disabuse us of our arrogance in supposing that man is his own maker and determiner of his own destiny, and will bring the socialists and liberals of the world back to a more realistic view of man's utter dependence on transcendent forces—a view that has been long ago . . . presented by the great religious traditions. The egocentric illusions, created by a nonscientific interpretation of man's new technological power to do what he pleases, will pass as the traditional religions begin to recognize that the new sciences are on their side in saying that man is a creature who must adapt, rather than that he is Lord of creation.[28]

Does this mean that science and classical theology deny the experience of choice? Not at all. The compatibility noted earlier between determinism and choice is pointed out by each of these theologians (although their concern is with divine determination, not natural determinism). While Jonathan Edwards assumed that "nothing ever comes to pass without a cause" and that to think otherwise is "repugnant to reason," he also accepted freedom as the opportunity to do what one wills or chooses.[29] Whether the will is determined does not enter into the definition or the experience of freedom, he contended. *Free acts are uncompelled, not uncaused.* Augustine believed the same: "It does not follow that, though there is for God a certain order of causes, there must therefore be nothing dependent on the free exercise of our own wills, for our wills themselves are included in that order of causes which is certain to God."[30]

The Argument for Divine Determination

But, we may inquire, why did Luther, Calvin, and Edwards oppose so strongly the freedom of the will? A quick review of the biblical and theological bases for this emphasis will indicate how the theologian's struggle to incorporate moral responsibility within the context of divine omnipotence parallels the philosopher's struggle to understand moral responsibility within the bounds of orderly causation.

God's foreknowledge. It is assumed throughout Scripture that God is omniscient, that he knows the future. Both moral and immoral conduct are foreknown by God. The selling of Joseph into slavery, the evil acts of the Pharoah, Peter's denial and Judas' betrayal of Christ, and the crucifixion are all foreknown. This evidence moved Luther to conclude:

If we believe it to be true that God foreknows and foreordains all things; that He cannot be deceived or obstructed in His foreknowledge and predestination; and that nothing happens but at His will (which reason itself is compelled to grant); then, on reason's own testimony, there can be no 'free-will' in man, or angel, or in any creature.[31]

There would appear to be no free will, in the indeterminate sense suggested in our thought experiments, because free will seems to imply that the future could not be known until the instant of decision—a refutation of God's foreknowledge.

This argument against free will is the least compelling. Philosophers have shown that divine foreknowledge is not logically incompatible with free will.[32] Many of us have developed our own objection: perhaps God *knows* the future without destining it, because all time is an eternal now in the timelessness of God, enabling God to *know* our freely willed choices before we decide them, and without controlling what they will be.

God's sovereignty. More relevant to the issue of free will is the biblical assertion of divine omnipotence: all things take place according to God's sovereign plan.[33] God's covenant promises are rooted in his sovereignty: "For thine is the Kingdom and the power." As it was expressed in the Westminster Confession of 1649: "God from all eternity did by the most wise and holy counsel of his own will, freely and unchangeably ordain whatsoever comes to pass."

One of the suggested definitions of *Yahweh*, the Hebrew name for God, is "the one who causes to be what is." For example, God's identification to Moses as "I am who I am" has also been translated as "I cause to be what comes into existence."[34] In this age of emphasis on the personal God, the very human God with whom we are pals and to whom we sing little ditty songs, it is well that we renew our sense of the awesomeness of God. His mystery, majesty, and sovereignty need to be reemphasized. It is no accident that Martin Luther, who had this sense of the transcendent God, has given us hymns of praise and worship which affirm the power of God so vividly.

What would free will imply concerning God's sovereignty? If human will is indeterminant—spontaneous, autonomous—then God is dependent on our unpredictable actions and is therefore "constantly changing his mind and intentions; altering his measures, relinquishing his old designs, and forming new schemes and projections," in order to achieve his purposes.[35] Jonathan Edwards could not give so much as an inch on the matter of free will, it being his contention that single acts of will could affect the course of history, thereby invalidating God's sovereignty. God alone is self-moved, he argued; all other beings have "causal ancestors." "They who thus plead for man's liberty, advance principles which destroy the freedom of God himself."[36] Antony Flew makes the same logical point: "To suggest that God might himself have limited his power is to fail [to take the theological doctrine of creation seriously]: for if the limitation is real it must involve that the Universe is now to that extent out of control, and contains things independent of God; which is precisely what the doctrine of creation denies."[37]

However we are to understand the biblical notion of human responsibility we at least must not understand our responsibility as something that takes over where God leaves off. Human will is not added to God's will such that the two together equal 100 percent. As Jonathan Edwards contended, nothing about human moral agency requires "the adoption of loose notions concerning the governance of God."[38] There is, as C. S. Lewis put it, no corner of the universe in which humanity may say to God, "This is our business, not yours."[39]

God's grace. A third reason why some theologians have objected to the popular assumption of free will is the biblical doctrine of grace. Nothing good that a human being does is deserving of credit; everything is a result of grace. As Paul stresses over and over, salvation is God's choice.

> He chose us in him before the foundation of the world,
>   that we should be holy and blameless before Him.
> He destined us in love to be his sons through Jesus Christ,
>   according to the purpose of his will. . . .[40]

Luther believed the bondage of the will to be the very cornerstone of the gospel, the foundation of the doctrine of grace. By denying free will, Luther was affirming our complete inability to save ourselves, and the totality of God's sovereignty and grace. His was not a doctrine of causal determinism but of our enslavement to sin and our salvation from it. We can perform no meritorious action independent of God. All such events are expressions of the omnipresence of God's sovereign will. Believing in human free will erodes the core of the gospel, asserted Luther.

Still, Christians have been tempted throughout church history to glorify human dignity by assuming the freedom of the will. They have often presumed that God and the individual person both make a contribution to salvation, for God offers his love, yet the receipt of this love is finally dependent on the person's freely willed acceptance of it. In this way, justification by faith came to mean that God justifies us contingent on our act of faith. But for Luther, Calvin, and Edwards, faith itself is the gift of God, leaving us nothing of which to boast.[41] "Nothing, however slight, can be credited to man without depriving God of his honor," wrote Calvin.[42] "There can be no virtuous choice, unless God immediately gives it," reasoned Edwards.[43] "God has taken my salvation out of the control of my own will, and put it under the control of His," said Luther.[44] So also states the Lutheran Small Catechism: "I believe that I cannot by my own reason or strength believe in Jesus Christ, my Lord, or come to Him." What then is left of free will? "Nothing! In truth, nothing!" insisted Luther.[45] Calvin was just as forceful: Because the term free will "cannot be retained without great peril, it will . . . be a great boon for the church if it be abolished."[46]

Objections to Divine Determination

Perhaps you agree to most of the foregoing argument but are bothered by some of what it seems to suggest. For example, is God, being the author of all that is, the author of sin and evil as well? Is it not blasphemous to suggest that Idi Amin's vicious slaughter of tens of thousands of Ugandans was part of God's plan? Surely, the guilt for human evil is ours, not God's.

To this familiar objection, Jonathan Edwards offered several replies. First, the problem of evil is not unique to those who take the determinist position; it is shared by Christians of all persuasions. The world could be other than what it is, for God is not limited by the laws of his own universe. As Augustine reasoned, either God cannot abolish evil or he will not: if he cannot, he is not all-powerful; if he will not, he is not all-good. John Stuart Mill saw this as an "absolute contradiction" at the center of the Christian faith. It is a mystery with which *all* Christians must live.

Edwards went on to grant that God *is* "the author of sin" in the sense that he permits sin as a temporary consequence of his ultimate good purpose, as, for example, when Joseph was sold into Egypt, or when Pharaoh's heart hardened, or Christ was crucified. These events are horrid in themselves and expressions of evil in those who perpetrated them.[47] Yet each is a part of God's wise plan. But in these instances, God was the agent or producer of sin only in the sense that the sun is the cause of darkness. Finally, Edwards reasoned, events will either "be ordered by something" or "disposed by chance." Better then "that the good and evil which happens in God's world should be ordered, regulated, bounded and determined by the good pleasure of an infinitely wise being . . ."[48]

The corollary to the problem of evil is, of course, the dilemma of human moral freedom and responsibility. Antony Flew's words are to the point: "Certainly it would be monstrous to suggest that anyone, *however truly responsible in the eyes of men*, could fairly be called to account and punished by the God who had rigged his every move. All the bitter words which have ever been written against the wickedness of the God of predestinationism—especially when he is also thought of as filling Hell with all but the elect—are amply justified."[49] It therefore seems that if we are to be held accountable for moral freedom and responsibility and credited with the potential for moral good, God must limit his own freedom by the freedom he confers upon us.[50] But even this limitation on divine omnipotence does not enable us to escape the dilemma. If it is still inevitable that every person sin, we are not free not to sin. How then are we to be considered responsible for sin? Reinhold Niebuhr recognized the Christian doctrine of responsibility for sin as a seeming absurdity, which he could only answer with paradoxical statements such as "the proof of our freedom is our recognition that we are not free to choose between good and evil."[51] So again we see that what at first glance seems a special problem for those like Luther and Edwards who attribute nothing to freedom of the will, is in the last analysis a mystery with which all Christians live.

Determinism and Divine Sovereignty

This discussion of divine sovereignty parallels the discussion of determinism. The two concepts are not, however, identical. What we understand as faithful, orderly, natural causation is certainly one way by which God might achieve his purposes, so determinism could be incorporated within the notion of divine sovereignty. But it is conceivable that God also acts through unpredictable interventions into the natural world. If there are occasional miracles this should not, however, deflect our attention from the conviction that *all* events, whether seemingly miraculous or not, are equally dependent on God's creative power.

It also may be that God ordains the future as a playwright ordains the last act of a play. The outcome is created by and foreknown to the author, but indeterminate to members of the audience, even after they have closely observed the preceding acts. Thus the playwright is sovereign, but his or her ends are unpredictable. To return to the thought experiment with which we began this chapter, divine sovereignty need not imply that identical circumstances will yield identical outcomes. God is free to script different outcomes. He is not bound by the laws of his own creation or obliged to conform to our understanding of cause and effect. G. C. Berkouwer makes this point emphatically:

Divine determining is utterly different from what is generally understood by determinism. It is not that there is a material similarity between the confession of God's Providence and determinism and that the only difference between them is the formal difference that in determinism the first cause stands at the end of the series of causes, while in the confession of Providence God stands there. . . . The essential error of identifying the Providence doctrine with determinism is the depersonalization of the God-concept. God is looked on as the beginning of a sequence out of which all things emerge.[52]

Here, then, is a second reason for questioning physical determinism. The introduction of chance uncertainty and the conviction that nature is open to divine initiative both suggest that the universe is not a mechanical clockwork. (Bear in mind, chance and Providence are not mutually exclusive categories any more than are nature and Providence.)[53]

The concepts of determinism and divine sovereignty do, however, converge in their common rejection of autonomous freedom of the will. They both affirm our dependence on forces beyond our knowledge. They thus share the common problem of accommodating the idea of moral responsibility. Just as it is tempting to loosen our concept of determinism to accommodate free will within the gap, so also is it tempting to soften our notion of divine sovereignty to accommodate at least a dash of human autonomy. God's sovereignty does not extend all the way down to the discrete level of what I ate for breakfast this morning, it is argued; God ordains only the ultimate ends. This argument not only weakens our concept of a God who is immanent throughout the creation, sustaining and upholding all events, but it also makes little apparent sense. How are the ends fixed apart from the means? A limited concept of divine sovereignty has to maintain that the discrete acts—what I eat for breakfast—have no ultimate effects, which seems plainly false. Jesus' view of divine sovereignty seems not to have been of this variety: not even a sparrow "will fall to the ground without your Father's will."[54] So also the Heidelberg Catechism: "Without the will of my Father in Heaven not a hair can fall from my head. . . ."

Indeed, this conviction of the total, absolute sovereignty of God is evident throughout the Scriptures.

> Man plans his journey by his own wit, but it is the
> Lord who guides his steps.[55]

> Everything that happens in this world happens at the
> time God chooses.
> He sets the time for birth and the time for death,
>   the time for planting and the time for pulling up,
>   the time for killing and the time for healing,
>   the time for tearing down and the time for building.
> He sets the time for sorrow and the time for joy,
>   the time for mourning and the time for dancing,
>   the time for making love and the time for not making love,
>   the time for kissing and the time for not kissing.
> He sets the time for finding and the time for losing,
>   the time for saving and the time for throwing away,
>   the time for tearing and the time for mending,
>   the time for silence and the time for talk.
> He sets the time for love and the time for hate,
>   the time for war and the time for peace.[56]

> A word with you, you who say, 'Today or tomorrow we will
> go off to such and such a town and spend a year there trading
> and making money.' Yet you have no idea what tomorrow will
> bring. Your life, what is it? You are no more than a mist,
> seen for a little while and then dispersing. What you ought
> to say is: 'If it be the Lord's will, we shall live to do this
> or that.'[57]

> You must work out your own salvation in fear and trembling;
> for it is God who works in you, inspiring both the will and
> the deed, for his own chosen purpose.[58]

God acts as the first cause of all things, we as the second. "Not the ability to will alone, but the willing and doing themselves are accomplished by God," concludes Berkouwer; God's "doing, like his willing, pertains to *all* activities of man."[59] So also Hendrikus Berkhof: "The fact is that the same deed is in its entirety both a deed of God and a deed of the creature. It is a deed of God in so far as it is determined from moment to moment by the will of God. And it is a deed of man in so far as God realizes it through the self-activity of the creature."[60] These insights are confirmed in our own experience. At any given moment, we perceive ourselves in control of our decisions and actions. Yet, later looking back on our experience, we can often recognize the providence of God at work.

My point in raising these enormously complicated issues is not to resolve them, or even to contribute anything original. It is simply to remind us that most Christians already accept moral responsibility within the bounds of divine sovereignty and that some theologians have felt it necessary to reject freedom of the will in order to affirm God's omnipotence and grace. Christian belief, therefore, does not, as is so often presumed, necessarily move us toward a humanistic psychology which is based on the notions of human autonomy and free will.

The Paradox: Human Responsibility and God's Purpose

It is evident from the foregoing that our assumptions of divine omnipotence and human responsibility are not logically harmonious. The Bible simultaneously affirms God's overarching will and plan for human history *and* human accountability within it. Jesus held Judas responsible for his betrayal—"Woe to that man by whom the Son of man is betrayed!"[61]—yet the act is foreordained, as Jesus was well aware. Presumably, an instant replay of Judas' decision would find him again behaving in the same predictable fashion. Judas was not externally compelled to act as he did, but he would not have chosen otherwise. The mystery reaches its climax in the crucifixion. The Word-made-flesh, the epitome of loving concern, becomes the object of the most passionate evil that human freedom can choose. All this was part of God's ultimate plan from the beginning of time. In the biblical account, it seems clear, human freedom and responsibility are not to be understood as a limitation upon God's sovereignty. To think of Judas (or ourselves) as partly free and partly determined underestimates both the reality of choice and responsibility *and* the completeness of God's governance.

We must also remember that nothing in the account of divine sovereignty implies that we should think ourselves mechanical puppets. Donald MacKay argues the point this way:

Even if we accept that the 'foreknowledge' of our Creator extends to every atomic event of His creation, past, present and future, including all the acts of all the agents in it, and that all is of His 'determinate counsel', it would nevertheless be logically erroneous to interpret that 'foreknowledge' as *knowledge of a determinate specification* which would be binding upon us whether we knew it or not, and whether we liked it or not. In our language, no such determinate specification *exists* until after the events to which it refers.[62]

That is, even if some omniscient mind knew our present and future brain states, meaning that from this external perspective we were determinate, it cannot be said that we would be bound to comply with the omniscient mind's predictions *whether we knew them or not*. This is because once we knew the prediction, our brain state would be different from what it was when the prediction was made. If I predict that you will choose coffee rather than tea, it makes a great difference whether you are aware of this prediction. Whereas if I say to a mere physical object, like a baseball, "you will drop two feet during the next twenty feet," my prediction is not invalidated by its announcement.

This is one reason why Kenneth Gergen has argued that social psychology is history. "The dissemination of psychological knowledge modifies the patterns of behavior upon which the knowledge is based."[63] The predictions we make about social influences on people may no longer hold once they become aware of these influences. I tell students that one of my objectives in teaching social psychology is to provide increased insight into the operation of social influences in their own lives and thereby a decreased vulnerability to undesired social manipulation. I hope, for example, that knowing that a person is less likely to help someone in distress when there are many other bystanders will increase the student's willingness to help under such conditions, thereby invalidating the principle for that student. Peter Berger makes the point beautifully:

We see the puppets dancing in their miniature stage, moving up and down as the strings pull them around, following the prescribed course of their various little parts. We learn to understand the logic of this theater and we find ourselves in its motions. We locate ourselves in society and thus recognize our own position as we hang from its subtle strings. For a moment we see ourselves as puppets indeed. But then we grasp a decisive difference between the puppet theater and our own drama. Unlike the puppets, we have the possibility of stopping in our movements, looking up and perceiving the machinery by which we have been moved. In this act lies the first step towards freedom.[64]

The only sensible perspective on our own present situation for us to take is to assume responsibility for our actions, even though an omniscient mind looking in from the outside may foreknow our choices. Our experience joins the Scriptures in simultaneously affirming the reality of responsibility, from the human perspective, and of divine omnipotence, from God's perspective. The future is in God's hands, and yet responsibility for the future is ours. In other words, "Work as if all depended on you, pray as if all depended on God." Paul senses this paradox when he writes, "I . . . : yet not I, but the grace of God which was with me."[65] Both divine sovereignty and human responsibility must be asserted.

We must therefore walk in reverence before the mystery of sin and evil within God's sovereignty.* Paul recognizes the difficulty in holding a person responsible for what God has ordained. "You will say, 'Then why does God blame a man? For who can resist his will?' " Note Paul's reply. He does not attempt to rationally demys-

---

* The problem of evil arises, as we have seen, from three seemingly incompatible assertions of Christian doctrine: (1) God is good; (2) God is sovereign; and (3) Real evil exists. Attempts to resolve the problem of evil generally soften or deny altogether one of the three assertions, but doing so creates new problems.

Some have denied God's perfect goodness, acknowledging God as the source of both good and evil. The blasphemy this creates is sufficiently obvious that few Christians would agree. For Christians, the first ground rule in this discussion is that we do not excuse our moral evil by blaming God.

A more attractive option, which seems to take God off the hook, is to limit God's omnipotence to allow for autonomous creatures who are the ultimate source of their own freely chosen evil. C. S. Lewis exemplifies this view:

> The sin, both of men and of angels, was rendered possible by the fact that God gave them free will; thus surrendering a portion of His omnipotence . . . because He saw that from a world of free creatures, even though they fell, He could work out . . . a deeper happiness and a fuller splendour than any world of automata would admit (*Miracles* [New York: Macmillan, 1947], p. 147).

But this makes God spectator to a creation that is out of his control to the extent that its creatures have free will. The ultimate end of arguments for human free will is to push God out of history. This denies the many biblical assertions of God's total sovereignty. Moreover, how does this resolve the problem of natural evil (those catastrophes which insurance companies call "acts of God")? And why, if God is good and if he knew evil would result from our freedom, did he allow it, and why does he not stop it and achieve his good ends without natural and moral evil?

The third solution maintains total divine control but softens the harshness of evil. Temporary evils are subsumed under a larger ultimate good, or else evil is said to exist by virtue of being defined by the very existence of Good, even as darkness is defined by the existence of light. This seems insensitive to the horrible reality of some evil. How can the slaughter of six million Jews or the abuse of even a single innocent child be seen as the necessary means to an ultimate good?

A fourth possible response is not to resolve the problem of evil, but to stand by all three assertions, even though doing so violates the law of noncontradiction. This is the response for which I opt in the remainder of this chapter. In doing so, I fully recognize the logical contradiction inherent in this response, but feel that the problems created by denying any of the three assertions are even greater. I will be satisfied if these chapters on freedom do no more than to encourage some Christian theologians and philosophers to continue working toward the resolution which has eluded me.

tify God's justice, but instead suggests that creatures ought not to question their creator. "Who are you, sir, to answer God back? Can the pot speak to the potter and say, 'Why did you make me like this?' Surely the potter can do what he likes with the clay."[66] "The reason (God) did not sustain man . . . lies hidden in his plan; sobriety is for us the part of wisdom," wrote John Calvin.[67]

Luther also recognized that asserting the bondage of the will left a profound mystery:

> By the light of grace, it is inexplicable how God can damn him who by his own strength can do nothing but sin and become guilty. Both the light of nature and the light of grace here insist that the fault lies not in the wretchedness of man, but in the injustice of God; nor can they judge otherwise of a God who crowns the ungodly freely, without merit, and does not crown, but damns another, who is perhaps less, and certainly not more, ungodly. But the light of glory insists otherwise, and will one day reveal God, to whom alone belongs a judgment whose justice is incomprehensible, as a God whose justice is most righteous and evident— provided only that in the meanwhile we *believe* it. . . ."[68]

The possibility of a higher level of justice which is incomprehensible to us mortals is credible for those familiar with Lawrence Kohlberg's research on moral reasoning.[69] Kohlberg has identified a series of developmental stages of moral reasoning through which individuals pass. We all travel the same highway, he contends, though we travel varying distances down the road. We can look back over the path we have traveled and understand the stages of moral reasoning through which we have passed, but we cannot grasp the moral reasoning that lies more than a stage or two ahead. Thus a child cannot comprehend conventional adult morality (e.g., doing one's duty) any more than can the conventional adult grasp the postconventional morality of abstract universal principles.

There are some interesting implications of Kohlberg's theory. One is that Kohlberg and other moral theorists must themselves be capable of formulating moral reasoning processes only a small step ahead of their own moral thinking. If God's justice is several levels beyond, it will be as incomprehensible to us as is adult moral reasoning to a child.

Kohlberg's theory is linked to the work of Jean Piaget, which can be used to make the same point. Piaget's primary contribution has been to show us that the child's mind is not just a miniature of the adult mind. It perceives the world and processes information in ways that are qualitatively different from the adult mind. (Christian educators who assume that preschool children will grasp anal-

ogies or be able to infer the meaning of Bible stories fail to appreciate the significance of Piaget's observations. Little children do not
think as their teachers do.) Recognizing the enormous difference
between adult and child minds can lead us to humbly contemplate
that God's reasoning may be at least as much superior to our own
as is ours to a young child's. Just as some things that are obvious
to us are unfathomable mysteries to a small child, even after the
truth is directly explained, so also some aspects of God's plan may
have to remain unfathomable mysteries to us. We had therefore
best be wary of assimilating God's system of justice to our own system of reward and punishment, as if to create God in our own
image. God's moral reasoning is surely not that of our local District
Court judge.

Like Job, we cannot understand what divine justice is. Conventional religious ideas about God's judgment seem inadequate. It is
good, then, that we remember that God did not answer Job's questions about the nature of his justice. He instead overwhelmed Job
with a picture of his infinite power and wisdom—to which Job
responded with a renewed sense of humility. Such is our response
to a vision of who God is; those who catch a glimpse of God's
power and perfection become humble. Even as little children need
to have basic trust in parental judgments they cannot understand,
so should we trust the unfathomable justice and goodness of God.
As Martin Luther concluded:

If His justice were such as could be adjudged just by human reckoning, it
clearly would not be Divine; it would in no way differ from human justice.
But inasmuch, as He is the one true God, wholly incomprehensible and in-
accessible to man's understanding, it is reasonable, indeed inevitable, that
His justice also should be incomprehensible; as Paul cries, saying: 'O the
depth of the riches both of the wisdom and knowledge of God! How un-
searchable are His judgments, and His ways past finding out!' (Rom.
11:33).[70]

Paradox in Science

It is discomfiting to be left with a mystery which our minds cannot penetrate. This is why Christian thinkers have long sought to
resolve this paradox of Christian doctrine. Some have started with
a concept of God's sovereignty as practically absolute and then limited freedom accordingly. Others have glorified the self-sufficiency
of human will and diminished the extent of God's sovereignty and
grace so as to leave room for human autonomy.[71] J. I. Packer states
the dilemma well:

People see that the Bible teaches man's responsibility for his actions; they do not see (man, indeed, cannot see) how this is consistent with the sovereign Lordship of God over those actions. They are not content to let the two truths live side by side, as they do in the Scriptures, but jump to the conclusion that, in order to uphold the biblical truth of human responsibility, they are bound to reject the equally biblical and equally true doctrine of divine sovereignty and to explain away the great number of texts that teach it. The desire to oversimplify the Bible by cutting out the mysteries is natural to our perverse minds, and it is not surprising that even good men should fall victim to it.[72]

Rather than diminish either divine sovereignty or human responsibility, we might take a cue from modern physical science. Although it was suggested earlier that the principle of indeterminacy does not provide an obvious place for moral responsibility, it does imply some logically contradictory pictures of nature with which most scientists have learned to live. Baffled physicists once sought by every conceivable means to reinterpret one picture or the other so as to achieve logical consistency, just as theologians have done with the biblical paradoxes. But most scientists have now concluded that no one law is capable of describing all phenomena. Niels Bohr labeled this "the principle of complementarity," which he understood to imply something significant about the very nature of physical universe.[73] The principle is summarized nicely by William Pollard:

Striking and apparently irreconcilable contradictions, instead of beginning to yield before the determined assault being made upon them, were rather more and more firmly established with each new step in research. . . . One entirely convincing set of experiments proves that light and electrons are both particles, while another equally extensive and convincing set of experiments proves that they are both waves. . . . Thus, this principle asserts that the experimental situation is not to be regarded as a paradox capable of being resolved by further work, but rather looked upon as reflecting an essential characteristic of reality.[74]

Like the ancient Chinese yin and yang, complementary opposites make the whole. "There are trivial truths and great truths," wrote Bohr. "The opposite of a trivial truth is plainly false. The opposite of a great truth is also true."[75] Reinhold Niebuhr defined a paradox as "an expression of faith that a rationally irresolvable contradiction may point to a truth which logic cannot contain."[76]

To be sure, calling something a paradox is intellectually unsatisfying and most of us would gladly junk the concept if a more satisfactory resolution should ever emerge. Yet, for the present, our situation is like that of a man stranded in a well with two ropes dangling before him. He grabs onto one, but no matter how fast he pulls himself up, he sinks still further into the well. So he grabs onto the other, but this rope lowers him still further. Only when he holds both ropes at once can he climb out of the well, because at the top, beyond where he can see, they come together around a pulley. Grabbing the rope of only determinism (natural and/or divine) or of only human responsibility leads us inevitably to the bottom of a well.[77] Recognizing the seeming absurdity in grabbing both, we are compelled to squint upward to catch a glimpse of how they might come together beyond where we can now see. But the light is dim; we see through a glass, darkly. Like Job, "I have spoken of great things which I have not understood, things too wonderful for me to know."[78] I can live with the mystery because I do not demand of God that I be able to totally comprehend his being.

In the middle of the night my young son calls out in distress, awakening me from the unreality of a dream. Climbing back in bed, I am frightened, while the dream is yet vivid, at the recognition that my perception of reality can be so confident and yet so wrong. "I said, 'I am resolved to be wise', but wisdom . . . lies beyond our grasp, deep down, deeper than man can fathom."[79] This causes me to look forward with a mixture of fear and hope to awakening from my death—fear about discovering how silly and distorted my thinking has been, yet hoping to see at last the solutions to some of the great mysteries of our existence.

As Søren Kierkegaard so clearly recognized, reason cannot reconcile the irrationalities of faith. But human reason is itself finite and socially conditioned, he argued (an assertion documented in Chapter 7), so let us not be intimidated by it. Kierkegaard thus "leaves us with 'the most frightful act of decision'. The choice is between unbelief, which sees sheer madness in the affirmations of faith, and belief, which sees in that madness the divine wisdom."[80]

> For my thoughts are not your thoughts
>   neither are your ways my ways, says the Lord.
> For as the heavens are higher than the earth,
>   so are my ways higher than your ways
>   and my thoughts than your thoughts.[81]

NOTES

1. William James, "The Dilemma of Determinism," in *The Will to Believe*, ed. William James (New York: Longmans, Green & Company,

1896), pp. 145–83. James noted that the evidence is not sufficient to decide for determinism or indeterminism since the mere fact that something has happened is no grounds for assuming that something else could not have happened. Imagine that after winding back the time clock of the universe, as in our mental experiment, you proceeded to make a different choice than you had the first time. "Either universe after the fact and once there would, to our sense of observation and understanding, appear just as rational as the other."

2. John B. Watson, *Behaviorism* (Chicago: University of Chicago Press 1958), p. 104 (Copyright 1930).

3. Joseph Wood Krutch, *The Measure of Man* (New York: Grossett & Dunlap, 1954), p. 261.

4. Thanks to John Barlow for this illustration.

5. From Edward Fitzgerald's "Rubaiyat of Omar Khayam."

6. As Leslie Weatherhead wrote: "We blunt the edge of social purpose until men mutter the slogan, 'God's will be done,' when the very opposite of God's will is being done, and when, if men had seen more clearly into the divine purpose and tightened up their loose thinking, they would have become the instruments of God's purpose and swept away the evil which they complacently regarded as the will of God" (*The Will of God* [Nashville: Abingdon Press, 1944], p. 16).

7. Gal. 6:7, NEB.

8. R. E. Hobart, "Free Will as Involving Determination and Inconceivable Without It," *Mind* 43 (1934): 1–27.

9. Prov. 22:6 RSV.

10. Exod. 20:5, 34:7; Num. 14:18; Deut. 5:9.

11. Barry Schlenker, "Social Psychology and Science," *Journal of Personality and Social Psychology* 29 (1974): 1–15.

12. J. G. Kemeny, *A Philosopher Looks at Science* (Princeton, N. J.: Van Nostrand, 1959), p. 226.

13. R. E. Hobart, *op. cit.* This provocative article was the stimulus for some of my illustrations.

14. J. S. Mill, *An Examination of Sr. William Hamilton's Philosophy*, Chapter 26, 1867, reprinted in J. A. Gould, ed., *Classic Philosophical Questions* (Columbus, Ohio: Merrill Publishing Co., 1971), p. 133.

15. John Dewey summarized this point well: "Courses of action which put the blame exclusively on a person as if his evil were the sole cause of wrong-doing and those which condone offense on account of the share of social conditions in producing bad disposition, are equally ways of making an unreal separation of man from his surroundings, mind from the world. Causes for an act always exist, but causes are not excuses" (*Human Nature and Conduct: An Introduction to Social Psychology*, [New York: Holt, 1922], p. 18).

16. As in Galatians 5:1 RSV: "For freedom Christ has set us free."

17. Cited in American Psychological Association *Monitor* 3, no. 9 (1972): 4. The contention that free will is necessary for jurisprudence is disputable. "There are two ends which, on the Necessitarian theory, are sufficient to justify punishment" wrote John Stuart Mill: "the benefit of

the offender himself, and the protection of others" (Mill, *op. cit.*, p. 131). Whereas if the will is indeterminate, then punishment cannot discourage repetition of the act or inhibit others from doing the same evil and the only justification for punishment is retribution. Considerations such as these led Bertrand Russell to conclude: "While, therefore, as a philosopher I hold the principle of universal causation to be open to question, as a commonsense individual I hold it to be an indispensable postulate in the conduct of affairs. For practical purposes we must assume that our volitions have causes, and our ethics must be compatible with this assumption. Praise and blame, reward and punishment, and the whole apparatus of the criminal law, are rational on the deterministic hypothesis, but not on the hypothesis of free will" (*Human Society in Ethics and Politics* [New York: Simon & Schuster, 1955], p. 79).

18. Marion Steininger and Kathleen Voegtlin, "Personality Variables and Beliefs about Psychological Issues," *Teaching of Psychology* 3, (1976): 51–54.

19. Malcolm A. Jeeves, *Scientific Psychology and Christian Belief* (Downer's Grove, Ill.: InterVarsity Press, 1967), p. 26.

20. Paul Ramsey, Editor's Introduction to Jonathan Edward's *Freedom of the Will* (New Haven: Yale University Press, 1957), p. 31.

21. William Pollard, *Chance and Providence* (New York: Harper, 1958).

22. Prov. 16:33 RSV. *The Living Bible* converts this to a modern idiom: "We toss the coin, but it is the Lord who controls its decision."

23. Pascual Jordan, *Science and the Course of History* (New Haven: Yale University Press, 1955), pp. 112–113.

24. See, for example, Sir Arthur Eddington, *The Philosophy of Physical Science* (New York: Macmillan, 1939), p. 182.

25. Richard H. Bube, *The Human Quest* (Waco, Texas: Word Books, 1971), p. 170.

26. Eddington, *op. cit.*, p. 183.

27. Erwin Schrodinger, *Science and Humanism: Physics in our Time* (Cambridge: Cambridge University Press, 1951), pp. 62–63.

28. Ralph Wendell Burhoe, "The Control of Behavior: Human and Environmental," *Journal of Environmental Health* 35 (1972): 247–58.

29. Jonathan Edwards, *Freedom of the Will*, ed. Paul Ramsey (New Haven: Yale University Press, 1957), pp. 181; *ibid.*, p. 185.

30. Augustine, *The City of God*, bk. 5, chap. 9.

31. Martin Luther, *The Bondage of the Will*, trans. J. I. Packer and O. R. Johnston (Old Tappen, N.J.: Fleming H. Revell Co., 1957), p. 317.

32. For example, Alvin Plantinga, "Necessity and Possible Worlds," a BBC lecture, 1976.

33. There is plenty of food for a good Bible study on God's sovereignty. The Old Testament pictures God as sovereign over Israel (Jer. 18:1–10) and all nations (Isa. 10:5–7, 15–17), over believing and unbelieving individuals (Isa. 45:1–2 and Dan. 6:26–27), and over events (Exod. 15:1–3 and Gen. 20). His sovereignty extends to the selection of certain chosen groups and individuals, such as the descendants of Abra-

ham (Gen. 15:12–21 and Deut. 7:6–11), the priestly line (Num. 25:12–13) and the Jewish nation (Exod. 19:5–6; Deut. 7:6; and Hos. 11:1–3). The New Testament also speaks of the sovereignty of God (as in Matt. 11:25–26; 1 Timothy 6:15; and Rev. 19:6) and of God's plan for the life and death of Christ (Gal. 4:4, Luke 1:30–33, Luke 22:22, Acts 2:22–23, and Acts 4:27–28). The emphasis on God's sovereignty as evidenced by his mercy toward those who cannot achieve their own salvation by freely willed acts of merit is clearly expressed in the writings of Paul (as in Rom. 8:28–30, Eph. 1:1–12, and Rom. 9–11).

34. B. W. Anderson in *The Interpreter's Dictionary of the Bible*, vol. 2 (Nashville: Abingdon Press, 1962), p. 410. I am grateful to my colleague, Francis Fike, for pointing this out to me.

35. Edwards, *op. cit.*, p. 253.

36. Cited by Ramsey, *op. cit.*, p. 27.

37. Antony Flew, "Divine Omnipotence and Human Freedom," in *New Essays in Philosophical Theology*, ed. Antony Flew and Alasdair MacIntyre (London: SCM Press, 1958), p. 168.

38. Ramsey, *op. cit.*, p. 3.

39. C. S. Lewis, *The Problem of Pain* (New York: Macmillan, 1973), p. 68.

40. Eph. 1:4,5.

41. See Eph. 2:8.

42. John Calvin, *Institutes of the Christian Religion*, II, II, 1 (John T. McNeill, ed., Ford L. Battles, trans.), (Philadelphia: Westminster Press, 1975), p. 255.

43. Cited by Ramsey, *op. cit.*, p. 34.

44. Luther, *op. cit.*, p. 268.

45. *Ibid*.

46. Calvin, *op. cit.*, VI, II, 8, p. 266. There is disagreement over exactly what Calvin and Luther meant in rejecting the freedom of the will. Their primary concern was not to argue a philosophical position, but to emphasize our dependence on God and our inability to do good and to achieve salvation apart from God's grace. But can these matters be disconnected from the rest of our existence? Some contend—while others deny—that the doctrines of Calvin and Luther have metaphysical implications which Calvin and Luther recognized. Luther's "bombshell" was "that God does *all things* according to God's infallible will, . . . that God necessitates all things" (David Ray Griffin, *God, Power, and Evil: A Process Theodicy* [Philadelphia: Westminster Press, 1975], pp. 104–5). Calvin believed it "wrong to suggest that human affairs are due partly to God's providence and partly to human free choice. We have no free choice. . . . God does everything" (*ibid.*, pp. 117, 126). My own limited reading of Luther (*The Bondage of the Will*) and Calvin (especially the *Institutes* chapters on Providence and will) inclines me to agree with Griffin's understanding of Luther and Calvin.

47. Indeed, "It is not the will of my Father who is in heaven that one of these little ones should perish" (Matt. 18:14 RSV).

48. Edwards, *op. cit.*, p. 405.

49. Flew, *op. cit.*, p. 163.

50. See Alvin Plantinga, *The Nature of Necessity* (New York: Oxford University Press, 1974), especially pp. 166, 190; or Georgia Harkness, *Understanding the Christian Faith* (Nashville: Abingdon, 1947), p. 63. I confess to not having fully studied the philosophical defense of this view of divine sovereignty. A simple analogy may nevertheless convey its plausibility: our genes have created us with an enormous capacity for adaptation and choice; our genes are sovereign, but in their wisdom, they have engineered our flexibility. So also the sovereign wisdom of God may permit free will.

It is easy to understand the problem which this view must resolve. The idea that God limits his power to permit our free will

> suggests that God allows the sinner to decide in freedom against God's command. God is, then, in His Providence, a balcony observer of a contest whose outcome is never certain. It suffices Him to create a playground and leave the decision to man whether it will be the scene of sin or of obedience. Sin, then, lies ultimately in man's power of decision and God's action becomes mere reaction to man's decision (G. C. Berkouwer, *The Providence of God* [Grand Rapids: Eerdmans, 1952], pp. 149–50).

Calvin was more blunt: "They babble and talk absurdly who, in place of God's Providence, substitute bare permission—as if God sat in a watchtower awaiting chance events, and his judgment thus depended upon human will" (*op. cit.*, Book I, Chapter XVIII).

51. Reinhold Niebuhr, *The Nature and Destiny of Man*, vol. 1 (New York: Scribner's, 1964), p. 258.

52. Berkouwer, *op. cit.*, pp. 163–64.

53. Clifton Orlebeke points out that one can therefore reject physical determinism but still accept a metaphysical determinism which includes unpredictable divine interventions ("Donald MacKay's Philosophy of Science," *Christian Scholar's Review* 7 [1977]: 51–63).

54. Matt. 10:29 RSV.

55. Prov. 16:9, NEB.

56. Eccles. 3:1–8, Good News.

57. James 4:13–15, NEB.

58. Phil. 2:12–13, NEB.

59. G. C. Berkouwer, *op. cit.*, pp. 143, 148.

60. Cited by Berkouwer, *ibid.*, p. 145.

61. Mark 14:21 RSV.

62. Donald MacKay, "The Sovereignty of God in the Natural World," *Scottish Journal of Theology* 21 (1968): 13–26.

63. Kenneth Gergen, "Social Psychology as History," *Journal of Personality and Social Psychology* 26 (1973): 309–20.

64. Peter Berger, *Invitation to Sociology: A Humanistic Perspective* (Garden City, N.Y.: Doubleday Anchor Books, 1963), p. 176.

65. 1 Cor. 15:10, KJV.

66. Rom. 9:19–21, NEB.

67. Calvin, *op. cit.*, I, XV, 8, p. 196.

68. Luther, *op. cit.*, p. 317.

69. Lawrence Kohlberg, "Development of Moral Character and Ideology," in M. L. Hoffman and L. W. Hoffman, ed., *Review of Child Development Research,* vol. 1 (New York: Russell Sage Foundation, 1964).

71. As in the Pelagian ideas of the early fifth century, which Augustine refuted, and the Arminian thought of the early seventeenth century, which was rebutted by the Synod of Dort and Jonathan Edwards, among others.

72. J. I. Packer, *Evangelism and the Sovereignty of God* (Downer's Grove, Ill.: InterVarsity, 1961), p. 16.

73. Niels Bohr, "On the Notions of Causality and Complementarity," *Science* 111 (1950): 51–54.

74. William Pollard, *op. cit.,* pp. 140–41.

75. Quoted by William McGuire, "The Yin and Yang of Progress in Social Psychology: Seven Koan," *Journal of Personality and Social Psychology* 26 (1973): 446–56.

76. Niebuhr, *op. cit.,* pp. 262–63.

77. Thanks to Robert Coughenour for this illustration.

78. Job 42:3 RSV.

79. Eccles. 7:23–24, NEB.

80. Merold Westphal, "Kierkegaard and the Logic of Insanity," *Religious Studies* 7 (1971): 193–211.

81. Isa. 55:8–9 RSV.

CHAPTER 10

Psychology and Human Freedom

In Chapter 9 we explored the philosophical puzzle of human freedom within the natural order and the theological puzzle of human responsibility within the bounds of God's providence, sovereignty, and grace. We concluded that there seems to be a mysterious paradox: we are part of God's order and yet responsible. Viewed from the outside or in retrospect, decisions and actions can be seen as caused; viewed from the inside, we must see ourselves as free in the present moment.

Now we are in a position to analyze the concept of human freedom within psychology. First, I will note how the assumption of freedom or determinism influences psychological research and application. Then I will present some new theory and research demonstrating the far-reaching consequences of our implicit assumptions about our own and others' freedom. This evidence will not bear upon the deep philosophical and theological mystery. It will, however, point to an analogous paradox which is not so logically mysterious: just as we must simultaneously live with both divine sovereignty and human responsibility—without shrinking our concept of either in order to accommodate the other—so also psychological research simultaneously affirms the enormous power of genetic and environmental determination *and* the reality of our capacity for personal control. Moreover, it does so in such a way that personal determination and external determination cannot be seen as mutually exclusive powers which sum to 100 percent, just as divine power and human power are not separate powers which sum to unity.

FREEDOM AND DETERMINISM AS CONTROL BELIEFS

What we psychologists believe about human nature controls what we choose to study and what social technologies we develop. Nowhere is this better illustrated than in the issue of environmental control versus personal control over ourselves. This involves a distinction between "backward" analysis of how past conditions determine the person and "forward" analysis of how people determine their own futures. Both views are valid; at any moment we are both creatures and creators of history. Niels Bohr identified this as another instance of the complementarity paradox, for it is entirely correct to say we are the products of our genes and environment even while in an equally correct sense we may claim that both our heritage and our future are the result of human determination.[1] Figure 11 summarizes this important point.

Figure 11.

Many behavioral scientists tend, however, to emphasize either environmental control or personal control to the exclusion of the other. This is more than a philosophical issue. "It affects which human potentialities will be cultivated and which will be underdeveloped."[2] Psychologists' emphasis on environmental control leads them to analyze the person and to propose general propositions about the effects of environmental manipulation.[3] They see the person more as a reactor than as an actor. We need not deplore this, because the scientist's task, unlike that of the novelist, is not to capture the richness of an individual's existence, but to gain understanding and rational control of social forces.[4] The importance of environment and the benefits of understanding its effects are recognized by anyone interested in improving schools, churches, homes, or any other social setting.

We must recognize, however, that in gaining some detachment on our subject—by objectifying persons—we risk viewing the person *only* as an object.[5] One evident result of such a view is a growing public image of persons as passive, helpless, determined objects. Anna Russell's "Psychiatric Folksong" parodies this image:

> At three I had a feeling of
>   Ambivalence toward my brothers,
> And so it follows naturally
>   I poisoned all my lovers.
> But now I'm happy; I have learned
>   The lesson this has taught;
> That everything I do that's wrong
>   Is someone else's fault.

The folksong expresses a valid point. Observers of juvenile delinquents have noted that many delinquents exhibit an amazing grasp of sociological and psychological explanations for their behavior. Although these youths may be quite correct in pointing out the causal role of their poor environment, viewing oneself as acted upon rather than acting prepares the way for further delinquency.[6] Although the deterministic perspective may be valid for an external observer, it is fatal when adopted as a self-image.

Another result of objectifying persons is the development of social technologies appropriate to the image, such as behavioral control through conditioning. Although we can apply behavior modification in ways that enhance our self-control, as in programs for managing our environment in order to lose weight or to stop smoking, behavioral technologies applied to *other people* have generally been coercive. Although the conditioning of people and pigeons seems on the surface to be the positive, nonpunitive affair described by B. F. Skinner and his disciples, we hear less about the fact that the first step in behavioral conditioning is for the caretaker to starve the pigeon in order to gain control over satisfaction of a pigeon need. The behavior manager deprives the person of something he or she needs so that the manager may gain the power to reward desired behavior. This prerequisite is why behavior control strategies tend to have been applied in relatively totalitarian institutions—prisons, mental hospitals, homes for the retarded, schools—where the management may manipulate constraints ("contingencies") appropriate to its own purposes. We see, then, that the technique is not value free; it tends to define an authoritarian relationship between the controller and the animal or person controlled.

This illustrates the point that thinking of control as a one-way street—from environments to persons—can lead to social technologies which minimize social freedom.[7] We therefore need to keep the reciprocal relationship between environments and persons clearly in mind. Recognizing the equal importance of *personal control* will lead us to also develop our capacities for self-direction and our sense that we are responsible for our behavior and its consequences. There is a two-way relationship between environment and people, making both responsible. We must, therefore, study and appreciate both environmental control and personal control. The recent calls for increased self-reliance and responsibility within the black community by Jesse Jackson and others reflect this awareness. So also do some recent developments in psychological research, as we shall now see.

THE WISDOM OF BELIEF IN OUR OWN FREEDOM

Environmental control—that is what psychology is mostly about. By using powerful techniques of reinforcement, by manipulating the brain through electrical stimulation, drugs, or surgery, by altering the social environment, we attempt to bring a wide range of responses under stimulus control. Studies based on these attempts all emerge, as we have seen, from the deterministic assumption that environments control persons. The complementary assumption—that persons control environments—suggests a complementary line of research on the consequences of a person's sense of personal control and, if there be such consequences, on how to cultivate this conviction of freedom. Several strands of research pertaining to personal control have recently emerged. Collectively, they make an impressive case for the importance of a person's conviction of personal freedom and self-determination, and they reinforce the biblical witness regarding freedom and responsibility. As this research becomes more widely known, I believe it will provide a needed counterbalance to the passive image of persons to which psychology has contributed during this century. Here is a quick overview of these interesting investigations.

Locus of Control

During the last ten years psychologists have developed an enormous research literature exploring the consequences of people's belief that they control their own destiny (internal locus of control) as opposed to assuming that their fate is beyond their control, determined by chance or by powerful others (external locus of control). The more than one thousand studies exploring this concept have used several measures. Here are a few sample items from the most widely used scale.

Do you more strongly believe that:

In the long run people get the respect they deserve in this world.	or	Unfortunately, an individual's worth often passes unrecognized no matter how hard he tries.
What happens to me is my own doing	or	Sometimes I feel that I don't have enough control over the direction my life is taking.
The average person can have an influence in government decisions.	or	This world is run by the few people in power, and there is not much the little guy can do about it.[8]

Unlike most measures of personal traits, the way people answer questions like these on locus of control predicts some of their behavior in other situations.[9] The well-known Coleman Report on Equality of Educational Opportunity reported that disadvantaged children with a strong internal locus of control achieved more than did students with a weak sense of personal control. People with a strong sense of personal control are also more likely to be nonsmokers, to wear seat belts, and to practice birth control (instead of trusting fate). They are more independent and resistant to influence, better able to delay instant gratification in the service of larger, long-term goals, and they make more money. By and large, all the research converges on the same conclusion: people benefit from a strong sense of personal freedom and control. Lower income and minority persons, who typically have a lesser sense of personal control, are handicapped by their sense of powerlessness. But this, of course, illustrates again the reciprocal relationship of environment and person, for they are probably realistic in seeing less connection between personal effort and payoff.

One striking finding has been the steady decrease in sense of internal locus of control among college students since the early 1960s. Today's students feel more powerless to change the world and to control their own destinies than did students ten and fifteen years ago. This change has been attributed to a sense of political powerlessness resulting from the Vietnam era. But I think it is also a plausible conjecture that teaching in psychology courses the importance of environmental control over personal control has itself contributed to the growing feelings of external control. A remarkable increase in the study of psychology has coincided with the increased sense of personal powerlessness among college students. Do you think this is mere coincidence (the number of color television sets, beef consumption, and a host of other variables also increased during this time), or might there be some causal connection?

Recent literature not only demonstrates the importance of a sense of personal control, it also reveals factors which affect it. Cultures vary in the extent to which they locate causation within the person. Our individualistic culture trains children to inhibit their early tendencies toward external locus of control. When my younger son recently unscrambled "gate the sleeve caught Tom on his" into "The gate caught Tom on his sleeve" his teacher, applying the western cultural assumptions of the curriculum materials, marked this wrong. The "right" answer located cause within Tom, not the gate: "Tom caught his sleeve on the gate."

People with a strong internal locus of control tend to come from warm, democratic homes where a child's actions lead to predictable consequences—engendering a sense of choice and personal control. The importance of a sense of personal efficacy has also been demonstrated in animal research. Dogs which learn a sense of helplessness (by being taught they cannot escape shocks) will later fail to take initiative in another situation when they *could* escape or avoid the punishment. By contrast, animals which are taught personal control by successfully escaping their first shocks adapt easily to a new situation. The investigator who conducted these experiments, Martin Seligman, notes similarities with human situations, such as when depressed or oppressed people become passive because they believe that their actions make no difference.[10] Like Job, they feel helpless when rewards seem not justly contingent on their actions.[11] Making positive reinforcement contingent on behavior is, from one perspective, manipulative. But one can argue that from the person's perspective it increases freedom, because personal action controls outcomes. If outcomes are not contingent on behavior, people feel helpless—unable to control their rewards and punishments. The evidence suggests that this is especially true of certain population groups—blacks, the elderly, and women, for example.

Learned helplessness is the reverse of the illusion of control discussed in Chapter 7. Just as we sometimes erroneously believe in the power of our acts—manic optimism being the extreme case—so we also sometimes underestimate our ability to help ourselves—reactive depression being the extreme of this. Helpless dogs and depressed patients both suffer paralysis of the will, passive resignation, even physical immobility. Here is a clue to how institutions—whether malevolent, like concentration camps, or benevolent, like hospitals for the physically and mentally infirm—can unwittingly dehumanize people. A sense of personal choice, a perception of control over one's situation, is now known to be linked to health and survival.[12] Several diseases have been connected to feelings of helplessness and diminished choice and so has the rapidity of decline and death in concentration camps and nursing homes. New experimental evidence indicates that hospital patients who are induced to believe in their ability to control stress require fewer pain relievers and sedatives and are seen by nurses as exhibiting less anxiety.[13]

In related experiments, elderly patients in a highly rated nursing home were treated in one of two ways.[14] One treatment stressed the patients' opportunities for choice, their possibilities for influencing nursing-home policy, and their responsibility "to make of your life whatever you want." They were also given small decisions to make and responsibilities to fulfill. Over the ensuing three weeks, 93 percent of this group showed improved alertness, activity, and happiness. With the other patient group the benevolent caregivers stressed "our responsibility to make this a home you can be proud of and happy in." The patients were treated as passive recipients of well-intentioned, sympathetic care. A substantial majority of these elderly persons were rated by themselves, by interviewers, and by nurses as further debilitated three weeks later. These observations of subjects ranging from helpless dogs to residents of institutions confirm the extreme consequences of losing one's sense of personal control over the environment.

The implications of this research are decidedly pro-democratic. Systems of governing or managing people which maximize perceived freedom will be most conducive to health and happiness. Managers may have to make hard decisions about basic priorities, but within these bounds there is usually room for many choices. If institutionalized patients are allowed choice in such matters as what to eat for breakfast, when to go to a movie, whether to sleep late or get up early, they may live longer and certainly will be happier than if these decisions are made for them.

Achievement Motivation

The recent studies on locus of control were preceded by David McClelland's well-known investigations of achievement motivation.[15] The need to achieve has typically been assessed by asking people to make up imaginative stories about ambiguous pictures and then analyzing the content of their stories for achievement-related themes. The procedure is sufficiently objective that a computer has been programed to score the stories. People with a high need for achievement seem to strive for an internal standard of excellence. Children and college students with strong achievement motives set difficult, but reachable, levels of aspiration when challenged with laboratory games. Adults with high need for achievement set their sights on moderately difficult occupations, especially on entrepreneurial occupations in which their initiative and performance controls their earnings.

McClelland and his associates have identified cultural variations among levels of achievement motivation. One study found that the strength of achievement themes in fourth-grade texts from countries all over the world predicted economic growth in these countries during the ensuing twenty years. Another study rated achievement imagery in children's readers in the United States since 1810. Achievement imagery declined from 1810 to 1830, then rose until 1890, and has been falling ever since. Interestingly, the annual number of patents per capita issued by the U. S. Patent Office follows by a few years the curve of rising and falling achievement imagery.

The need to achieve is related to internal locus of control, but differs in that the former is a *motive* or desire to succeed, whereas the latter entails a belief or *expectancy* that, with effort, one *could* succeed. High achievement motive coupled with internal locus of control therefore breeds optimism; high motivation coupled with external locus of control breeds despair. Both high motivation and internal locus of control contribute to high actual achievement: increases in a person's internal locus of control predicts increased achievement, and so also do increases in the achievement motive.

McClelland and David Winter discovered that the need to achieve was lower among small businessmen in India than in America.[16] To test whether achievement motivation could be learned, a sample of Indian businessmen was taught to think and act in ways characteristic of businessmen with high achievement motivation. Two years later, those who experienced the achievement motivation training were found to have started four times as many new businesses, invested twice as much new capital, and created more than twice as many jobs as had an untrained, but otherwise comparable, group.

Personal Causation

Richard deCharms blends ideas from both the achievement and locus of control literatures in his theory of personal causation.[17] His postulate is that our basic motive is to be a causal agent, effective in producing change in the environment. This is reminiscent of Robert White's earlier concept of competence motivation and of Jack Brehm's theory of psychological reactance.[18] Competence motivation is an inborn drive evidenced in both primates and children to explore and manipulate the environment. Reactance theory is based on the idea that if our freedom is threatened, we will react to restore the freedom. People resist being coerced and manipulated. Experiments that support reactance theory demonstrate that choices which are threatened by a loss of freedom take on more value than they had before the threat. This human tendency to assert freedom of choice is exemplified when parental interference intensifies feelings of romantic love (the Romeo-and-Juliet effect) and when we use reverse psychology on our young children by commanding the opposite of what we wish. Wise parents therefore direct their children in ways that allow the child to maintain a sense of personal freedom. Better to ask, "When do you plan to practice your piano?" than to attempt to coerce the child on the spot. You may recall that this advice also follows from a central theme of Chapter 5—that greater internalization results from *chosen* action than from coerced action.

In order to study personal causation, deCharms used the terms *origin* and *pawn* as a way to characterize both persons and situations. People who have a strong internal locus of control and who are motivated to initiate behavior which changes their environment are referred to as "Origins." People who view themselves as pushed around by external forces rather than originating their own behavior are referred to as "Pawns." Situations may likewise be characterized in terms of the relative amount of freedom and compulsion which they prescribe: sometimes people are treated as Origins and sometimes as Pawns.

An ambitious study tested the assumption that treating people as Origins—helping them to take responsibility for their own behavior—would enhance their sense of personal causation, which would, in turn, result in more competent and satisfying behavior.[19] Black sixth- and seventh-grade teachers in an inner-city district received personal-causation training—a week-long residential training session designed to promote Origin rather than Pawn behavior. During the ensuing year the teachers were also assisted in designing classroom exercises to increase children's self-concept, achievement motivation, and sense of personal responsibility. The results: personal-caustion training affected both teachers and students. Trained teachers were more likely than untrained teachers to advance within the school system and to treat their students as Origins. The children in the experimental classrooms revealed an increased sense of personal causation in imaginative stories they wrote and, unlike untrained children, they did not fall behind in scores on a national test of academic achievement.

Intrinsic versus Extrinsic Motivation

An interesting controversy in psychology today concerns the effects of extrinsic rewards on intrinsic motivation. The evidence suggests that the more you pay people to do what they would do anyway, the *less* favorable becomes their attitude toward that activity.[20] People (and monkeys) who are rewarded for an enjoyable activity, such as playing with puzzles, subsequently like the puzzles less than when extrinsic incentives are not attached to the activity. Promise children a reward for what they intrinsically enjoy and you will turn play into work. (An *unanticipated* reward afterwards does not diminish intrinsic interest, apparently since people can still then attribute their behavior to their own motivation.)[21]

One year my younger son voraciously consumed six or eight books a week from our public library—until a reading club was started which promised a party to those who read ten books in three months. About two weeks after the reading club had been formed he began checking out only one or two books during our weekly visit. Why? "Because you only need to read ten books, you know." As Mark Twain demonstrated with Tom Sawyer's adventure of whitewashing the fence: "Work consists of whatever a body is *obliged* to do. . . . Play consists of whatever a body is not obliged to do."

One explanation of this effect is that external rewards cause people to lose their feeling of personal causality, and instead to feel like pawns to the rewards. In one experiment, students tried to convince others that students should have some say about course offerings in their college—a position in which all believed. Half were paid to espouse this position and half did so without pay. Those who were paid indicated later a *decrease* in the strength of their belief. This demonstrates that rewarding people for supporting something they believe in may undermine their belief.[22] Extrinsic incentives can lead a person to attribute causality to the environment rather than self, thereby undermining the person's sense of self-determination.

This explanation is closely related to the emphasis of Chapter 5 on the necessity of perceived freedom of choice if behavior commitment is to engender attitude change. (The corresponding biblical witness is that the more we give of ourselves without thought of gaining external rewards, such as appreciation and public esteem, the more we internally know abundant life. By emptying ourselves we become filled.) Although controversy surrounds this new research literature, the importance of personal causation and the danger of preoccupation with environmental control is underscored by this growing interest in the intrinsic ("cognitive") sources of human motivation.

Popular Applications

An additional indication of the importance of belief in our own freedom comes from popular books and courses instructing people how to become more sensitive to the effect their actions and communications have on others. In self-assertion training the individual is taught to *choose* how to act in a given circumstance and then led to rehearse assertive responses which enable effective expression of feelings, desires, and thoughts. By practicing freedom of choice, first in a group situation and later in everyday situations, some people exchange their sense of helplessness for an increased ability to exercise social power—personal control over their environment. Even the respected behavioral psychologist Albert Bandura now proposes that effective psychological procedures, whatever their form, serve as a means of creating and strengthening expectations of personal efficacy:

The strength of people's convictions in their own effectiveness is likely to affect whether they will even try to cope with given situations . . . [and] determine how much effort people will expend and how long they will persist. . . .[23]

Although this research on the origins and effects of personal control is unprecedented, the emphasis on realizing one's potential for personal control is hardly original with recent psychology. The Horatio Alger theme is an enduring American myth, and one that has surfaced recently in what may be called the theology of "The Little Engine that Could," which stresses self-reliance and "possibility thinking." Since I am writing these words in my office in Hope College's Norman Vincent Peale Science Center, it is fitting that I sum up this survey of recent theory and research by recognizing that there *is* a power to positive thinking![24]

Conclusion

Our survey of recent investigations of personal control reveals the importance of a belief in personal freedom and the benefits of maximizing individual freedom. There is a deep tendency in us to become what we imagine ourselves to be. It is, as we have seen, a matter of considerable practical importance if human beings think of themselves as devoid of intentionality, responsibility, and freedom. Our belief in our own freedom—our feeling strong, capable, and self-confident as against feeling weak, helpless, and defeated—has substantial effects on our destiny in life. Freedom is not just a matter of minimal coercive pressures upon us, but also of our own internal beliefs. If I assume that I have the power to make significant choices, I am more likely to exericise to the limit my potential for choice. People who believe they have responseability act with more responsibility. Unlike some of the research summarized in previous chapters, the research we have just reviewed *confirms* our traditional beliefs. Whether you look at dogs or people, those who persevere with hope do better than those who sink into cynicism, despair, and defeatism.

Humanity's unique achievement is its ability to control the environment for its own purposes. Have dominion over the earth, the Scriptures tell us; "Don't let the world around you squeeze you into its own mold," as the environment does to lower organisms.[25] Humanity, to a much greater extent than any other species, is master of its environment and hence responsible for its own future. Our mind's ability to foresee, choose, and control events places us at the apex of the creation.

But this is only half our story.

THE WISDOM OF ASSUMING THAT OTHER PEOPLE ARE CONTROLLED

We have seen how vital it is that we understand our own actions to be substantially under our personal control. To view ourselves as passive billiard balls in a complex universe of forces is a recipe for helplessness and, in extreme cases, defines a mental disorder. But when we shift our perspective from looking at ourselves from the inside to observing others from the outside, we do well to also shift our assumption about the locus of causality to the complementary emphasis on environmental control. I will support this assertion with two lines of argument. First, I will argue that, as a matter of objective truth, environmental regulation is far more extensive than most people realize. Second, I will advocate that this assumption be made for its practical wisdom: Christian attitudes and actions toward others are more likely to result from assuming external control than from assuming that other people act of their own free will.

The Great Lesson of Social Psychology

If I were to summarize all of social psychological research in a single statement, it would be that social behavior depends primarily on present and past social situations, including how these situations affect a particular personality type, *not* on pervasive personality traits which are consistently evident across situations.* Although it often does make a difference who a person is and how he

---

* This statement needs four qualifications. First, there are exceptions. For example, intellectual competencies (IQ and its relatives) have much more consistent effects across situations than do nonintellective personality traits.

Second, it is inappropriate to pit the social situation against individual differences and assign weights to each for the same reason as it is difficult to weigh the relative

or she interprets the situation, it is nonetheless true that we cannot predict social behavior if we know *only* about a person's general personal dispositions.

The role of social situations in behavior does not deny the importance of genetic endowment. The genetic endowment of our whole species and the genetic sources of individual differences within our species are, as was noted in Chapter 3, of enormous consequence, especially to such traits as emotionality and intelligence. Without contradicting these truths, we can nevertheless recognize that part of our genetic endowment, which is more than 99 percent the same as that of every other human being, consists of our being "wired up" to respond to our environment in certain ways. The clearest example of this is the phenomenon of "imprinting." Ducklings, chicks, and goslings exposed to a moving object during a certain few hours after birth become attached to that class of ob-

contributions of heredity and environment to intelligence. The relative importance of the two factors depends on the amount of variation in each of them. One could prove the importance of personality variables by selecting subjects from psychiatric extremes and comparing these trait differences to trivial situational differences. Or one can make a point for the importance of the social situation, as I am about to do, by showing how powerful situational differences overwhelm a normal amount of personality variation.

Third, as I tried to indicate in the statement above, the effect of a social situation will often depend upon the attributes of the individual. Psychologists refer to this as the "interaction" between persons and situations. The interplay between personal and external influences is apparent in recent research on obesity and eating behavior. The effect of food stimuli varies from person to person. Obese people are quite responsive to external food stimuli. Slim people are more responsive to internal ones, such as stomach contractions.

Finally, while the recent literature does emphasize the great importance of the social situation as over against personality traits, we must not forget that the social situation is a human creation. Often, we create or select the very situation which affects us. For example, when two people are interacting, what Person B will do may depend on what Person A did the moment before—A's behavior elicits B's reaction. Person A is generating the situation to which he or she then responds. People who cynically perceive other people as hostile may therefore be realistically perceiving how other people treat them, as in laboratory games where hostility begets hostility. The reciprocal influence of persons and situations was demonstrated in a recent experiment. Men students had a phone conversation with women who they believed were either attractive or unattractive. Analysis of only the women's contributions to the conversations revealed that women who were thought (unknown to them) to be attractive, came to behave in a more friendly, likeable, and sociable manner than the women who were perceived as unattractive. Obviously, the men's perceptions acted as a self-fulfilling prophecy, leading them to act in ways which influenced the women to confirm the stereotype. (See M. Snyder, E. D. Tanke, and E. Berscheid, "Social Perception and Interpersonal Behavior: On the Self-Fulfilling Nature of Social Stereotypes," *Journal of Personality and Social Psychology* 35 [1977]: 656–66.)

jects (normally their own species). This phenomenon is, in a sense, entirely genetic, but it is also entirely environmental.

Human genes are permissive, not prescriptive. While measurable variations in individual traits certainly exist, they have been inferior predictors of many social behaviors when compared to past and present aspects of the social situation. In research studies, global personality traits generally predict only about 10 percent of the variation in observed behavior, just as global attitudes predict only about 10 percent of the variation in behavior.[26] (See Chapter 5.) The degree of honesty, conformity, and aggression a person exhibits, for example, depends substantially on features of the specific situation.

In early 1976, 75 percent of Americans surveyed said they preferred to cut down on their car's fuel consumption by forming carpools, but only 10 percent were actually doing so. When President Nixon called for energy conservation during the Arab Oil Embargo of 1973–74, people's expressed support for the president and for the energy conservation policiy was unrelated to their actual conservation behavior. Situational aspects of the crisis, such as its personal impact or financial incentives for conservation, were much stronger predictors of who conserved and who didn't.[27] Shortly after taking office President Carter declared that combating the energy crisis was "the moral equivalent of war." Americans heard this, but during the following summer automobile gas consumption nevertheless rose to record levels.

The capacity of personal trait or attitude scores to predict social behavior is improved if we average behavior across different situations, but this is like predicting a baseball player's batting average across a whole season of different games. Even if we could do so, it is still true that in any particular time at bat the behavior of the batter depends substantially on such factors as the attributes of the pitcher, and how the situation interacts with the attributes of the batter.

Rather than looking at complicated interactions between situations and persons, I will demonstrate the impact of the social situation with some simple examples of the effects of social environment on social behavior. We are all unique individuals, yes, but our similarities in responding to social situations often overshadow the unique personalities we bring to the situation. Every person is in some respects like all other persons and in other respects like no other person. It is the magnitude of the former which we fail to appreciate.[28]

This illusion concerning the magnitude of our uniqueness enables astrology and graphology to thrive. Ask some friends their birthdates. Then read them each this "astrological description" and have them each judge how well it fits.

You have a strong need for other people to like you and for them to admire you. You have a tendency to be critical of yourself. You have a great deal of unused energy which you have not turned to your advantage. While you have some personality weaknesses, you are generally able to compensate for them. Your sexual adjustment has presented some problems for you. Disciplined and controlled on the outside, you tend to be worrisome and insecure inside. At times you have serious doubts as to whether you have made the right decision or done the right thing. You prefer a certain amount of change and variety and become dissatisfied when hemmed in by restrictions and limitations. You pride yourself on being an independent thinker and do not accept other opinions without satisfactory proof. You have found it unwise to be too frank in revealing yourself to others. At times you are extroverted, affable, sociable, while at other times you are introverted, wary and reserved. Some of your aspirations tend to be pretty unrealistic.

If your friends are like my students they will agree that it fits amazingly well. As P. T. Barnum once said, "There's a sucker born every minute." The gullibility which results from the many illusions of human thought makes people easy prey for entrepreneurs in astrology, psychology, and even religion. Moreover, the clients are likely to be satisfied with what they receive, thus increasing the professionals' confidence in what they market.

The impact of the social situation is already well-known to any student of anthropology or cross-cultural psychology. I can recall visiting Indian reservations during my boyhood in the Pacific Northwest. The apparent unemployment, alcoholism, and lack of achievement motivation was generally attributed to the Indian disposition, thereby relieving us of guilt for their condition and creating a handy rationale for perpetuating discrimination. Yet we all know that things were not always this way for Native Americans. In an earlier age, in a different situation, they were a different people.

A tragic example of the degeneration of a culture in response to changing situation is reported by Colin Turnbull in *The Mountain People*. The Ik people of northeastern Uganda were at one time a peaceful, cooperative society. But when the Ugandan government made the Ik's tribal grounds into a national park and moved them to a new mountainside area, they developed into a "passionless, feelingless association of individuals." They would laugh when a young child grabbed a hot coal, beat their elders, and, as starvation set in, hoard food and abandon old people to die. It seems, concluded Turnbull, that "those values that we all hold to be basic to humanity . . . are not inherent in humanity, not a necessary part of human nature."[29]

There is not room to communicate here the vast additional social psychological evidence of the importance of the social situation. But four examples will illustrate the point. First, recall Stanley Milgram's obedience experiments described in Chapter 5. These experiments dramatically demonstrate how easy it is for ordinary, well-meaning people, simply doing their jobs without any particular hostility, to become agents in a terrrible, destructive process. As a result of experiments like Milgram's, popular explanations of Nazi obedience in terms of "German national character" now seem less convincing than situational explanations. Were the actors in the My Lai massacre all suffering personality disorders? As our nations' leaders occasionally demonstrate for us, evil deeds are often not the product of uniquely evil people acting from consciously malevolent movites, but of good bureaucrats simply performing their role.

Another well-known series of experiments demonstrates the same point. When Kitty Genovese was murdered in New York in front of thirty-eight apathetic bystanders, most observers explained the apathy in terms of personal factors such as alienation and dehumanized character. Subsequent research has clearly shown, however, that situational factors—number of bystanders, whether the victim is known, ambiguity of the situation—are major determinants of a phenomenon most people thought best explained in terms of personal disposition. An illustrative experiment was suggested by the parable of the Good Samaritan.[30] Princeton Seminary students on their way to record an extemporaneous talk either about an irrelevant subject or about the Good Samaritan parable encountered a shabbily dressed person slumped by the side of the road. Neither the religious disposition of the passers-by nor their contemplation of the parable had much impact on the likelihood of their helping. But a situational manipulation—being told or not told to hurry to their destination—had a substantial effect on helping.

A third example: Why are prisons so laden with conflict and bitterness? Is the institution dehumanizing because it attracts evil people as inmates and guards or because of the corrupting effects of evil dynamics which are inherent in the prison situation? (The way to reform prisons is "to convert the jailer," says one famous preacher.) In a widely publicized demonstration, Phillip Zimbardo nullified personality trait factors by randomly assigning some exemplary students to be guards and others to be prisoners in a simulated prison.[31] After several days the students were thinking and acting like real guards and prisoners. The pathological characteristics of the prison situation elicited extreme antisocial behaviors (guards brutally harassed the prisoners, for instance) which were not related to pre-existing personality traits. The destructive hostility was therefore attributable to the role relations inherent in this powerful situation rather than to personal dispositions.

The same point is even more powerfully evident in Langdon Gilkey's fascinating description of the Shantung Compound, a World War II internment camp into which the Japanese military herded foreigners residing in China.[32] The internees were provided only bare essentials but were not subjected to torture or starvation. The situation elicited a pervasive self-centeredness which was evident in *all* types of people—missionaries, doctors, lawyers, professors, business people, junkies, and prostitutes.

These observations—and many others besides—reveal that manipulations of the social situation have substantial impact, often much more than global personality differences. I witness this directly when I teach classes at both 8:30 A.M. and 7:00 P.M. The freshly scrubbed faces are silent at 8:30 A.M.; at 7:00 P.M. it nearly takes a bullhorn to break up the party. There are some individual differences in talkativeness, to be sure, but the difference between the situations far exceeds the differences among people.

If all the scholarly evidence does not convince you of the enormous power of social influences, then I urge you to breach some significant norm, to "not be conformed to this world."[33] Just as a fish becomes aware of its water as it jumps out of it, so do we become aware of the power of culture when we attempt to violate some simple norm. There are people who have chosen to die in a burning building rather than run outside naked. Says Milgram:

Embarrassment and the fear of violating apparently trivial norms often lock us into intolerable predicaments. And these are not minor regulatory forces in social life, but basic ones. If you think it is easy to violate social constraints, get onto a bus and sing out loud. Full-throated song now, no humming. Many people will say it is easy to carry out this act, but not one in a hundred will be able to do it. The point is not to *think* about singing, but to try to *do* it. Only in action can you fully realize the forces operative in social behavior.[34]

Having emphasized the enormous impact of the social environment, we nevertheless must remember that *both* the environment and the individual are basic for human behavior because they dynamically interact. The locus of control is *both* in the social environment *and* in the individual persons who create and constitute the social environment. Psychology must therefore study *both* environmental factors and person factors and the complex ways in which these interact.

Attributing Responsibility to Self and Others: The Science of Pride

The human tendency to overestimate the importance of personal disposition and to underestimate the significance of the social situation has recently become the subject of considerable scientific scrutiny. This is one aspect of what has recently been the hottest area of research in social psychology: attribution theory.[35] Attribution theory involves analysis of the amateur psychology that people use in trying to understand their own and others' behavior. It holds that we are always looking for the causes of behavior. We are naive scientists, sifting and simplifying the complex events of our environment in order to ultimately locate the cause for a person's action either within the person (an internal disposition) or in the environmental situation (an external locus of control). Attribution theorists seek to identify the rules that govern when we will attribute responsibility to personal dispositions and when to the external situation.

Several fascinating findings have emerged from this research. First, we are not very good scientists; systematic errors bias our interpretation of causality. For example, we tend to attribute others' actions to their personal dispositions ("John was angry because he is a hostile person") even when we would attribute a same similar act on our own part to environmental factors ("I was angry because everything was going wrong").

In the experiments which make this point researchers do not ask people to directly rate the extent to which their behavior is externally determined—most people will simply assert their freedom—but rather they ask a more neutral question about the *reasons* that prompt certain actions. Students in one study attributed their own choice of a major about equally to the environmental situation (e.g., "Chemistry is a high-paying field") and to personal causes. But when asked to list reasons for their best friend's choice, they listed personal causes three times more often. A number of experiments have also demonstrated that when someone performs an act which someone else observes, the actor will likely explain his or her own behavior in terms of the situation, but the observer will hold the actor personally responsible.

We have all experienced this in moments of conflict with someone close to us. When my wife and I are upset with each other, I understand my own feelings as a just response to the situation, but attribute her feelings to an evil disposition. Her perception is, of course, just the reverse. Still, the better we know another's situation, the more likely we are to find environmental causes, which is why marital partners often become more understanding and accepting with time.

Another example of attribution error is the "Peter Principle" that people tend to be promoted to their level of incompetence. People who excel at a job may be promoted until they reach a position where they no longer excel. The manager's mistake is attributing the employee's previous success to personal traits rather than to the happy fit between the situation and the person.

A dramatic demonstration of this powerful human tendency to overestimate others' freedom helps us to understand the differing perceptions of Watergate-related activities by persons inside and outside the Nixon White House. Why did the principal actors in the Watergate drama portray their own acts as morally justified while most outside observers interpreted the same acts as reprehensible corruption? Was the President coldly calculating in his protestations of innocent motives, or were there sincere differences in causal attributions by actors and observers of the Watergate drama? To find out, Steven West and several colleagues induced people to agree to commit an illegal activity similar to the Watergate burglary.[36] Subjects were approached by a private investigator and asked to assist in burglarizing a local advertising firm on behalf of the Internal Revenue Service. After an elaborate justification for this activity was created and immunity from prosecution guaranteed (strong situational pressure!), approximately one-half agreed to participate. All subjects were then debriefed (there was no actual burglary) and asked why they had decided as they did. Other people were told about the experiment in great detail, and then they too were asked to explain the behavior of those who had agreed to participate. Can you guess the results? The "actors" tended to attribute their participation to environmental factors, whereas the "observers" were more likely to attribute the actors' decisions to personal dispositions. This experiment demonstrates that an actor's sincere interpretation of reality can be quite different from that of outside observers, including the press, *even when both have identical information concerning the action and its outcomes*.

Consider Patricia Hearst: Should responsibility for her criminal acts have been attributed to her situation or to her personal disposition? Even if we knew the complete truth about what led her to act as she did, we may be sure that outside observers would still be more likely to assume personal causation than would Ms. Hearst.

This exemplifies many conflict situations—parent and child, society and its offenders, wife and husband: "You are to blame, and you must be punished," versus "It wasn't my fault, and you have no right to punish me."

Why these differing attributions? Attribution theorists point out, first, that we generally have more information about our own behavior and its inconsistencies than we have about that of others, which makes us more sensitive to the events which influence our own actions. Second, we have a different perspective when observing than when acting. When we watch another person act, that person occupies the center of our attention and so seems to cause whatever happens. When we act, the environment commands our attention. Finally, it appears that as observers, we derive some benefit from assuming that the accidents, failures, and faults of others have an internal locus of control, for this relieves our own sense of vulnerability. To invoke environmental factors is to admit we might do the same. Whereas, by believing that this is a just world, that victims deserve their fate (as Job's three friends insisted to him), we may compliment ourselves that we are not so evil and negligent.[37] For these reasons we are much less understanding and accepting of others than of ourselves. It seems that just as professional scientists' perceptions are biased by their beliefs and values, so also are the perceptions of the masses of "naive scientists."

This conclusion is driven home by one more fascinating discovery: The inclination to interpret our own acts as situationally induced but the acts of others as personally caused depends on the nature of the act. While we readily blame the environment for our failures, we are somewhat more likely to take credit for our successes. Here is human pride! Since, by contrast, we tend to attribute *others'* negative behaviors to personal traits, this is a recipe for social problems, as when the policeman attributes ghetto violence to the personal traits of the residents, but attributes his own defensive behavior to the threatening situation. The residents respond in reciprocal fashion—attributing their toughness to the survival demands of the situation, but perceiving the policeman's behavior as due to an arrogant and brutal disposition.

This tendency to assume responsibility only for our successful acts has been experimentally demonstrated in various ways. In conflict simulations, students tend to see themselves as responsible for their winnings, but hold their opponents responsible when they fail. Other experiments indicate that teachers take credit for their successful students, but blame poor performance on the student. The archsymbol of this human attribution tendency is, of course, Adam's excuse that "the woman you gave me . . ." You may be able to demonstrate the principle by asking some student to recall a recent failure (e.g., a D on an exam) and indicate the reasons for it. Next, have this person analyze a recent success. Is the success more likely to be attributed to personal causation?

The same dynamic is evident with college faculty. When frustrated in our attempts to publish scholarly material, we are inclined to attribute responsibility to the situation: "With these horrible teaching loads and inadequate resources, it is nearly impossible to be a productive scholar."[38] When we do publish, we are considerably less inclined to attribute responsibility to the environment and more inclined to take personal credit.

The pervasiveness of human pride has been evident in other experimental situations as well. In both the Milgram obedience experiments and the simulated Watergate experiment just described, people who are told the situation in detail rarely predict they would accede to the immoral act. But they flatter themselves, for the experiments have already shown that many of them would. I have observed a similar self-flattery time and again in my own research. As a demonstration, answer the following story problem. Your task is to advise our protagonist, Henry, how much risk he should be willing to take:

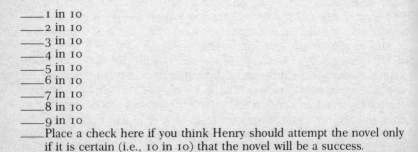

Henry is a writer who is said to have considerable creative talent but who so far has been earning a comfortable living by writing cheap Westerns. Recently, he has come up with an idea for a potentially significant novel. If it could be written and accepted it might have considerable literary impact and be a big boost to his career. On the other hand, if he was not able to work out his idea, or if the novel was a flop, he would have expended considerable time and energy without remuneration.

Imagine that you are advising Henry. Please check the *lowest* probability that you would consider acceptable for Henry to attempt to write the novel.

Henry should attempt to write the novel if the chances that the novel will be a success are at least:

_____1 in 10
_____2 in 10
_____3 in 10
_____4 in 10
_____5 in 10
_____6 in 10
_____7 in 10
_____8 in 10
_____9 in 10
_____Place a check here if you think Henry should attempt the novel only if it is certain (i.e., 10 in 10) that the novel will be a success.

Now that you have decided your own response, guess how your average peer would respond to this item.

If you are like 75 percent of the participants in our studies, you guessed your own response to be more in the socially preferred direction (writing the novel, even if the odds of success are low) than your average peer. This turns out to be a pervasive human tendency—people tend to see themselves as better than average. Surveys have repeatedly shown that most American business people believe themselves to be more ethical than the average business person and that people perceive their own views as less prejudiced than the norm of their community. An exhaustive series of investigations with adolescent and adult French people confirms the same strong and consistent tendency: people tend to perceive themselves as superior to the average members of their groups.[39] A large body of recent experimental research indicates that individuals in successful groups see themselves as more responsible for the group's performance than do individuals in groups which fail. Moreover, these members of successful groups perceive themselves as more responsible for the outcome than their fellow group members.[40] All these perceptions are, of course, distorted; the average person cannot be better than the average person.

We can bring this even closer to home. In situations where you have worked with others did you see yourself as more or less effective than your average fellow employee? Few among us see ourselves as average or less. Many of us therefore tend to feel at least a small injustice has been done when merit raises are announced and half receive less than the average increase. Note that our perceptions of injustice do not necessarily depend on actual injustice. Even if, unknown to us, God himself prescribed the salary increases according to his most perfect justice, many of us would still be upset—unless our self-perceptions distributed themselves in conformity with the true distribution of employee excellence, which they surely do not. (Where pay is determined by a fixed salary schedule, I venture the prediction that many secretly feel that equal pay is, for them, inequitable pay, since they are more competent and committed than most others.)

To sum up, I have argued in this section that we should generally assume *others'* actions to be externally controlled. If the truth be known, there is a deep human tendency to underestimate the environmental sources of others' behavior. Social behavior is more dependent upon the specific situation than upon general personal dispositions. But we typically see it just the other way around. We err in making attributions of causality. What the Christian knows as the basic sin of pride is evidenced in a wide variety of experimental situations. This evidence that we attribute our failings to the situation, even while we blame others for their failings, documents Kierkegaard's contention that becoming aware of our own sin is like trying to see our own eyeballs. Goethe put it delightfully: "People n'er feel the devil's touch—e'en tho he has them in his clutch."

The Nature of Sin and Evil

If all this is true, does it not follow that most sin is *not* a product of conscious temptation, *not* a deliberate decision to do evil? As James Burtchaell has suggested, we are likely to see our own evil as something that "happens to us," if we see it at all. "When bent upon our own self-aggrandizing purposes, we confuse ourselves with double-talk of the mind, we emit a cloud of 'if's' and 'but's', we never look ourselves in the eye. Evil is hardly reflective. . . . Remember that in Christ's parable on judgment the condemned are sent away for offenses that were unwitting."[41] The net result of this self-deceit is that when looking for sins to confess, we trivialize sin. Sin becomes the little impulses to which we consent, not the lovelessness and corruption of motives which unconsciously infect all our action.[42] This is one reason we cannot elect to save ourselves from our sin—our sin is seldom a deliberate choice to do evil.

The trivializing of sin is evident in the way the public evaluates presidential candidates. Is candidate X a decent person? Does the candidate refrain from lying, graft, and excessive profanity? Well and good, but the Scriptures join attribution research in reminding us that sin and evil run deeper than deliberate personal evil. History is filled with examples of people who perpetrated or perpetuated human suffering for what they perceived as laudable motives. The more significant question of presidential morality therefore concerns the public morality of each candidate. Whose policies will best fulfill the biblical mandates of love and justice?

The first implication of this analysis, then, is that sin and evil are not limited to knowing, guilt-producing choices to do evil. Human evil is rarely described as such by its doers. "No one can see his own errors," noted the Psalmist.[43] "Every man," William Saroyan wrote many years ago, "is a good man in a bad world—as he himself knows."

These are not easy words to hear. We would much rather listen to election year schmaltz about the American people being so good and decent and sinless or to the humanist illusion of the inherent goodness and morality of human nature than to realize that "if we claim to be sinless, we are self-deceived and strangers to the truth."[44]

But we had best not deceive ourselves. Better to be grounded in reality than in falsehood. Irving Janis has noted that one source of destructive international conflict is the tendency of both sides to believe in the inherent morality of their acts.[45] If we build missile bases near the Russian border in Turkey this is to protect the free world from communism, but if Russia puts missiles in Cuba this is an aggressive threat to our security. Their attribution of motives tends, of course, to be the reverse. This phenomenon of "mirror-image perception" is a characteristic of most human conflicts.

The second implication of our analysis is that evil is collective as well as personal. My emphasis on the extent to which individual acts are a function of the situation may disturb some because it helps pass the buck for evil to the social context in which evil occurs. If the experimental demonstrations of situationally-induced evil do not convince you that this is appropriate, if historical occurrences such as Nazi Germany, the My Lai massacre, and Watergate leave you still unconvinced, then consider the biblical evidence. In Revelation there are images of evil transcending individuals, while institutions and political systems become bestial and demonically corrupt. These biblical images of evil power convey a profoundly important meaning. In Rudolph Bultmann's words, the concept of Satan and the evil spirits

rests upon the experience . . . that our own actions are often so puzzling; men are often carried away by their passions and are no longer master of themselves, with the results that inconceivable wickedness breaks forth from them. . . . The conception of Satan as ruler over the world expresses a deep insight; namely, the insight that evil is not only to be found here and there in the world, but that all particular evils make up one single power which in the last analysis grows from the very actions of men, which form an atmosphere, a spiritual tradition, which overwhelms every man. The consequences and effects of our sins become a power dominating us, and we cannot free ourselves from them. . . . The evil for which every man is responsible individually has nevertheless become a power which mysteriously enslaves every member of the human race.[46]

My first main reason for urging an operating assumption that other people are determined has been because we underappreciate the truth of this assumption. My second reason will be more pragmatic, for our assumptions about human nature can also be examined in terms of their practical consequences.

Christian Belief and Racial Prejudice

No aspect of religion has been subject to more social psychological scrutiny than the relationship of Christian faith and ethnic prejudice. The mass of studies can be simply summarized:

1. Church members evidence more racial prejudice than non-members, and
2. Racial prejudice is directly related to the degree of adherence to traditional Christian beliefs.[47]

These findings have proved constant no matter where and when the study was conducted or what type of ethnic prejudice was studied. Although these facts are indisputable, it is not clear what they mean. Knowing the relationship between two variables—religion and prejudice—tells us nothing about their causal connection; in fact, there might be no causal connection at all. One interpretation is that strong religious commitment causes prejudice. But three newer sets of studies clearly indicate that this popular conclusion is wrong, or at least greatly oversimplified:

3. Among church members, high levels of participation (e.g., weekly attendance) is associated with greater tolerance than found among occasional attenders,
4. Intrinsic commitment to Christian faith as an end in itself is associated with greater tolerance than found among those whose religious commitment is motivated by self-serving, extrinsic benefits (comfort, inner peace, social benefits), and
5. The views of Christian clergy are more compassionate than the views of their laity.

These findings suggest that it is *not* the depth of one's piety, but the conservatism of one's religious content that is associated with bigotry. The very devout are actually less prejudiced than the more superficially religious.

Still, we may inquire, why this connection between conservative belief content and racial intolerance? Might belief in free will or determinism affect a person's sensitivity to suffering and injustice? Charles Glock and Rodney Stark conclude from their extensive surveys of California church members that a central aspect of popular doctrine—the concept of free will—contributes directly to race prejudice.[48] Another recent study found that belief in free will predicts prejudice, even when orthodoxy is held constant.[49] Why is this so? If other people are presumed free agents, capable of rising above miserable circumstance, in control of their own destinies and thus responsible for their fates, then it follows that impoverished minorities can be held to blame for their lot in life and for any undesirable behavior traits which are perceived. A radical belief in free will allows one to put the blame for disadvantage upon those who are disadvantaged and to accept credit for one's own achievements; judgment of others and pride in oneself are facilitated by a strong belief in free will. Thus, to the extent that Christians accept the concept of free will, they reject one of the premises of the battle against prejudice and discrimination. The point can be extended to poverty in general. Linking poverty with moral failure can keep us from feeling guilty about the poor and reassure us that it is unlikely we will ever become poor.

Determinism and Christian Attitudes

The practical consequences of our implicit philosophy can also be seen in the attitudes of those who assume that human thought and action are determined. The working assumption of behavioral scientists is that human behavior is not capricious—causes are ultimately to be found in one's genetic endowment and social environment. The importance of an individual's own "willpower" is not denied; indeed, personal control is, as we have seen, a part of the process of reciprocal control between persons and environments.

Although the evidence for personal control very strongly confirms the importance of belief in our own freedom, it also indicates how *situations* can create a sense of helplessness and external control. Both the conservative and the liberal are right—the conservative in emphasizing the importance of individual initiative and sense of responsibility, and the liberal in emphasizing the constraints of social situations. Doctrinaire liberals and doctrinaire conservatives both propound only half truths. For every chicken discovered by an environmentally oriented liberal, the conservative can discover a prior egg in personal slothfulness, and vice versa. Note also that the model of reciprocal causation between persons and environments is dynamic. This is in contrast to one-sided mechanistic-behavioristic models, which depict the environment as an autonomous force (e.g., Skinner: "A person does not act upon the world, the world acts upon him"), and to individualistic political and theological views which are preoccupied with personal decisions and self-initiatives.[50] Preoccupation with personal freedom nourishes the sins of pride; overemphasizing external control nourishes the sins of slothfulness.

The working assumption of determinism always moves the behavioral scientist to look behind a person's depression or violence or laziness to ask what brought the person to act thus and so. Thus alcoholism is now seen as a medical problem rather than as a moral failure. Instead of ending the inference chain at personal disposition, the human sciences go a step further to ask about the sources of that personal disposition. Spinoza expressed this well: "I have made a ceaseless effort not to ridicule, not to bewail, nor to scorn human actions, but to understand them."[51] It is therefore not surprising that behavioral scientists are among the strongest advocates of social change. And what would you guess to be the prevailing political identification of political scientists, sociologists, and psychologists? Surveys indicate that Democratic party leanings outnumbered Republican leanings by nearly a five to one ratio![52] Philosophical and religious doctrines are not just abstract truth claims; they are also proposals for the construction of personal attitudes and social orders. This is why reflection on our implicit doctrines of human nature is essential.

We can now tie our analysis of psychology and human freedom back to the earlier theological assertions, for the practical consequences of our assumption about others' freedom can also be expressed in biblical language. Social psychology and the Bible both reject the popular modern idea of an independent, autonomous, self-created person. The biblical conviction of divine determination—of God's foreknowledge, sovereignty, and grace—has implications for our personal attitudes. The first implication is that we should have a sense of *humility and gratitude*. If our response to God is, at bottom, the work of God in our lives, then our proper response is glorification of God, not self. Since we deserve no credit, there is no ground for self-righteous comparison of brownie points. Suppose, suggested Calvin, "the same sermon is preached to one hundred men. Twenty accept it in faith. This does not mean that the eighty are more wicked than the twenty, but that God comes to the aid of the twenty. Thus the distinction in men is found in God's grace alone."[53] Surely this is why Jesus also instructed us to *not judge*. If I were that person whose action I despise I would be acting the same. "There, but for the grace of God, go I." Hate the sin but love the sinner is the root principle.

Throughout history we human beings have been loathe to admit our own dependence. Pelagius, Erasmus, Arminius, and we who today emphasize our capacity to decide freely our own conversion, are all willing to risk getting blamed for our evil (which we see as minimal, anyway) in order to gain credit for our perceived goodness, or at least for our smart decision, and to rest assured that all the evil *other* people do will ultimately be punished.[54] This choice is profoundly at odds with the humility, gratitude, and acceptance of others which grow from a sense of God's complete sovereignty and grace. Pulpit talk about self-determining, self-made humans is hardly conducive to these Christian attitudes. When covenantal theology (as found, in varying degrees, in the Presbyterian, Reformed, Episcopalian, and Lutheran traditions, among others) recognizes baptized infants as full members of the covenant family, it acknowledges that a free human act of faith is not a prerequisite for God's grace. Rather, God's gracious action in Christ precedes one's response in faith. God initiates and the child later chooses to respond as enabled by God's Spirit.

One other consequence of divine determination is our sense of *trust*. To believe that God is in control is a tremendously comforting thought in times of stress. If we do not believe in "the necessary foreknowledge of God and the necessity of events," wrote Luther, "Christian faith is utterly destroyed, and the promises of God and the whole gospel fall to the ground completely; for the Christian's chief and only comfort in every adversity lies in knowing that God does not lie, but brings all things to pass immutably, and that His will cannot be resisted, altered or impeded."[55] Calvin agreed: "Gratitude of mind for the favorable outcome of things, patience in adversity, and also incredible freedom from worry about the future will necessarily follow upon" the knowledge of divine providence.[56]

CONCLUSION

There can be no doubt that the philosophical issue of freedom and determinism has important practical consequences, not only for our view of justice and punishment, but also for our attitudes. We are all naive philosophers with implicit assumptions about our own and others' freedom. An analysis of these assumptions and their effects brings us to a paradoxical conclusion: it is important to see ourselves and to help other people see themselves as free agents because the stream of causation does truly run through our next choice and because to assume otherwise creates a self-fulfilling prophecy of personal impotence. But we also need to more fully appreciate that other people do not autonomously will their own destiny; the truth is that we often overestimate the importance of personal dispositions and doing so contributes to counter-Christian attitudes.

This paradoxical conclusion is at a different level of discourse from the deep mystery of human responsibility within the bounds of divine omnipotence and grace. Our distillation of the psychological research literature has therefore not resolved the deeper philosophical and theological mystery. It does, however, enable us to better understand an analogous paradox from practical theology. The model of reciprocal causation between environments and persons allows us, at any moment, to see either ourselves or others as *object* of external causation or as *agent* of personal causation. Each perspective is correct and complementary to the other, for we are *both* the products and architects of our histories. In one sense, it is wise to understand ourselves as determined, lest we become proud of our achievements and decisions, and to see others as free agents, lest we become paternalistic and manipulative.

I have stressed, however, the complementary views of *self as agent* and *other as caused* in order to cultivate the practical fruits of self-discipline and self-initiative as we view ourselves, and of a quest for understanding and social justice as we relate to others. This also seems to be the emphasis of the Scriptures. When the Bible talks to us directly, it emphasizes our responsibility for our own failings. When it talks about *others,* such as the poor, it generally advocates the complementary perspective: act with compassion toward the oppressed, we are told; take the beam out of your own eye before worrying about the motes in others'; let judgment begin with the house of the Lord.

Consider Proverbs. When speaking to us directly, Proverbs urges self-control of one's passions, receptiveness to instruction and correction, and hard work. But when we turn our attention from ourselves to other people, Proverbs reminds us that "he who oppresses the poor insults his Maker," that "he who despises the hungry man does wrong," and that "the righteous man is concerned for the cause of the helpless, but the wicked understand no such concern."[57]

We generally reverse this wisdom—excusing our own failures, while blaming the poor for their slothfulness. Just as divine sovereignty and human responsibility are warp and woof in the fabric of Christian doctrine, so also an awareness of environmental control and of personal control are warp and woof to a personal existence which steers between the sins of pride and sloth.

Now we are ready to summarize the mysterious picture of human freedom and dependence which has emerged from our review of the theological and scientific literatures.

1. Christian and scientific perspectives share a common ten-

dency to reject the "autonomous self." We are not the first cause of our actions; our acts do not emanate from us merely as a bolt from the blue. The presumption that we are ultimately our own makers, the self-created sources of our own destinies, is an arrogant illusion.

The Christian and scientific perspectives make this assertion for differing reasons. Many theologians have rejected the freedom of the will because this seems to erode one's sense of the completeness of God's providence, sovereignty, and grace and therefore to undercut an attitude of childlike humility. Rejecting free will does accentuate the problem of evil and ultimate moral responsibility, but these mysteries remain even if you grant free will; God could have made things other than they are. Research psychologists are likely to reject human autonomy for different reasons. They do so because of their working assumption of determinism and because the successes of the behavioral sciences reinforce this assumption (although they also point to the bewildering complexity of human action).

The biblical emphasis on divine sovereignty and human dependence does not directly imply a causal determinism. Nevertheless, the biblical view of orderly movement in nature and history from creation to the end of time and the conviction that the created order at every moment reflects the activity and faithfulness of God should prompt Christians to presume the orderliness and regularity of nature and to explore it. Christians are open to the possibility of miracles and mysteries which defy a causal determinism. Yet they are not in need of them because they are convinced that *all* events, whether seemingly miraculous or not, are equally grounded in the power of their Creator.

2. There is ample room for a rich, full-bodied concept of human freedom within the regularity and order of nature and even within determinist science. In fact, recent research *strengthens* our awareness of the magnitude of human freedom, of the importance of our conviction of personal freedom, and of the conditions which are conducive to this conviction. I am talking here not about ultimate free will but about the freedom everyone cares about—the opportunity to choose and shape our personal destinies. This freedom is no mere illusion—it is real and should be maximized.

3. We generally underestimate the extent to which others are externally controlled. This contributes to self-serving attitudes such as prejudice and pride. Viewing others' shortcomings as an understandable product of their life histories and current situations seems closer to truth and more congenial to the practical theology of the Scriptures.

If we feel humbled by the abundant evidence of human dependence and self-deceptive pride, we can nonetheless take heart. The bad news has been heard, yet we can still celebrate, for the final word on our subject is good news: the dignity and value which our lives possess is not conditional upon our voluntary escape from evil or upon our achievement of a pure and loving nature. The ground of our self-acceptance is instead the unconditional affirmation of our creator. "You shall know the truth and the truth will set you free."[58] This is the liberation Pinnochio experienced when, floundering in self-doubt and struggling to justify himself, he turned to his maker, Gepetto, and confessed, "Pappa, I am not sure who I am. But if I'm all right with you, then I guess I'm all right with me." Lacking Pinnochio's experience of grace, we are driven by our insecurities to attempt self-justification. Self-deceptive pride is the inevitable result. Fortunately, establishing our goodness is not the only route to self-acceptance. As we read in the United Presbyterian Confession of 1967:

All human virtue, when seen in the light of God's love in Jesus Christ, is found to be infected by self-interest and hostility. . . . [Yet] new life takes shape in a community in which men know that God loves and accepts them in spite of what they are. They therefore accept themselves and love others, knowing that no man has any ground on which to stand except God's grace.

NOTES

1. Niels Bohr, "On the Notions of Causality and Complementarity," *Science* 111 (1950): 51–54.

2. Albert Bandura, "Behavior Theory and the Models of Man," *American Psychologist* 12 (1974): 863.

3. For more discussion of this see Herbert Kelman's paper: "Manipulation of Human Behavior: An Ethical Dilemma for the Social Scientist," *Journal of Social Issues* 21 (1965): 31–46.

4. Though opponents of empiricism rightfully recognize the inherent limitations of the human sciences, those who would make psychology into another humanities discipline fail to appreciate the importance of the existing humanities and the desirablity of keeping some boundary conditions on what we shall understand the word *psychology* to mean.

5. So fears Paul Jewett: "For me the great threat of psychology to a true and adequate understanding of man is that in its concern to be scientifically objective, psychology may reduce man to mere object" ("A Response to Doctor R. Gorsuch" in *The Nature of Man: A Social Psychological Perspective*, ed. R. Gorsuch and N. Maloney, [Charles Thomas, 1975], p. 99).

6. Gresham M. Sykes and David Matza, "Techniques of Neutralization: A Theory of Delinquency," *American Sociological Review* 22 (1957): 664–70.

7. The application of behavior technologies is, however, sometimes considerably more humanizing than existing alternatives. It has, for instance, considerably enhanced the social freedom of many retarded persons. The positive, individualized aspects of educational applications, such as in computer-assisted instruction, often makes behavior technology substantially more humanizing than existing educational practice.

8. Rotter's Internal-External Locus of Control Scale. See J. P. Robinson and R. P. Shaver, *Measures of Social Psychological Attitudes* (Ann Arbor: Institute for Social Research, 1973), pp. 227–34.

9. I draw these conclusions from the following reviews of the literature: E. Jerry Phares, *Locus of Control in Personality* (General Learning Press, 1976); and A. P. MacDonald, "Internal-External Locus of Control," in Robinson and Shaver, *op. cit.*, pp. 169–243.

10. Martin E. Seligman, *Helplessness: On Depression, Development and Death* (San Francisco: W. H. Freeman, 1975). A short summary is available as "Submissive Death: Giving up on Life," *Psychology Today* 7, no. 12 (May, 1977), pp. 80–85.

11. For an analysis of Job's behavior in terms of research on learned helplessness, see James H. Reynierse, "A Behavioristic Analysis of the Book of Job," *Journal of Psychology and Theology* 3 (1975): 75–81.

12. Herbert M. Lefcourt, "The Function of the Illusions of Control and Freedom," *American Psychologist* 28 (1973): 417–25.

13. Ellen J. Langer, Irving L. Janis and John A. Wolfer, "Reduction of Psychological Stress in Surgical Patients," *Journal of Experimental Social Psychology* 11 (1975): 155–65.

14. Ellen J. Langer and Judith Rodin, "The Effects of Choice and Enhanced Personal Responsibility for the Aged: A Field Experiment in an Institutional Setting," *Journal of Personality and Social Psychology* 34 (1976): 191–98.

15. David C. McClelland, *The Achieving Society* (Princeton, N.J.: Van Nostrand, 1961).

16. David C. McClelland and David G. Winter, *Motivating Economic Achievement* (New York: Free Press, 1969).

17. Richard deCharms, *Personal Causation: The Internal Affective Determinants of Behavior* (New York: Academic Press, 1968).

18. Robert W. White, "Motivation Reconsidered: The Concept of Competence," *Psychological Review* 66 (1959): 297–333; Jack W. Brehm, *A Theory of Psychological Reactance* (New York: Academic Press, 1966); J. W. Brehm, *Responses to Loss of Freedom: A Theory of Psychological Reactance* (Morristown, N.J.: General Learning Press, 1972).

19. Richard deCharms, "Personal Causation Training in the Schools," *Journal of Applied Social Psychology* 2 (1972): 95–113.

20. Edward L. Deci, *Intrinsic Motivation* (New York: Plenum Press, 1975).

21. For a review of many studies see John Condry, "Enemies of Ex-

ploration: Self-Initiated Versus Other-Initiated Learning," *Journal of Personality and Social Psychology* 7 (1977): 459–77.

22. Carl Benware and Edward L. Deci, "Attitude Change as a Function of the Inducement for Espousing a Proattitudinal Communication," *Journal of Experimental Social Psychology* 11 (1975): 271–78.

23. Albert Bandura, "Self-Efficacy: Toward a Unifying Theory of Behavioral Change," *Psychological Review* 84 (1977): 191–215. In line with Chapters 5 and 6, Bandura summarizes evidence indicating that successful *action* is more conducive to perceived self-efficacy than is observing others, verbal persuasion, or emotional arousal.

24. The official name of the building is the Peale Science Center, named in honor of Ruth Stafford Peale and Norman Vincent Peale.

25. Rom. 12:2 Phillips.

26. For an extensive discussion of this see Walter Mischel, *Personality and Assessment* (New York: John Wiley & Sons, 1968), and Walter Mischel, "Toward a Cognitive Social Learning Reconceptualizing of Personality," *Psychological Review* 80 (1973): 252–83. Mischel does not deny the importance of internal factors. His argument is against the generalizability of global personality traits, not against the complexity and uniqueness of each individual. He assumes that the unique history of each person contributes to his or her unique and seemingly inconsistent responses to various situations. My own argument here is not against the reality of individual differences or against their genetic basis. It is rather that social behavior cannot be predicted without knowing the situation.

27. Steve Ferber, "More on Energy: A Look at Research," *APA Monitor*, April, 1977, pp. 10–11.

28. We have all observed how *differences,* however small, command attention; similarities get ignored. If in our college, denomination, or community we are confronted with a great diversity of opinions and life-styles, these catch our attention and small differences are easily tolerated. If the group is more homogeneous, small differences of belief or behavior can be a source of great tension. The extent to which our differences from others around us shape even our self-concepts was demonstrated in a recent study of sixth-grade students. When simply asked to describe themselves, the children were most likely to spontaneously mention their distinctive attributes, not their shared traits. Thus foreign born children were more likely than children born in this country to mention their birthplace, redheads were more likely than black- and brown-haired children to volunteer their hair color, and light or heavy children were more likely to make a reference to their body weight than were children of average weight (William J. McGuire and Alice Padawer-Singer, "Trait Salience in the Spontaneous Self-Concept," *Journal of Personality and Social Psychology* 33 [1976]: 743–54).

29. Colin Turnbull, *The Mountain People* (New York: Simon and Schuster, 1972).

30. John M. Darley and C. Daniel Batson, "From Jerusalem to Jericho: A Study of Situational and Dispositional Variables in Helping Be-

havior," *Journal of Personality and Social Psychology* 27 (1973): 100–108.

31. P. G. Zimbardo, C. Haney, and W. C. Banks, "A Pirandellian Prison," *New York Times Magazine,* April 8, 1973, pp. 38–60.

32. Langdon Gilkey, *Shantung Compound* (New York: Harper & Row, 1966).

33. Rom. 12:2, RSV.

34. Quoted in *Psychology Today,* June, 1974, p. 72.

35. A good introduction to this research literature is provided by Kelly G. Shaver, *An Introduction to Attribution Proceses* (Englewood, N.J.: Winthrop Publishers, 1975); and by Edward E. Jones, "How Do People Perceive the Causes of Behavior?," *American Scientist* 65 (1976): 300–305.

36. S. G. West, S. P. Gunn, and P. Chernicky, "Ubiquitous Watergate: An Attributional Analysis," *Journal of Personality and Social Psychology* 32 (1975): 55–65. (The investigators were more sensitive to ethical issues raised by this experiment than my brief summary can indicate.)

37. An interesting program of research on this "just world" phenomenon has been carried out by Melvin Lerner. An accessible summary of his research appeard in "All the World Loathes a Loser," *Psychology Today* 5, no. 1 (June, 1971): 51–54, 66. These studies demonstrate again how prevalent is our tendency to impute causal connections where none exist (see Chapter 7).

38. When I succumb to this excuse I sometimes prod myself with the reminder that Jonathan Edwards wrote his massive *Freedom of the Will* in just eighteen weeks, while serving as missionary to the Housatonnuck Indians, pastoring a small church, and being father to a large family.

39. Jean-Paul Codol, "On the So-Called 'Superior Conformity of the Self' Behavior: Twenty Experimental Investigations," *European Journal of Social Psychology* 4 (1975): 457–501.

40. See Barry R. Schlenker and Rowland S. Miller, "Egocentrism in Groups: Self-serving Biases or Information Processing," *Journal of Personality and Social Psychology* 35 (1977): 755–64.

41. James T. Burtchaell, *Philemon's Problem* (Chicago: Acta Foundation, 1973), pp. 149–150, 82. If the offenses of the condemned were not entirely unwitting, they were at least unaware of who they had sinned against (Matt. 25).

42. Some sociobiologists have reasoned that self-deception has survival value because it facilitates the self-serving deceptions we perpetrate on others. Cheaters, for instance, can give a more convincing display of honesty if they see themselves as honest.

43. Psalms 19:12 Good News Bible.

44. 1 John 1:8, NEB.

45. Irving Janis, *Victims of Groupthink* (Boston: Houghton Mifflin, 1972).

46. Rudolph Bultmann, *Jesus Christ and Mythology* (New York: Scribners, 1958), pp. 20–21.

47. For a recent review of this literature see Richard L. Gorsuch and

Daniel Aleshire, "Christian Faith and Ethnic Prejudice: A Review and Interpretation of Research," *Journal for the Scientific Study of Religion* 13 (1974): 281–307.

48. Glock and Stark have written a number of books and articles. See, for example, "Prejudice and the Churches," in *Prejudice USA*, ed. C. Y. Glock and Ellen Siegelman (New York: Praeger, 1969), pp. 70–95.

49. Donald T. Matlock, *The Social Psychology of Prejudice: The Religious Syndrome and a Belief in Free Will* (Ann Arbor, Mich.: University Microfilms, 1973).

50. B. F. Skinner, *Beyond Freedom and Dignity* (New York: Alfred A. Knopf, 1971), p. 211. See Albert Bandura's analysis, "Reciprocal Determinism," in his *Social Learning Theory* (Englewood Cliffs, N.J.: Prentice-Hall, 1977) for an excellent discussion of this subject.

51. To some extent this view characterizes educated people in general, which may be one reason why people with higher levels of education tend, on the average, to express more acceptance and understanding of those who are different.

52. C. G. McClintock, C. B. Spaulding and H. A. Turner, "Political Orientations of Academically Affiliated Psychologists," *American Psychologist* 20 (1965): 211–21; Malcolm G. Scully, "Faculty Members, Liberal on Politics, Found Conservative on Academic Issues," *Chronicle of Higher Education,* April 6, 1970, pp. 1, 4–5.

53. Quoted in Charles Partee, "Calvin and Experience," *Scottish Journal of Theology* 26 (1973): 180.

54. The "I found it" billboards and bumper stickers which plastered the United States during our bicentennial year, for instance, seemed to imply that we, by our act of faith, make a decisive contribution to our own salvation and therefore share the credit with God. On the other hand, although most Americans say they believe in hell, many fewer see themselves going there. Hell is the place for all those wretched other people.

55. Martin Luther, *The Bondage of the Will,* trans. J. I. Packer and O. R. Johnston (Old Tappen, N.J.: Fleming H. Revell, 1957), p. 84.

56. John Calvin, *Institutes of the Christian Religion,* I. XVII (John T. McNeill, ed., Ford L. Battles, trans.), Westminster Press, 1975.

57. Prov. 14:31, 14:21, 29:7, NEB.

58. John 8:32, NEB.

Conclusions

The purpose of this book has been to explore human nature from the perspectives of psychological research and Christian belief. I proposed to distill the human image emerging from several different areas of research and to relate this to the human image discerned by biblical scholars and theologians. After wading through hundreds of research studies and after scrutinizing the insights of Scripture and of dozens of biblical scholars and theologians, it is time now to briefly reflect upon the picture of human nature which has been portrayed.

I began by arguing for the appropriateness of relating psychological research and Christian belief. In contrast to those who see nature and spirit as separate realms and who therefore sense an intrinsic competition between natural and spiritual understandings of human nature, the historic Hebrew-Christian view sees God acting and revealing himself through all events of his creation. The Spirit of God is understood as something greater than merely another force which sometimes intervenes in nature. Christians can therefore see psychological research in Christian terms—as exploration of the natural revelation.

If, indeed, the natural as well as the biblical data are a part of God's revelation, then Christians should be open to the insights that come through either, remembering that scientific and religious explanations generally operate at different levels and answer different questions, making them complementary, not competing. If all revelation has a common source, then a fundamental unity must exist among the different levels at which human nature can be understood. A challenging adventure therefore awaits those who, in search of a coherent world view, would probe both the essential unity and the apparent tension between religious and scientific views of human nature.

Relating science and theology has sometimes meant putting one at the mercy of the other. Since it is increasingly evident that both scientific and theological theorizing is shaped by the beliefs and values of the theorist, we must be wary of efforts to absolutize any given human interpretation of either nature or Scripture. When scientific concepts are congenial with Christian belief, we can celebrate the apparent coherence. When there appears to be tension, we should explore the apparent conflict with humility and openness.

With this framework established, the primary agenda of this book was to relate Christian belief to four different areas of psychological research.

1. Investigations at the rapidly changing frontiers of biopsychology point to the intimate, mysterious union of mind and body. The evolutionary emergence of mind, the genetic foundation of our individual differences, and the correspondence between our brain states and our emotions, thoughts, and actions, all point to the unity of mind and body. Our minds do not occupy our bodies; they are manifestations of our bodies.

This holistic picture of human nature is congenial with the ancient holistic understandings of the Hebrew people. The idea that our human essence is pure spirit or pure mind is nearly as foreign to biblical thinking as to current scientific thought. In contrast to the dualistic body-soul image which has shaped Western thought, the Old and New Testaments consistently convey a unity of mind and body. No sharp distinction is made between the two. This holistic image is reinforced in the Christian idea of human mortality (in contrast to Plato's concept of the immortal soul) and in the Christian hope that ultimately the mind-body unit will, in some form, be resurrected. One's view of human nature—as a body-soul duality, as has been popular since the ancient Greeks, or as a holistic entity, as seems to be the growing consensus of scientific and biblical scholarship—has important practical implications for one's view of salvation, of ministry, and of one's own body.

2. What is the relationship between people's attitudes and the way they act? Although most attempts to influence people assume that causation proceeds from internal attitudes to external action, thus implying that one had best start by changing people's hearts and minds, the evidence is at least as strong for the reverse assumption. Diverse research findings indicate that we are as likely to act ourselves into a way of thinking as to think ourselves into action. Attitudes and actions have a spiraling, reciprocal relationship, each feeding on the other.

This insight regarding the effect of action on one's attitudes and beliefs is congenial with the Hebraic understanding of religious knowledge and faith. Throughout the Old and New Testaments we are told that full knowledge of God comes through actively doing the Word. Faith is enhanced by obedient action. This is consistent with the biblical image of persons as whole beings and contrasts with the more rationalistic views which follow from viewing human nature as a body-mind duality. Practical implications of these insights regarding behavior and belief can be derived for church renewal, for worship, and for Christian nurture.

3. Having noted with satisfaction an emerging unity to scientific and biblical perspectives on human nature, we must also openly probe areas of apparent tension. One area of tension is suggested by recent research which demonstrates the prevalence of superstitious thinking. Human rationality is riddled with biases, errors, and distortions. We are, for example, remarkably inclined to perceive causal connections among events which are merely correlated, to perceive relationships between events even when there is no relationship, and to think we can control events which are beyond our control. These illusions of thought confirm the biblical image of the finiteness of the human mind, but they also prompt one to wonder whether superstitious thinking might penetrate religion, giving people an inflated perception of the manipulative power of their prayers.

Given the psychological needs which are satisfied by superstition, true religion seems as likely to be displaced by superstition as by secularism. Although being overly sensitive to superstition can move a person to cold, cynical skepticism, being aware of possible superstitious infections of petitionary and intercessory prayer can serve two healthy purposes. First, it can move Christians to explore other deep purposes of prayer and meditation. Second, it may alleviate some of the arrogance which so often accompanies a confident declaration of prayer's manipulative effects. When Christians begin to think that nature is out of control except when their prayers induce God's intervention, they have begun to shrink their concept of God to a small caricature of the great Creator-Sustainer God of the Bible. The truth which Christianity proclaims is not magical solutions to problems, but the way of the Cross and the hope that nothing can separate us from God's love. The peace which flows from this conviction runs deeper than the fragile comforts of our illusions.

4. The preceeding contentions—that there is a fundamental unity to what we understand as nature and as supernature, that body and mind are also a unity, that there is a reciprocal union between action and attitude, and that our beliefs are both subject to distortion and amenable to scientific scrutiny—lead inevitably to the deep issue of human freedom. Although conventional thinking seems nearly always to emphasize the freedom of the will, theo-

logians and scientists have often been inclined to reject the "autonomous self." Theologians sometimes remind us that when we see ourselves as ultimately our own makers we are likely to have already seriously eroded our sense of the completeness of God's providence, sovereignty, and grace. Research psychologists tend to reject human autonomy partly because of their deterministic working assumption and partly because of the wealth of evidence pointing to genetic and environmental influences upon behavior.

Nothing in these theological and scientific views denigrates the practical reality of human choice or our capacity to shape our destinies through responsible choices. Since persons and environments exist in a reciprocal union, each affecting the other, one can insist that environments determine people *and* that people create environments. Just as divine sovereignty and human responsibility are warp and woof in the fabric of Christian doctrine, so also a simultaneous awareness of environmental control and of personal control are warp and woof to a personal existence which steers between the sins of pride and sloth.

In summary, I have contended that a holistic view of God and nature and of human nature integrates the human sciences with the Hebrew-Christian world view. We are, however, still left with some profound mysteries. For example, although there is abundant evidence concerning the dynamics of human evil and our consequent need to find redemption from it, it is difficult to understand why human beings should ultimately be held morally accountable for their evil. Some of these mysteries will forever remain beyond the grasp of human intelligence. We see now through a dark glass, only faintly and imperfectly detecting the human and divine images. But the glimpses we have gathered are exciting, and the mysteries of human nature and of the divine nature prompt us to accelerate the exploration. Probing the mysteries of the human creation is part of our worshiping God with our minds. It is a way by which we may come not only to know ourselves better but also to draw closer to our creator and sense the awesome mystery of his being. Our hope is that the divine revelation is not static, but ever-continuing. In the second of C. S. Lewis' *Chronicles of Narnia*, the young child Lucy meets the great lion Aslan after several months of separation.

"Welcome, child." he said.
"Aslan," said Lucy, "you're bigger."
"That is because you are older, little one," answered he.
"Not because you are?"
"I am not. But every year you grow, you will find me bigger."

INDEX